Marriage

Building it to Last

Bob and Paige Bingham

U-Build Enterprises LLC
PO Box 1510
Spirit Lake, ID 83869

Marriage: Building it to Last ©

Original Copyright © 2010 Bob & Paige Bingham

1st Printing February 2011

Publisher
U-Build Enterprises LLC
P.O. Box 1510
Spirit Lake, ID 83869
www.u-build.com

Bingham, Bob and Paige
Marriage: Building it to Last / Bob and Paige Bingham
1. Marriage. 2. Intimacy. 3. Relationships. 4. Family.

ISBN *978-0-9832542-0-1* Suggested Retail *$21.99 USD*

Printed in the United States of America

Each authorized copy of this book comes with a printed serial number
inside the front or back cover. Register your copy at www.u-build.com

---

Quotations appearing in text box frames that do not contain a referenced author were created by Bob or Paige Bingham. When quoting, reference the title of the book and the publisher's web site.

Acknowledgments –

Grateful thanks to cousin Mary Bingham, for her time, talent and patience in the many initial edits of our handbook. Mary helped align our thoughts to our words.

Sincere thanks to the talent of our freelance final proof editor, Barbara Fandrich, for her professional proofing work and for letting our style prevail. Barbara offers very reasonably priced editing for authors and can be reached at bjfandrich@hotmail.com

A sincere thank you to Paige's OB/GYN who provided a sanity check examination of our sexual intimacy chapter.

To our awesome daughter who had to live with us while we were learning how to be married and how to be parents. We love you!

And finally we also wish to thank our prerelease content readers who performed the first-pass read of our draft version. Your feedback was invaluable.

CONTENTS

MARRIAGE FRONT and CENTER

THE BLENDING of HUSBAND and WIFE

SEX and LOVE

PREFACE

We love it when the light bulb comes for a couple when they realize their marriage has turned a corner and new hope begins to flood their relationship. It's that "we get it" moment and joy just starts to bubble up.

I'm not sure when the light bulb came on for us, but it was years into our married life when we realized that the concepts I used in construction were very similar to what was required to build a solid marriage. Both home building and marriage building start with an idea, both require good materials, both require tools, and both need to be built to last. Speaking as a Neanderthal type male, never before had I understood that I had to "build" my marriage, but it became very clear that lasting marriages are indeed a building process. The trouble for any marriage is not necessarily with one spouse or the other, but trying to build a marriage without using the correct materials and tools.

With 30 years of marriage behind us, Paige and I thought it was time to share on a broader scale what we believe are valuable and time-tested marriage building practices with other couples to help them navigate the not so intuitive process of building a great marriage. Good marriages don't just happen, and if you are like us, the concept that you actually have to build your marriage never occurred to you. We've traveled this road and found married life presents many twists and turns, some of which are really beneficial and others that are detrimental to building a great marriage.

> My wife and I know each other so well I can start a sentence and she will finish it. Like the other day I said, *"Our marriage is forever and forever,"* implying she is stuck with me no matter how messed up I get, but then she responded with a grin, *"until death do us part!"* ☺

As guys we like to build stuff: we build homes, cars, shelves, shops and other things. You give us some tools and parts and we'll see what we can put together. And we like to build things well! We love it when someone, especially our wife or kids, tell us we did a great job. There is something inside of men that is keyed into building. And guys this is the revelation for us: *we have to build our marriages too!*

[Paige jumps in] Likewise, we women like to live in what our men build. Once our man gets his car built, we like to go for rides in it; once the house is built, we like to live in it. The fact is neither the car nor the house is truly complete until we join our husbands in them. When a wife joins with her man in the man-car, it transforms the "drive" into a "joy-ride"; when a man marries and brings his bride into the house, it transforms the "house" into a "home." We take the house and turn it into a completed work by living in it and decorating it. Our presence and touch makes a house a home, a place our husbands want to retreat to after slaying the dragons all day. In a well-built marriage both the husband and wife are very much part of the marriage building process, but it's a process no one ever seems to talk about.

Akin to building a house, we will take you step by step and explain the concepts and the processes in terms both husbands and wives can use and apply. You'll not only understand what it takes to have a great marriage, but we'll explain it in a way that helps you comprehend and intuitively apply what you've learned, with plenty of humor thrown in. By using our marriage-building concepts and techniques, couples will easily understand what it takes to build your own unique home. It's really quite liberating once you realize that building a great marriage is a process. With that realization and some solid guidance a couple can be comforted in knowing the results will be the great marriage they envisioned.

There is no magic wand for obtaining a great marriage but we believe with all our heart that the information you now have before you will provide a path to achieving your goal of an enduring, happy marriage. But you will gain much more than an enduring marriage. Imagine that your home becomes a refuge because it has become a secure, peaceful, and nurturing environment as a result of building your marriage. Your home can be free of excess stress and tension, a place you and your spouse desire to retreat to, rather than escape from.

While writing this handbook took over a year and was one of the most laborious tasks we have ever undertaken, it was a labor of love. We truly enjoy helping couples have better marriages. We are excited knowing that the vast majority of you will literally change your lives for the better after following this handbook. Within these pages we've poured out our heart and soul, to give you the best of what we have to offer. We sincerely thank you for the trust you are placing in us to help you in building this most important of all relationships.

Bob & Paige

INTRODUCTION

You Are Not Alone

In addition to your marriage there are millions of other married couples around the world and perhaps hundreds of millions of other marriages preceded ours. So while your marriage might be new to you, marriage is not new to humanity. All marriages have much in common, yet your marriage is unique. All marriages will go through various stages of marital bliss and marital struggles. Yet a rather discouraging statistic indicates approximately half of current marriages will not endure longer than two decades. Will your marriage be one that survives?

Some of you were given this handbook because you are planning to get married. Someone who cares for you wants to make sure your eyes are wide open as you cross that threshold into matrimony. And rather than reject the notion you need to learn how to build your marriage, you have embraced the idea that indeed you could use some help. Kudos to you, and we hope to get you off to a great start.

Some of you are happily married and are reading this handbook just to get a tune-up. It has always been your practice to invest time and effort in nurturing and remodeling your marriage and as a result your marriage is doing well. Good for you; we hope to offer you some new perspectives to help your marriage flourish.

Others of you are in some struggle right now and you are looking for answers. Your marriage may be in the midst of a fierce storm or just the opposite, it seems to be drifting with no purpose. The spark seems gone and you're merely living one day to the next. In this group some of you are angry, some of you are hurting, and others are indifferent and have given up on your marriage. But all of you are reading this handbook in the hopes there may be some answers for you. We're gonna do our best to give you a lift up and get you moving in the right direction; a marriage remodel lies ahead of you. You've got a little fight left in ya, and we can work with that. *"Hi-five."*

Another group of you have moved beyond a marriage and are now divorced. Dismayed, yet inside you know you are not the type that can live alone. You're asking yourself, "Did I do something wrong?" If so, "What did I do wrong?" and "How can I do it better the next time?"

We extend a hug to you and congratulate you on your quest for answers and improvement.

But you ask, *"Is a great and enduring marriage possible?"*

The answer is yes, and it's a YES FOR YOU! You can have a great marriage and with this marriage-building handbook you're going to learn how. We are going to give you the information you need to build or, if necessary, remodel your marriage so it will indeed stand the test of time.

What is different about our approach? Well 1st it's proven! 2nd it will work for anyone who is willing to apply the concepts. And 3rd, the concepts will become intuitive and easy to apply. Great marriages are built, hurting marriages are remodeled, and healthy marriages still require regular maintenance to remain healthy. No matter what group you fit into, you're on a journey to establish a lasting marriage and we are here to help you accomplish your goals.

To understand where these concepts and methods are coming from Bob & I only have to think back to those early years when we got married. We knew how to "get" married, but we were in fact clueless about how to "remain" married. Let us explain.

At the time we became engaged, my original blood parents had four marriages between them; Bob's blood parents had seven marriages behind them. Since our wedding day our combined two sets of parents have experienced an additional three more marriages. All totaled to date, there have been **fourteen** marriages in just our two sets of blood parents, which means there have been a corresponding quantity of divorces as well. In addition, other members of our family have experienced infidelity, while others fought constantly and bitterly, and still others rarely expressed love by words or deeds. Two other sets of relatives separately confessed to us that they had not been intimate in over six years. One aging relative stated that in over 40 years of a contentious marriage they had been sexually intimate only <u>three</u> times.

As Paige just described above, we had many marriage examples, just none that seemed to be working. We didn't and don't blame our parents, indeed we love them. They obviously chose the path they desired, but we passionately desired to do marriage just once and we truly wanted to grow old together. But I think deep down neither of us really thought we could have an enduring marriage—nothing around us provided any confirmation that it would be possible.

iv

Was your family upbringing as handicapped as ours?

We are certain that no one, not even our parents, enters into marriage hoping to divorce several years down the road. We gradually came to the understanding that we and our parents were missing the tools and instructions on how to build a marriage and keep it healthy. It was obvious if our marriage was going to survive, we needed to figure out how to do it. Along our journey of learning, we experienced disagreements, fights, annoying habits, and trials that we had to work through. Those are all components of married life, *every* marriage has these. Married people will have many things to work through and as you'll learn in later chapters, there are no perfect people, not even people who write books about marriage. But enduring and great marriages don't just happen. Sadly, going with the flow is very likely going to end in divorce.

Paige and I knew if we were going to have any success in being married we would have to diligently apply ourselves and seek information from outside our family tree. Over the years we found ourselves sharing our experiences and our advice with other couples as we continued to mature in our own marriage relationship. This journey of learning brings us to here, our first book, in what we are calling the *Building it to Last* series of marriage relationship books. We've been happily married for 30 years; we are indeed each other's best friend.

For those of you who are divorced or have more than one marriage behind you, some of the material may cause a few of you to feel a bit defensive as you read it. Please resist the feeling that we might be picking on 'you', we know nothing about your circumstances so that can not be an accurate appraisal. What ever your past is, it's behind you, this is a new beginning and all of us have one job to do and that is to build the marriage we are in.

Congratulations, You're on Your Way!

Please congratulate yourself; you have begun the most critical of steps, you are searching for instruction. Your journey began when you went looking for a resource to help you and your spouse, not only to preserve your marriage but to help it flourish. Many couples will refuse needed help until they have completely melted down. Another whole group of people will be married, get divorced and still think the problem was with their spouse. They mistakenly believe they only need to find a better one the next time.

The fact that you have picked up this handbook is a very good sign. Really! You care enough about your marriage to seek help in making it better. *"Way ta go, booty bump to ya."*

Marriage failures happen for a variety of reasons, but much of what's missing is the understanding that marriages like homes are built, and after they are built they still require regular maintenance to keep them in shape. Divorced people can be some of the most hurting people around. They trusted in an institution called marriage that is supposed to bring happiness but for some reason turned very sour. Divorced folks can suffer a unique kind of loneliness and some really spiral down with ever decreasing self-esteem. If you are divorced, own up to your failures, and then forgive yourself. Really forgive yourself! This is a new beginning. Today you commit to learning everything you can to do your next marriage correctly.

While you'll laugh with us and hopefully learn some new things, we will not let you remain as you are. Initially, you will feel uncomfortable and maybe a little fearful as you begin working on your marriage, and we will push you to apply yourselves. Building a marriage or remodeling a marriage will take some of the same hard work building or remodeling a home entails. The tasks will be different, but sometimes huge amounts of effort and persistence will be required.

But rest assured, the discomfort will give way to joy as your marriage takes shape and becomes secure, healthy and vibrant. You'll learn why ignoring damaged areas (issues) never works. We will ask you to be real, to really give your marriage some thought and to care for your marriage. It is worth it, it is really worth it. With three decades of marriage behind us, we've had to be real as well; it's the only way to make it better.

If your marriage is already built we will help you perform an inspection, looking for areas that may be damaged and thus need remodeled before structural damage occurs. Termites can do a lot of hidden damage—they need to be found early. Before we can fix anything, we first have to admit it's damaged. It is common that one spouse may not even be aware of damage while it is very obvious to the other spouse. Finding damage is not particularly a joyous event. Admitting there is damage can be hard for men as we do not like to admit we have neglected routine maintenance tasks. Paige and I hope to break down that "fear of failure" wall by going before you. We will be real and pave the way for you to follow.

If no one else on earth is willing to call it as it is, let it be our marriage and yours that says, *we might be messed up but we are going to make every effort to make it better*. We are going to help you see the damaged areas that need remodeling. Then we'll give you an understanding of various building concepts so you can go to work at building a great marriage. In our marriage we've had to deal with a lot of crap, and you'll read about that in later pages. Over the years we've learned it was better to remove the crap rather than allow it to pile up.

Not a One Stop Fix-all

While the concepts in this handbook will help many couples to greatly improve their marriage, it is not a one stop or one time fix-all. Marriage self-help books come in many different flavors, providing instruction and guidance on a variety of topics. If this handbook doesn't meet your needs *(and even if it does)* go after another, there is much to learn.

We do not personally know you or your spouse, yet you are both jointly responsible to build and care for your marriage. Because we are writing to a limitless audience of personality types this information is offered in a generic format and we do not represent that it will fit your particular needs or blend with your individual personalities. Apply what you feel works best in your situation, and if need be get help that specifically applies to your marriage issues; seek professional one-on-one counseling. You'll learn in chapter 9 we all need a network of support to help us build anything of value, and indeed your marriage is very valuable.

The reason there are so many different how-to books in home improvement centers is because they each address different areas that may need work. The same is true for your marriage; no one book, no one conference or one trip to a counselor is going to provide everything you need to build a marriage or to make all the repairs that might be required. However, in this, the first in a series of marriage-related books, we are going to cover the main concepts of marriage building and briefly expand on those concepts. For now, we will not be going into a lot of detail but you should walk away with enough of an understanding to begin building or remodeling your marriage.

Are you still a bit fearful of dealing with the issues in your existing marriage? Have you avoided going into areas that you know need work? Let us make the point more clearly by asking you a question. Would you find it more embarrassing or more of a failure to be miserably married or to get one-on-one counseling and end up with a better marriage? The answer is obvious, but frankly why would you care what other people think anyway? In chapter 1 we're gonna show you that all those other marriages are far from perfect too.

We wish our parents had sought help. Paige and I will never know what it is like to be raised in a normal, one-set-of-parents' household. We missed that boat, and it will never come along again. However, we did see to it that our child would have what we missed, one set of happily married parents *"until death do us part."* In a phrase it's called "leaving a legacy." We made a very deliberate effort not to follow our parents' examples with regard to marriage. We are hoping you will decide to <u>very purposefully</u> make sure your marriage is built well and regularly maintained.

Don't take everything in this handbook or yourself too seriously; there are some jokes, dry humor, little teasers, and the like to make sure you are engaged and thinking. If occasionally we make you drop your jaw saying *"Omigosh,"* or you laugh out loud, then you're on your way to living life as we do. You'll learn that we, like you, have encountered the storms of life along the way.

A good portion of this handbook deals with remodel work or related damage repair. It would be rare that every type of damage mentioned would apply to any single marriage so you may read various portions and say "that doesn't apply to us" but it will still be worth reading as you will gain an understanding of what other couples are struggling with.

We are going to ask you to verbally repeat some expressions to each other as you progress through this handbook. Speaking these words out loud to each other may not seem that important to you at the time, but speaking them to your spouse is very important for their hearing and for the growth of your communication skills and your relationship. Consider this a requirement; you must follow our requests as we ask you to engage throughout the handbook. We will go before you, helping you and your spouse say some things you may never have said to each other before. After you've done this, you'll be more able to continue expressing yourselves to each other in a loving and respectful way.

In addition to the building concept theme, an important underlying theme for how we made it work is based on the application of our moral compass, which for us is based on our Christian faith. We sincerely believe that if our marriage was not firmly based on our biblically based moral code, it would have already fallen prey to divorce. We will be sharing marriage building techniques and the path we followed in hopes you will find the information beneficial in building your own great marriage. Ultimately, history and our conscious will determine if we were true to our principles. Not born of money, nobility, or privilege (by U.S. standards) Paige and I want our legacy to be *"They loved God, they loved each other, and they had a great marriage."* What do you want your legacy to be?

As you read through this handbook we want both the husband or the wife to step in at any point and speak directly to your spouse with words like; "this really matters to me", or "this really affects us" or "this is important". Then we would like the spouse hearing the emphasis to respond back, "OK, I understand", or "OK, let's work on it". Misunderstandings occur when we fail to make sure our words are being heard or the significance of those words is missed. Make sure "you get it".

Not long after Bob & I were married he attempted to give me a couple of hickies (*you know—you suck hard on the neck, leaving a blood mark*), but I fought him off. He explained to me that I had to have them because hickies were one way men marked their territory so other men would know their woman was taken. Bob went on to say that either he had to give me hickies or pee on me (to leave his scent); which did I prefer?

I looked at Bob as if to wonder what planet he'd come from. With utter disbelief, and with a breath of exasperation, I shouted, *"You dork! What do you think this wedding ring I'm wearing means to all those other men?"*

Paige Goes One-on-One with the Ladies

Ladies, you would think the authors of a handbook about marriage would have had a PERFECT marriage for the last 30 years, but that would not be the truth. Our marriage has been a journey in phases, starting with infatuation, to naivety, to what the heck, to one of deep love and affection. We were two immature young people that fell in love, yet we had no idea what marriage was about. Raised as a fatherless adolescent (my dad didn't live near me), I had been searching for love in all the wrong places. Is that a song? By some amazing grace I found Bob. Bob was a very confident and perhaps cocky young man, and I was a young girl straight out of high school that had no self esteem and needed a lot of patient loving.

While it wasn't obvious to either of us, we both had a lot of maturing to do. We were two very dysfunctional people who had no idea what it might take to make a marriage last.

Our marriage journey has not been without roadblocks and speed bumps. We have had a lot to learn. Fortunately, we have given each other the time and patience to do so, while seeking advice wherever we could find it. Several times we could've thrown in the towel saying, "This is taking too long, he will never be sensitive enough," and "She is too needy." Like all newlyweds, we wanted a good marriage, but in those early years we stumbled along our way trying to figure it out. You will stumble some too.

I have had to learn to grow in many areas, one of which is to be open to what my husband has to say; likewise, he has had to learn how to approach me in love, not with a 2x4 (figuratively speaking). Men and women are wired differently; it took me years to understand those differences and not take things so personal, which would then take me into a spiral of self-condemnation. I had to learn that giving Bob the silent treatment is never a good option—thank goodness for maturity in that area. I had to learn that when I talk about my husband my words should never dishonor him. I used to think it was OK to take verbal jabs at Bob, in front of family and friends. It was funny and everybody laughed, humor is good for a marriage, right? Controlling this negative aspect of my behavior was and still can be a challenge for me.

Every morning I wake up and make a choice to love, honor and respect my husband, even on the days when I might not feel like it; you know, those days when our husbands act like shits! He in turn cherishes, protects, honors and lifts me up, and what woman doesn't want that? As a result we have a great marriage and a deep love from <u>nurturing each other.</u>

We are works in progress, but we have committed to building our marriage. Yes, we are human, we falter and make the same mistakes that all married people make. The difference is what we do in those situations. We don't always make the right decision the first time; we don't always remember who the real enemy is, but we always work it out. We talk it out and do our best to find the answers to the problems, without giving up on our marriage. It is a really wonderful feeling to know that our marriage is solid, that it will endure, and that we are forever on this journey together.

In any marriage there should be hope. Part of that hope comes from having answers, but you have to be actively searching for those answers and then you have to put them into practice. We've watched several marriages self-destruct when neither spouse cared enough to seek help. You have to ask for guidance and find mentors if need be. Regardless of what we feel our husband's failures are, ladies, we have to admit we come with our own baggage. You have to be open for change, even when that means you are the one that has to do the changing. A good marriage takes action, not indifference.

I wish we would have had the tools and resources that are being made available to you here, early in our marriage. My hope is that you will have a soft heart when you read this handbook, and that you don't condemn yourself or point fingers at your spouse, but come away convinced of the importance of "building" your marriage. Here is your chance to turn around your mistakes, failures, and hurts, and truly have the great marriage you desire. We've been there, and now we are sharing our journey with you in the hopes that you will skip some of the potholes we went through by applying what you are learning within these pages.

Ladies, on a final note you'll notice that most of the writing or perspective is from Bob throughout the handbook, but every word represents our combined knowledge and understanding. You'll learn about the two becoming one later, but Bob and I represent ourselves as a unit as much as practically possible. You'll notice too we jump back and forth in narrating the discussions in various chapters. Bob is the "talker" in our marriage so it should be no surprise he is also more gifted in doing the writing for our handbook. Besides, he is stronger and I couldn't pull the laptop out of his gorilla-grip hands!

And fair warning; be prepared to roll up your sleeves, get dirty, and yes, even sweat a little bit because when you build or remodel there will be messes and hard work involved!

One Last Point before We Begin

Your feedback will be very important to us, so after reading though the handbook please return the Feedback Form or otherwise contact us with your comments. This was written as a handbook and meant to be referenced again and again to keep the concepts and your own notes in front of you. Keep working on your marriage; do not let it fade again into the land of the forgotten, which is a terrible place. In the near future we will offer a workbook that will help you further apply what you've learned in this handbook.

Please help us in our journey to make this handbook a success. Recommend it to friends and family, give copies away, and get the word out about a great marriage-building handbook. By doing so you'll not only be building and repairing your own marriage, but helping other couples build theirs. And we thank you for your trust.

Bob & I decided our marriage would not be broken, but that resolution is common to many. This handbook is about the good and useful things we learned from our mistakes, our successes, pastors, marriage instructors, friends, books, our own experiences, and so on. Remember, none of us are born with the knowledge or intuitive ability to be great marriage partners; we had to learn and so can you.

To the Literary Critics

We need to ask those of you who have been trained in the linguistic arts to bear with us and accept our apologies. This is not a "literary work," rather it is a job site instructional handbook written to connect with an audience that is much broader than academia achievements. As such, we have taken certain linguistic liberties that we hope you can overlook as we seek to appeal to people across all educational and maturity levels. Neither are the pictures and drawings within our little handbook great works of art. In fact they are nowhere near the high quality of most books, but please do not let that distract you from the visual thought they were meant to convey.

We are going to beat the critics by saying upfront, we have several orphan words and sentences and no page design. If you cannot move beyond some annoying writing faults, it's certainly going to be tuff for you to accept some annoying traits that come with being married. Thus we freely admit the weakness in the writing, but there is marriage building power in the words and the message. If our handbook gets used as we intend, it will have spilled coffee and soda pop stains all over it and crumpled pages just like any other job site reference manual.

While this handbook is not a workbook (we will be producing a workbook in the near future) we want you writing notes and highlighting in it. As such, we tried to find a balance between leaving you enough space for notes and filling in the pages with text.

Let's get started!

Getting Started

CHAPTER 1

STOP! For those of you who normally skip the preface and introduction, please flip back and begin there, you'll be missing some very important info. We are here to help you, so please indulge us, thank you!

Marriage in Review, a Reality Check

What Is a Marriage?

If you look up "marriage" in a dictionary you are likely to find something like the following:

> *Marriage – the state of being united to a person of the opposite sex in a consensual and contractual relationship recognized by law, until such time they choose to dissolve it.*

Pretty sterile sounding, isn't it? It really doesn't express our idea of what a marriage is or should be.

Our definition is more along these lines:

> *Marriage – a state of union by two previously separate people of the opposite sex who have come together in a consensual and covenant (meaning never to be broken) relationship of unity. They pledge their love, respect, devotion, fidelity, and all possessions to build a single and united union of oneness. They agree to protect the union at all costs, giving up their individual desires for that of the union, and further agree to serve the other above self and to defend the union against all efforts and/or hazards that may seek to extinguish it. Each spouse continually seeks to do better and improve the union and to add a healthy dose of forgiveness and humor, which shall exist until such time as death occurs by one or both persons.*

How do you define marriage? Do you and your spouse have the same definition? If you are already married, does your marriage look and function as you intended?

Everyone without exception wants to have a "great" marriage otherwise they wouldn't get married. *(OK, make me a liar and be the first to write me and say you purposefully got married to be miserable!)*

It is not unusual that a couple has storms and trials to work thru, but what is hard to understand is some couples become comfortable in the misery. When the roof of the house is leaking into the home, a good first step is to place pots under the drips to catch the water, but it is insanity to continue this course of action for months when you have the ability to repair the roof. By the time you finish this book you'll agree that to be miserable in a marriage, a couple has to intentionally ignore their marriage. *(We refer to these couples as "M&Ms")* Because you're reading this book, we know being miserably married is not in your plans, and you are already taking steps to prevent and repair any damage. To survive, let alone be great, all marriages need attention. Any couple that wants a great marriage can have one—really!

Great Marriages or Perfect Marriages?

Why are there so many failures in marriages? What is the difference between those marriages that are great versus those that are not?

In the simplest terms, our observations can be summed up as *not giving the marriage the attention it deserves.* Ridiculously simple answer, isn't it? Yet, it's entirely true. If you work at building a great marriage, you will very likely have one. But most of us don't have the understanding when we get married that we indeed have to build the marriage relationship. Now that you have that understanding, the next question is "HOW?"

Because it's very rare that any of us intuitively know how to build a great marriage the very first step is admitting we need help.

As we proceed, we are going to accentuate some points we call "FACTOIDS." These are really important to help the two of you grasp facts relating to married life and they will be inserted midstream in any topic. When we give you a FACTOID, consider yourself hit with a 2x4 of learning; we want this imbedded into your head.

FACTOID – There is no such thing as a "perfect" marriage because there are no perfect people, but there are some "great" marriages.

Let's review this analytically. Given that the above statement is true, that means the people who have great marriages are imperfect people! That also means a great marriage is available to all of us imperfect people. If we reason this out a bit further, we can say: *There is nothing better than an imperfect marriage.* This statement is true because no perfect people and no perfect marriages exist, thus at best we all work within an imperfect marriage.

FACTOID – We all need help and instruction to have a great marriage.

We write this to give you hope because a "great" marriage is never perfect and it's made up of imperfect people, it is thus available to every couple, <u>without exception</u>, no matter what faults you or your spouse have.

Let's reason this out further.

Question: If "perfect" people were available, would you want to be married to a perfect person?
Answer: **No!** *(If your answer is yes, you'd be the only one in the marriage to blame for al the faults!)*

Let's take this yet another step further.

Question: Do you want to be married to yourself, i.e., someone exactly like you?
Answer: **No!** *(If your answer is yes, yer one sick puppy!)*

We want everyone to understand that it is our imperfections as people, as couples, and as families that make us unique. Given the choice we want neither a perfect person nor someone exactly like ourselves. However, many of us have not actually thought this out. We believe we want a near perfect spouse and/or we think we should find someone just like ourselves. Yet, the differences between you and your spouse are what make your marriage unique and unlike any other marriage. It is yours to shape and mold into what works for your imperfect union.

We've all heard one friend or another say "He's perfect for me" or "She's perfect for me." However, there is no upside to "perfect," as it is already the best it can be. With the expectation level already set at "perfect" that means the only direction the marriage can go is down. Can you see how some couples set themselves up for disappointments even before the marriage begins?

Are you still not convinced imperfect people can make the best spouses? Let's explore this a little deeper. Imagine if God created everyone perfect. The first thing that comes to my mind is that we'd all be exactly the same,

1

for anything other than the perfect model would be imperfect. In trying to visualize this perfect people scenario, all the women would look exactly like Barbie and all the men would look exactly like Ken. To complete this nightmare everyone would have perfect character, perfect morals, follow the same perfect predictable actions, and never do anything wrong. OK, we've just created the perfect society. Do you want to live in it? Doesn't it sound strange? Does it seem like we'd be missing something in all the perfection?

Did you ever see the movie *The Stepford Wives*? Perfectly programmed robot women, but not capable of real love, just the appearance of love. Toward the end we found out that the man running the program was also a robot. By the end of the movie all had shunned their perfect spouses for the real deal.

I'm telling you, my wife knew she wasn't getting perfection when she married me. If I was or am perfect at anything, it's being a dork. OK, a dork with a bad-ass biker look. It doesn't matter what neighborhood we've lived in, the neighbors might hear my wife shouting "*dork*" at various times of the day. I'd usually follow that up with "*wench*," to which she'd re-respond with "*mule*," to which I'd comeback with…er, well, uh, whoops, back to the topic at hand.

And consider this fact: Not only do we not want to be perfect; most of us will distance ourselves from so-called "perfect people." We actually prefer to be around people who are not perfect.

FACTOID – It is our imperfections that make us unique, desirable, and loveable.

Ever wonder why women pick some of the worst looking pets (usually dogs) from the pound? No matter what you feel your shortcomings are, no matter what your spouse's shortcomings are, you are coming into the marriage with the same stuff from which great marriages are made. In layman's terms we can label these imperfections as faults, annoying habits, physical imperfections, mental limitations, emotional baggage, etc.

My parents had troubles keeping track of us kids, but somewhere after the 7th marriage, I had troubles keeping track of all my parents.

6

How-to Books

As we mentioned in the introduction, every home improvement center has a section filled with "how-to" books. These how-to books help customers complete various building tasks correctly by giving the do-it-yourselfer the insight of professionals. Learning how to build a strong marriage, a marriage that will stand the trials and tests of time will put every couple on the road of discovery and learning and you can likewise reference this handbook as your how-to instruction manual.

Perhaps the difference between Paige and I and our parents is that we understood we knew very little about how to build a great marriage and we also knew we could not go to our parents for marital advice. *(Go back and read the introduction if you are wondering why)* We came into the marriage with the same hope that every couple does; we had that same dream of forever love. Time has proven we must have made a more purposeful effort to build and improve our marriage than our parents.

The need seemed very obvious to us, great marriages do not just happen; there is no magic wand. Great marriages must be "built" and the concept of building is going to be used throughout this book. It works for me because we men like to build things and after we are done, we like to stand back, slug down a beer and admire it. It works for Paige because she knows that while it will take some time to build, we none the less are moving in a common direction together. While we are building our marriage she can feel secure in it, she can decorate it and show it off to her friends because it's going to get better and better.

FACTOID – Great marriages are made, they do not just happen.

Let's begin with a self-assessment, you and your spouse are married, but very likely you have spent zero hours learning how to build it. And yet, if we asked you to build a house you'd spend hundreds of hours looking up info, hiring people who could help you, purchasing materials and tools, and all of that would be based on a plan of what you want the house to look like.

So if we have this right, you'd make all kinds of preparations to build your house that statistics say you will live in for about six to seven years, but you've made no preparations to build your marriage that you want to last a lifetime!

7

1   Let's get really real here. *"What have you done to build or maintain your marriage?"*

Couple's project—Pause here and discuss these last few pages with your spouse.

Building Is a Hands-on Activity

Throughout this book, we will employ the kind of approach that a typical new hire might desire if he were a rookie carpenter to the building trade, or if she were an apprentice interior decorator. Indeed this marriage handbook is about home building, for if you build a good marriage, you'll be well on your way to building a good home. Both the husband and wife will not only enjoy showing off their home, but they will have created a legacy of marital harmony to leave with their children.

Most people prefer to be "hands on learners." As men we understand and retain better with hands on instruction, hands on demonstrations, and tasks that employ "doing." Classrooms, and frankly book reading, can be a challenge especially when dealing with such fuzzy concepts as relationships.

And just so you don't think that this teaching method only applies to men, I'll put the same question to women. Would you rather learn a new dance by reading about it in a book or doing it with someone who knows how?

"Let's see, I am to divorce my wife if we disagree on some point that I'm unwilling to yield on. We shall divide and reduce all of our wealth in thirds between, my wife, myself, and the lawyers. At which time I can begin living alone in a small apartment in which I shall then have my freedom.

I can now begin dating other women from their failed relationships who are also as lonely as me, in the hopes that I will find one I can love as much as I did when I married the wife I just divorced! Then my new wife and I can start all over trying to get to know each other while we begin building our financial and emotional security—but all the time aware this new relationship might fail too.

Am I missing something or wouldn't it be better to nurture the marriage I am in?"

OK, I've made the point; we all like to learn by doing. However, since Paige and I cannot meet with all of you, you are going to have to read this book, but we promise to keep it interesting and we will have you regularly doing activities and talking with each other. We'll do our part and you both do yours.

Paige and I are going to help you develop a design for a great marriage. Then we are going to take you thru the steps one at a time from the ground up. While this is not the conventional way of marriage instruction, we think once you understand the concepts of building and maintaining, you'll be able to build the marriage you want. And because this is a book based on building concepts, both men and women will find it easier to remember. Keep this book nearby where you can reference it as the marriage building or marriage remodel work continues. Your marriage is the job site and you're both very important to the building or remodeling process. It's time to punch in and get to work.

Question: How many of us never make mistakes? Answer: **None of us!**

Just like working at a job site, you and your spouse will make mistakes, but none of these mistakes are insurmountable, nearly everything can be corrected and repaired. Mistakes can be bad, mistakes should be avoided, sometimes mistakes cost us, (getting a ticket or jail time), but mistakes will occur if we are doing anything worthwhile.

FACTOID – We all make mistakes, and we have to learn to accept them while learning how to make fewer of them.

Every person is different, every couple has unique circumstances, yet the keys and tools presented in the following pages are going to apply to nearly all of you, and you can safely apply them in your marriage. If you disagree with something mentioned in the following pages, then skip it and employ the other tools. If after reading this entire book you only find 10% of the material useful, then you're still on your way to a 10% improvement in the current status of your marriage. You will in fact be moving in the right direction.

FACTOID – Couples in a good marriage are always aware of areas that need improvement. A marriage does not rest on the successes of the past, dwell on the failures of the past, nor is it content to live only in the present. A good marriage has a vision for the future, which is to always improve the marriage and the recognition that it can always be better.

I cannot think of a property we've owned that we ever felt was totally complete, as in just exactly the way we wanted it. As such, we are always looking for ways to improve our home or land. The same is true for great marriages. Even when our marriage is good, we can still find ways to make it better.

When a builder goes to build a house, he must acquire five things to be able to finish the task. *This is a simplified list:*

- A <u>plan</u> of what the house is to look like.
- The required building <u>materials</u>.
- A crew of support to <u>help</u> in building.
- <u>Tools</u> to get the job done.
- An <u>understanding of the order</u> of tasks and when they are to occur.

With an appreciation of what it takes to build a house we can likewise understand that a marriage will also require; a plan, basic materials, support, tools, and knowledge to have it turn out correctly.

FACTOID – No one starts out hoping their marriage will fail, but nearly all start without the required items to accomplish what they desire. "Let's wing it" rarely gets a marriage or a house built.

Programmed for Failure

Paige and I began our marriage without much planning. We want you to be real and we will be real with you. Here is a list of some of the "crap" we either brought to the marriage or have since had to deal with:
- Hurts & memories from past relationships
- Financial troubles
- Raised in a non-traditional home by parents with multiple marriages between them
- Parents who were absentee parents
- No understanding of marriage other than *"living in the same house and having sex"*
- Wrong ideas of what intimacy is
- Wrong priorities – not balanced with work and family
- Pornography & romance novels
- Failed past relationships
- Low self-esteem
- Poor parental skills

- Anger – excessive pride – self-centeredness
- Poor conflict-resolution skills

Fortunately, we both had two things going for us, *a desire to learn and a desire to make it better.* We "loved" each other but perhaps more importantly we figured out we had to foster that love by seeking to grow our marriage union and keep it vibrant. We did get some good premarital counseling by my wife's pastor. *(He wouldn't marry us without it!)* Rob set us on the right road of being willing to learn how to be happily married. He gave us that ever so important initial understanding that we didn't know how to be married and we'd have to learn.

Collateral Damage

Children of broken marriages can carry a lot of baggage. We can have feelings such as these: our parents left us rather than the other spouse, we were partly to blame for the turmoil leading to our parents' divorce, or we were unloved. Thus, grown children of divorced parents find it can be hard to trust other people; we can be bitter, and a host of other issues. All of that "hurt" can wreak havoc in a marriage if we let it. Paige and I will never know what it is like to be raised in a loving home where both parents stayed together, but that didn't mean our child would have to experience what we had to. Like a master builder, we will never stop learning and never stop seeking to better our marriage.

FACTOID – No matter what your family background is, you can have a great marriage.

> *Hubby sputters with a sheepish grin, "Honey, a feeling has come over me, I'm in the mood and it starts with an "H,"... to which she replies, "Hey, I'm hungry too!"*

Ideally, we'd like you each to read this handbook at the same time or following within a chapter or two of the other. You are encouraged to use a highlighter, to write notes along the margins and to discuss the portions that seem to really fit into what you want for your marriage. Then share your notes, thoughts, and hopes with each other. If you like, the husband can make notes on one side of the margin about the things he felt were really important and the wife can make notes on the other. Sit down and discuss what you've learned in between chapters. Talk things out.

FACTOID – Couples tend to joust combatively back and forth when something troubling occurs in the marriage. Changing the tone to lighthearted bantering can be a way to lower the tone and make the discussion less threatening. Pretend you're both six years old, during your next argument.

We've designed this handbook to work interactively with couples by engaging you and your spouse in question/answer activities, emphasizing key points and tools, having you as a couple explore what you are seeking in your marriage, and providing a few exercises. It is imperative to mix the new knowledge and tools with action, for it is not enough to gain head knowledge, you must put into practice what you learn.

FACTOID – Head knowledge without putting what you know into action is similar to sitting on a toilet but not pulling your pants and underwear down. There's gonna be a mess, and because you're knowledgeable, you'll know why.

Safe Time

Before any work begins, you both must agree to a condition that is demanded on all home construction sites. What is that, you ask? That we work safely! Every builder huddles his crew for a job safety meeting. Same here. As you both open up and learn about each other's feelings, failures, and needs, you must agree that it will be a **SAFE TIME**. This allows you to be real about what you feel without fear of the discussion blowing up. You are about to begin a verbal journey of sharing feelings. We are going to ask you to be real. That means the barriers drop, and you set aside your feelings of insecurity and anger. You both must agree you will be open, vulnerable, and honest. No matter what is discussed, you'll keep your attitude and anger in check.

This handbook will help you find damage (if any) in your marriage, then it will help you learn how to cut out the rotten wood and rebuild it with solid materials. Don't get mad at your spouse; focus on exposing damage and repairing it. It's time for solutions, not anger. Some things we have to deal with will hurt, but like every bodybuilder knows, the pain always leads to building more muscle. It is OK to feel hurt, it is OK to need a few minutes or a few hours to come to grips with various issues you were not previously aware of, but it is not OK to lash out. If you do get angry, if you do say things you shouldn't have, as soon as possible ask forgiveness (it should be genuine) and seek to heal that wound.

When a master gardener prunes a bush, the pruning makes the bush better. Weaker branches are cut off, which is disruptive in the beginning. So it is when working on your marriage, think about how the critique can make you better, not weaker. Don't fight the change, embrace it; don't wonder that repairs are needed, rather focus on making the needed repairs. We are not going to make you repeat it out loud, but we'd like you both to verbally express that you agree to the **SAFE TIME** pledge.

SAFE TIME pledge: That you will not "act out" with curt or angry responses during any current or future marriage enrichment activity. Please agree that as you work through this handbook it will be a continual **SAFE TIME.**

We are not asking you or your spouse to give in to any matter, we are saying a marriage must deal with feelings as much as facts. It's OK to have trouble swallowing what a spouse says, but try to really see it from your spouse's viewpoint. How a person feels is equally as important as the facts are to the healing process.

To help you understand that both of you can be right while each thinks the other is wrong, we have a little exercise for you: Face each other, now reach over and hold each other's hands. Husbands ask your wife which is the "left" side? Husbands answer the same question: which is the "left" side? You will notice that both of you answered correctly but the answer was opposite from your spouse's perspective. Now, if we make this into an argument, one of you would be yelling, "No, this is the left side; you're wrong," while the other would be insisting they were right. All that is needed is for one or both of you to take a look at the issue from the other's perspective.

Couple's project—Pause here and discuss this with your spouse.

Are You an Iceberg or Skyscraper?

When Bob asked me to go out on our first date, his plan was to spend the whole evening just driving around talking. Gas was only about $1.25 a gallon back then! If it didn't go well, he could drive me back home at any time, but instead we spent about four hours of quality time getting to know each other. We could have done any number of functions for our first date, but I think our first four hours of doing nothing but talking, with no other distractions, jumpstarted our relationship more than a dozen dates could have. After our first date we continued opening ourselves up and helping each other get to know what others never see. Bob has an interesting analogy for this and I'll let him explain it to you.

I think I could get most of you to agree that when people meet, we are like icebergs in the respect that only a small portion of the real person is made known to others. About 10% of an iceberg is above the surface and visible; the other 90% is hidden from view. We agree with this protective aspect of human psychology to a point.

However, when we marry someone we have a decision to make regarding how much of ourselves we are going to reveal to our spouse, and conversely our spouses have the belief that we will reveal to them all that is hidden from others. Yet some spouses will never open up and let their spouse know the real person they married.

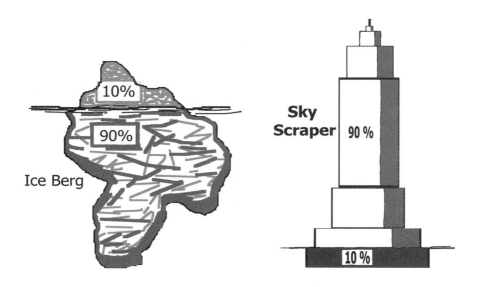

The reverse analogy to the iceberg is the skyscraper, where about 90% of it is visible and only 10% is hidden. These analogies are presented to you our readers because you and your spouse have decisions to make about how much of "you" you are going to be open and real about as you progress in your marriage.

How much of the real you did you reveal to your spouse by the day you were married? Some of you are going to respond "all of me" to which we'd respond "bull!" My question might lead you to another question:

Did you marry someone you didn't really know? As a society we have actually made an allowance for people who marry not really knowing each other; this is expressed in a legal document called a *prenuptial agreement*. It's an expression of doubt: *I may not really know the person I'm about to marry!*

We are not trying to say that everything not known is dark and evil, we are rather pointing out what may not be obvious to many couples: that when we marry, we are continuing a journey of getting to know just who we married. It is entirely possible you married someone you really knew very little about. Certainly you liked/loved what you could see, but what about what you can't see? Some of us will open up more than others, for some they may never truly open up to their spouse or anyone else for that matter. Yet, it is an interesting analogy that the "unsinkable" ship called the *Titanic* was sunk on its maiden voyage by what it couldn't see under the surface.

We know a couple that has been married for over 25 mostly difficult years and we believe they still have only let each other see a portion of who they are. Indeed, we believe it is what is hidden that keeps interfering in their relationship. So with all this said, we have to consider that a portion of our readers are likewise not going to open up. We will discuss this protective aspect in chapter 13 but we are hoping to prompt the "iceberg" personalities that they owe it to their spouse to let them know the real you.

So we ask, *does your spouse have a right to know "you"?*

How much of you have you let them see?

NOTE: Beginning with this chapter and throughout the rest of the book, we would like you each to grade how well you feel the content in each respective chapter was interesting and beneficial to you. This grading will accomplish two tasks. First, spouses can use this to see how each other perceives the information being taught. Second, it provides a feedback measurement of how well we presented the information and you will grade us at the end of the book. Each spouse will select (circle) a 1–5 value representing their opinion.

Did you learn anything? Yes / No
Chapter personal benefit appraisal: **HER 1-2-3-4-5 HIM 1-2-3-4-5**
1=not at all, 2=a little, 3=some good stuff, 4=fairly helpful, 5=very helpful

CHAPTER 2

Current State of Your Union Appraisal

As we ended chapter 1 we were making a point that your spouse deserves to know the real person they married. That dovetails into every chapter of this book because if you are only going to reveal 10% of the real you, and you are not going to apply the information contained in these pages to the hidden 90%, the outcome is not going to be very beneficial. Consider really opening up to each other as you proceed.

Crap! Right out of the gate, **it's a TEST!!**

For married couples—This very short appraisal is meant to take a snapshot of your marriage *"at this moment in time."* If the scores for one or both of you are low, then low is where we are starting from. It just means things can get a lot better! This is not a judgment or blame test, it's an expression by each of you of where you feel your marriage relationship is now. Please do not assume or believe that low scores are a bad reflection on one or the other of you. They most likely are not and I'll tell you why.

There is something your teachers didn't tell you when they gave you tests. Low scores are an indication of the combined effort of the teacher, the teacher's methods, the instructional materials, and the student. If one or both of you have had little or no marriage instruction, **then low scores are to be expected**.

FACTOID – How can anyone expect you to know what you have not been taught?

Low scores tell the teacher and the student where more emphasis is required and if new or different teaching methods are required. So a low test score doesn't necessarily indicate someone is not smart, it is merely an expression of what you've been taught and what you've retained at a point in time.

Let me explain this with a personal story. When my daughter was in her early teens, I took her aside and explained to her I wanted to know how she felt about "me as her father." Up to this point in her life, I had been working a lot of hours. Our father/daughter bond was very weak and I knew it.

I wanted to see if she would confirm the breakdown I believed was occurring in our relationship. I told my daughter that this was a "**SAFE TIME**." I would not get upset with her, I would not lecture her, and I wanted her to be honest. I'd like to tell you I scored high, but the facts were I scored low in her assessment. My daughter was honest and our relationship was failing in several areas. She was right and my inattention to fostering a close parental relationship with her *(as the adult and parent)* produced expected results. The poor score didn't mean I was a bad dad. It did mean that I really didn't know what I was doing, and what I had been doing was not working.

Just to show you how dense my wife and I were, while we understood we didn't have the knowledge and training to have a good marriage and went after learning that area of our life, we failed to understand that we also did not have the knowledge of how to raise children, and carelessly we ignored getting more help in that area.

See, we are real people too. We will make mistakes at times and in various areas of our lives just like everyone else. If you like, after you've completed the quiz, you can discuss the results with each other. Remember, this is just a snapshot of this moment in time. You are going to be moving your relationship to somewhere else, and you'll look back and see where you were.

> *"It seems to me that marriage is a lot like jail, when your day started out you were just looking for a little fun and a good time, the next thing you know, you're in it."*

We've put several answers or scores in for you, it is because we want you to begin at that point, **regardless** of where you think you are. As the authors, we make the rules!

The rating is based on a 1–10 scale for the first five questions:
      1 means it needs lots of work.
      5 means it's OK, but could be better.
      10 means great. A 10 is rare, so be honest.

Couple's project—CURRENT CONDITION TEST

Question	Him	Her
How would you rate your marriage as a whole?		
The degree I feel I am loved is about ?		
The degree I feel I am respected is about ?		

Question Answer (yes/true) or (no/false)	Him	Her
Our sexual intimacy is about ?	3	3
Our communication is about ?	3	3
I feel we already know everything we need to know about how to have a great marriage.		
I would rather be with my spouse for a weekend than doing just about anything else.		
Our marriage is better than most.		
I am 100% confident we will still be married in 10 years.		
I feel secure in our marriage.		
I fully trust myself and/or my spouse to never cheat because our relationship is very strong.		
When we have fights or disagreements, we limit our words to the topic at hand.		
My behavior in this marriage has been less than admirable with some frequency.	true	true
I put my spouse above all others including other family members and my children.	false	false

2

Remember, <u>do not feel hurt by low results</u>! A low score just means we have areas to work on. It is very important that each spouse understand this is a **SAFE TIME** while you work thru the items in this book. If you let your tongue slip, apologize, ask forgiveness, and start again.

For those who are recently engaged, the test doesn't apply.

> *"Jim said his <u>first</u> clue that his marriage was heading south was when he got served the divorce papers. He immediately called his wife who had been living her mother for the last year to ask her. 'what was up'?"*

Did you learn anything? Yes / No
Chapter personal benefit appraisal: **HER 1-2-3-4-5   HIM 1-2-3-4-5**
1=not at all, 2=a little, 3=some good stuff, 4=fairly helpful, 5=very helpful

www.u-build.com

CHAPTER 3

Understanding a Man

Women say men are: Barbarians, arrogant, egotistical, self-centered, selfish, liars, unloving, unromantic, insensitive monsters, who fart, belch, and are walking sex-craved bastards that are so underhanded they only get married to have sex without having to pay for it! And this is not a complete list!!

Good things about men—they kill spiders and can carry out heavy trash.

CHAPTER 4

Understanding a Woman

Men say women are: Emotional creatures driven by hormones that cause them to say things that do not make sense—like why am I in trouble for a dream my wife has in which another woman flirts with me?

And they cry when they are happy instead of drinking a beer.

Trying to understand her is like trying to program my home entertainment center. I think I'm pushing the right buttons but after hours of trying with no results I just give up. I could go on but it may get back to her somehow and she'll cut me off!

Good things about women—that's easy, body parts! But after we marry one, we never stop paying for it.

(We'd just like to point out that this handbook is such an easy read that you've just read two complete chapters in less than one minute! And hopefully you understand these last two chapters are a parody!)

CHAPTER 5

OK, We Start with a Level Playing Field

So in chapters 2 and 3 you've learned that men and women have a similarly high opinion of one another. We are different and those differences can be "painfully" contrasted as in the previous chapters or they can be embraced. At our own expense we enjoyed a laugh about the differences. Obviously the previous two chapters were not meant to be a scientific analysis; however, if you haven't said something like it out loud, you've thought about it!

> *"I went to a marriage ceremony once where I beheld a large group of people focused on a couple who was about to pledge to live their lives together.*
>
> *Given that half of all marriages will fail in less than 20 years, I supposed that most couples should be sent away before this grievous ceremony was allowed to continue, or perhaps something much more punishing should be done to make sure the union would endure. Maybe the threat of a five-year jail term or electric shock therapy if they failed in making it last. But alas my thoughts were interrupted by the preacher who was asking <u>me</u> to repeat after him…"*

We have two choices, we can enter into a relationship with an awareness that there is not much to work with on either side, thus <u>we both need to improve and change</u> or we can enter into the relationship thinking each other is the perfect prince and princess of marital bliss. The first option sets up everything that comes afterward as gain and improvements, while the second option sets us up for very large disappointments. <u>Making improvements and changes are the basis of this handbook, i.e., "building, remodeling, and improving" your marriage.</u>

So we each have issues; how do we deal with that? <u>Well, we focus on working on ourselves while we nurture our spouse.</u> Change must come from within a person. NEVER get married to someone with the thought or hope that you will be able to change them. You can only change <u>you</u>. If you've already made that mistake, get over it and focus on you. Even while reading this book, your focus should not be on force feeding chunks of this book to your spouse. The real work is making sure <u>you</u> are working on <u>you</u>.

5

A few optimistic spouses have married someone who was addicted to drugs or alcohol thinking they could change them, only to be painfully disappointed. The *12 Step Program* helps the alcoholic understand their condition <u>so they can acquire the desire to change</u>, and then they help the alcoholic bring the newfound desire for sobriety into reality. A person will not try to fix a problem they first are not willing to admit they have.

A marriage pastor once said that nearly every week when he starts a counseling session with a couple, one of them will say to him: *"I'm just here to be the moral support for my wife/husband."* The marriage is in crisis and they are just there for moral support? Get real!

We are <u>all broken</u> in various ways; we need to own up to our stuff and quit blaming others. You married your spouse because you thought he/she was nearly perfect for you, and then some years later you're claiming they soured? I'd point out to you that if they soured, they soured on your watch. Where the heck were you?

Is the quarterback or receiver out there just for moral support? No, he's working just as hard to make the team a success. Grow up! Get over "you," and get on with "us." Do you really want a <u>great</u> marriage? Then focus on getting <u>your</u> stuff in order so you will be an ass<u>et</u> to the team, not an ass.

So we have this problem, we were created in such a way that we are highly attracted to each other in spite of all the crap we both have going on.

Question: What does that tell us?

Answer: We have to figure out a way to blend our faults, differences, and contrasts into something that works. No, not just works, but "works beautifully." We want a "great" marriage not just one that survives.

FACTOID – A great marriage begins with two people of the opposite sex, usually with opposite interests, different personalities, and various degrees of emotional baggage. Watching them work thru all that over time is like sweet & sour sauce, the blend creates something better.

> *"She's got gaps and I got gaps, together we fill gaps."*
> Rocky Balboa from the 1976 movie *Rocky*

26

For the automobile enthusiasts let's use a car illustration. There is a difference between a big pile of auto parts and the car itself. That difference takes a pile of parts that can do nothing and changes them into a marvelous machine that is capable of transporting people from one place to another. When the car is assembled it has power and it has a much greater purpose than the individual parts.

Similarly, when a man and woman get married they have the opportunity to create something far superior than each other as individuals. The marriage they create can achieve a greater function and greater purpose than the sum of their own identities. Many couples start out shaping themselves into a completed car but stop at some point in the process. The result almost looks like a marriage, but it is non-functioning. If we convert the automobile illustration back to our house-building theme, it's like the materials show up on the job site, but no one takes them and builds them into the house.

I deduced that my wife had to be an intelligent woman. After all she married me when other women decided to pass. Paige regularly demonstrates how smart she is, not only in her work but in our marriage. For instance, when I got on a high horse and told her that she was *"a pain in the ass,"* she came back with, *"If I'm the pain, what does that make you?"* My feeble brain had to chew on this. If she's the pain, I must be the...er...ah...ass??? A smart woman can put you in your place anytime she wants.

Unrealistic Expectations

Most of the time, we tell people to aim high, to set the bar high and strive for high achievement. But when it comes to relationships, and more specifically the first few years of marriage, we think the initial expectation level should be a little "muted" while marriage maturity is developed. Couples need time to mature together and that usually occurs at different rates, which requires that allowances be made in goals. A house is not built overnight, a baby takes time to mature, and great marriages take time too. Let the early years be a period of learning and discovery, as you'll be in marriage school for a long, long time.

Kellie, an old boss of mine, use to say, *"Ya know how ya get 10 years experience? With 10 years."* There is no way to get 10, 20, 30 years' worth of marriage maturity unless you put in 10, 20, 30 years. Do not expect it to change overnight, just enjoy that it will get better over time.

It gives you something to look forward to as you grow and make it better each year.

FACTOID – Great marriages do not happen overnight. It is unrealistic to expect instant change; it occurs gradually over a period of weeks, months, and years.

If you "expect" your spouse will always open the door for you, or will always pick up after themselves, or never decline your sexual advances, well you're going to be disappointed. You've set the bar too high too soon.

If you expect that after your spouse reads this book or gets counseling that the heavens will part, the angels will sing. and your spouse will be magically converted into the perfect man or woman, then you're going to be disappointed. It's also clear we didn't get thru to you a couple of pages back, when we wrote *"focus on you"* not your spouse. If you are both willing, you'll make adjustments to yourselves and the many ways you interact with each other. Over time, you will have the marriage you desire.

For the sake of the artists among us, let's use an analogy. Consider yourselves lumps of clay, but your desire is to be formed into something beautiful. Even if your union as husband and wife looks nothing like a marriage now, if you let the master potter work with you, you can be shaped into something great. How quickly the work is completed has a lot to do with how much you are willing to conform to the master potter's hands. You've got lumps, your spouse has lumps, and they need to be kneaded out. The different clays are blended and molded together, shaped, and eventually each ball of clay is molded into one, perfect for the intended use. You'll learn more about becoming one in chapter 21.

> *"I've known no greater joy than to be in a loving happy marriage, and I've witnessed no greater marriage misery than two people living in a bad one."*

There are many good "tools" to start you off in the early years of marriage; they are a must. However, you'll not have the luxury of being "an old salty sailor" until you have put in the time. A salty sailor will try to avoid troubles on any given voyage. But with every storm, every breakdown, every injury, these events build and reveal the character of the sailor. With these trials comes the experience that everyone else looks up to.

Pretty soon, the salty sailor is not threatened by storms, he knows what to expect, and what to do to keep the ship safe.

We are not saying you have to embrace storms in your marriage, we are saying the more of them you work thru and the quicker you get thru them, the less threatening new storms will be. Instead of launching a rowboat to abandon ship *(or abandoning the marriage),* you'll confidently work thru the trials to come out victorious on the other side.

FACTOID – Trials and storms can work to make your marriage stronger. You don't have to enjoy them, but if you're willing your marriage can grow stronger as a result. Trials reveal our true character.

Bob told me a story of when he worked with his dad. Bob's dad gave him some wise advice when he was supervising construction crews. He said, *"Bob, would you rather hire ten carpenters who think, or ten carpenters who do not think but just do everything you say?"* Well, the answer seemed very obvious to Bob who responded: *"I'd hire the ten who think!"*

"OK" he said, *"you've hired ten carpenters that have demonstrated they are good at what they do, they have a set of plans, <u>let them do their job</u>. They may do it differently than you, but the house will look the same when they are done."* Bob's dad was right. As a superintendent Bob was too focused on "his" way, but there are more ways than just his way. Understand Bob truly felt his way was the best way, but that can be irrelevant when dealing with people. People, like our spouses, have feelings. They want to be trusted and have the sense that they are contributing and that their opinion matters.

Maybe you're like Bob and would say, *"Yes, Dad, but my way is best!"* On several occasions where they were framing up identical sections of a duplex, Bob's way of building indeed demonstrated a higher efficiency resulting in completion of the tasks sooner. That was relevant, but it was less relevant than <u>fostering respect</u> for the experience the tradesmen brought to the table. Obviously being competitive and getting tasks done faster was part of the goal, but not at the expense of <u>mutual respect</u>. The point here is to <u>have respect for your spouse's way of doing things</u> as long as it is not damaging or threatening to your marriage union. If he or she is a little messier, but otherwise relatively clean, it's OK, relax, enjoy the differences and contrasts between you rather than fight about them. Let them be a source of humor rather than contention.

5 Respect – *granting consideration for ability, wisdom, character, experience, a courtesy, an expression of value. When given, it is a positive affirmation of a person. To hold regard for, to value or show favor, an acknowledgement of acceptance or right.*

FACTOID – Respect does not require you to agree with each other; it does however, require that you treat each other nicely when you do disagree.

Disagreements are often just related to our unique perspective. Remember when we had you face each other in chapter 1 during the SAFE TIME topic to determine which was the left side? Just different perspectives! If I held up a dollar bill between you and I had each of you individually describe what you see, one of you would be looking at one side of the dollar bill and the other would be looking at the other side. Again, different perspectives but the same dollar bill. Often, all that is required to be in agreement is for one of you to make a little effort to move around and take a look from your spouse's point of view.

Couple's project—Each spouse turn to the other and say out loud, *"I'm part of the problem."* Ladies first, then the guys.

FACTOID – How is a great marriage built? It starts out needing lots of time and it's finished having demonstrated it stood the test of time.

> *"Every marriage is entitled to just one divorce, so the best marriages start with divorce. Each spouse will divorce themselves from all the selfish things that might later interfere with the couple's relationship. Once you get divorce in the proper order, your marriage has to last."*

Did you learn anything? Yes / No
Chapter personal benefit appraisal: **HER 1-2-3-4-5   HIM 1-2-3-4-5**
1=not at all, 2=a little, 3=some good stuff, 4=fairly helpful, 5=very helpful

www.u-build.com

30

CHAPTER 6

The Essentials of Every House; Get the Lay of the Land Before You Start to Build

To support the building structure and help the home stand against the elements, every house needs a solid foundation. The foundation is the most solid portion of the home; it has the strength to support everything that rests upon it. Without a solid foundation the walls have nothing firm to rest upon and they will easily give way to the elements, allowing the house to collapse. The same concept is required in a good marriage; it must be based on a solid foundation, something that will stand the test of time and all the trials thrown at it.

> In her first year of marriage Wanda shouted to her psychologist; *"My husband drives me crazy,"* to which the psychologist replied, *"Great!"* and sat silently as if waiting for Wanda to say more. The silence continued for several moments while Wanda alternated her gaze from the floor to the counselor's eyes. It was then that she began to understand, "crazy" is a part of love. We move back and forth from *"crazy in love"* to *"crazy I wanna kill you."* She then broke the silence and asked, *"This is love isn't it?"* To which the therapist responded, *"Yes. That will be sixty dollars if there's nothing else?"*

In chapter 7 that follows, we are going to review various designs for your marriage, but it is essential to understand that the type of ground you are going to build your house (marriage) on may determine and perhaps alter the basic building plan. The characteristics of the building lot will determine part of the requirements for the foundation.

The builder must consider: Is the lot sloping or flat? Are there trees, boulders, pits in the way, or was it an old dump site? Will the home rest on sand, gravel, solid rock, clay, or peat? Does it have a high water table? Are other buildings already on the lot? Has the building lot been surveyed so you are sure your home is built on your land? All of these factors are potential obstacles to building the new house.

OK, so you ask how this relates to your marriage. There are two simple points to understand:

31

First is that you and your spouse bring both desirable and undesirable things to the marriage that should be considered prior to building your marriage. Was one of you sexually abused? Was one of you physically abused? Did you come from a family that did not express love? Was one of your parents controlling? If this is your 2nd, 3rd, or 4th marriage, what "baggage" are you carrying that has never been dealt with? Compulsions, addictions, bad habits, dependencies? Are there going to be children in the house from a previous marriage? Are there mental or physical problems? **Second,** do you have the same moral code that forms the basis for your marriage?

Crap!

We <u>all</u> have crap in our lives, but it's best to consider how we are going to handle the crap prior to getting married, and if you're already married but have not dealt with the crap, you've noticed the smell has yet to go away. Some individuals have become so accustomed to the crap in their life, they consider it normal and may not even smell the stench or perceive there is a pile. Thus, there is a real need to discuss these things openly and fairly. Just because we have crap doesn't mean we are saying we should accept it. Crap is crap and both spouses should work to get rid of it rather than make it an integral part of their marriage.

You already know Paige and I are the products of parents who have a combined 14 marriages between them; we obviously had crap we had to deal with. Let me add a few details about my growing up and thus the resulting mayhem I brought into our marriage.

For most of her life my mom was addicted to prescription drugs and alcohol. She tried to commit suicide at least three times. I was given to my grandparents at age 11 after flunking 5th grade. Later after her third divorce and when I was about 13, I was allowed to move back in with my mom; however, just two years later I was kicked out of the house and kicked out of school at age 16. I didn't meet my real dad until I was 14 and he lived 1900 miles away.

My dad has a philosophy about love. Even today, occasionally when I talk to my dad he'll repeat to me that he doesn't think "love" should be part of a relationship. He says he prefers to say "I like you a lot." My dad's belief system is based on humanism and he says it's quite unnatural for people to remain married or monogamous. In explaining his rationale a bit more to the point, he says, "What drives men is the thing hanging between their legs." In different words, I've told my daughter just about the same thing.

While my mom has passed on, I do not ever recall talking to her about any of her marriages. Not long after I was kicked out of the house my mom quit talking to me and my grandma; this lasted for approximately 20 years. My mom believed in love, but she also used it like an on-off switch. She used love as a weapon, cutting love off when it suited her. Truthfully, my mom was a bitter person. I'm not sure why but based on her actions toward us, it appeared she always felt we were letting her down. My mom believed in God, but she didn't practice her faith. Like so many who say they believe in God, words rarely lined up with actions. My mom's second marriage lasted less than three months.

Shortly after I married Paige, I drove my new bride 1900 miles across the U.S. to introduce her to my mom. I called my mom when we arrived but my mom said she was too busy to meet us; she had shopping to do. It would be many years before my mom and Paige would meet and it only happened one time.

I want to let everyone know that I love and respect both my mom and my dad. Dad and I both have the curse of speaking perhaps too bluntly, but my dad taught me many valuable things as a young man, and I would not be where I am today without my dad's help. Yet, we differ 180 degrees on not only love and marriage, but also in other areas.

My mom could have given us kids up for adoption—she could have made her life much easier by getting rid of us. Indeed by the time she was 24, she had three young kids and was without a husband, had no job, and not much of a welfare program in those days (1961). While my grandparents helped out some, we were on state aid and food stamps in the years that would follow, except for those periods when she was remarried. There is a lot more I could go into, but won't at this time.

Do you think I came into marriage with a balanced marital or family outlook? Hell no! I had more than my fair share of crap I needed to deal with, and Paige brought her own dysfunctions to our new marriage. You may have begun your adult life with as much or more of a troubled upbringing. A difficult childhood can certainly bring challenges to a new marriage. That is why we are espousing that on your own or with a counselor or mentor couple, you and your spouse discuss the various land mines of crap that if not dealt with could one day explode. The sooner you deal with the crap in your life to get rid of it, the better your marriage will be.

FACTOID – If you do not deal with the crap, don't be surprised that while you've left it alone in its own little room, the smell alerts everyone around you that your house is not clean.

We all have some of those annoying little quirks, those things we learn to live with in a marriage, but then there are those more serious items that shouldn't or can't be ignored. These have to be dealt with. Some of the crap can be based on cultural or regional upbringing.

Moral Principles

Perhaps more challenging is the fact that people get married for different reasons; sadly some couples never discuss why they want to marry. Is it a correct assumption to think everyone marries for love? For some, being married is a means to obtaining tax breaks or legal citizenship and has nothing to do with love or commitment. Maybe some are marrying for money? Others might marry for security believing love is not a requirement. In some cultures marriages are arranged by the parents and do not begin with nor may ever contain "love." In yet other cultures women are sold to men. Perhaps you are merely seeking a spouse to procreate your gene pool?

How about an evolutionary humanist getting married to a born-again Christian? They have nothing in common regarding their moral compass, but are hoping to survive on love. What if a person's belief system is that women are always to be subordinate to the male? Some cultures hold certain animals in high esteem; they will not so much as slap the butt of a cow, but may be willing to beat a spouse or child for the slightest reason. Should you know what your husband thinks about polygamy before or after you marry him?

Your moral code (or the lack of one) forms the basis for everything you do in life. You may violate your moral code, but when you do so, you are forced to admit the error was with you, not your code. Not only do you get to judge your own actions against your moral code when you violate it, but so do those around you, which is important because others can help keep you true to your code. But when your foundational belief system or moral code is vastly different than that of your spouse, it's like building on two different types of soil. It is possible but it is often very difficult to accomplish. In addition it will present more trials, more tears, more arguments, and can result in more unresolved marital and family issues. Hopefully, you're getting an idea of what we mean by *"getting an understanding of the lay of the land."*

When couples with different moral codes disagree, who is to say which opinion or activity is more correct or more valuable than the other? And when disagreements are settled in a compromise, it is often far less satisfying to both parties. But if you enter into marriage with the same moral code you both measure your own actions and the actions of your spouse against that common code, and it becomes the plumb line to ensure you're building the home correctly. Our moral code is the biblically based Christian standard for our marriage. It serves to direct how our marriage will function, the things that are acceptable and that are not. Paige and I know that infidelity is wrong, we know that lashing out is wrong, we know that hitting one another is wrong, we know we must serve one another, that we must honor and respect one another because our biblically based moral code directs us that way.

> *"Let us with caution indulge the supposition that morality can be maintained without religion. Reason and experience both forbid us to expect that national morality can prevail in exclusion of religious principle."* George Washington

George Washington's comment is relevant from the perspective that he expresses a nation's morality will not survive without (religious) principles and our point is we have found that marriages must also be based on a moral code or moral principles to survive.

Nothing is impossible; we firmly believe nearly every marriage can become great. If you are already married to someone with a different moral code, it doesn't mean your marriage is doomed for failure or the repairs needed are insurmountable.

If you are not yet "a couple," ask yourself these important questions: Does your purpose for marriage, core principles, and belief system agree and how are you going to deal with any differences? Where does "your" moral code come from? Is it biblically based? Is it Eastern mysticism? Is it astrology? Muslim or Hindu based? From whence does your guidance come when you need to settle differences? What and who holds you accountable? What plumb line keeps the building true?

6

Straight up, for some of you, getting married is perhaps something you should not do or should not have done. If you use love to manipulate or as a weapon, or your core belief is that man is driven to mate and procreate with many females then perhaps marriage should be avoided. Ask yourselves, are these ideals and principles where you want to build, will they support your marriage? You must survey the land and build on ground that will support the marriage you're seeking to build.

While we have a strong conviction, we are not writing to debate the validity of one philosophy or creed in this handbook, but it is essential that you and your spouse have this discussion. If you have not yet tied the knot and your man says: *"This is me, take it or leave it,"* or your woman says: *"This is me, take it or leave it,"* then we'd suggest leave it. A person not willing to improve and/or negotiate in a marriage relationship is setting a course for a very troubled union. Better to say "no" in one minute, than cry "oh no" for the years to come.

However, for those of you who are married, but now find yourselves with vastly different foundational belief systems, we are not advocating divorce. Rather we'd advise you to take stock of what you do have in common, and work with that. There are going to be compromises and dealing with these types of foundational differences will require tact, humility, grace, forgiveness, and more. Apply what you'll learn in this handbook.

We address this topic because we have shared the tears and pains of couples who did not have the same foundational moral compass, and while this seems not to be a big deal in the lovey-dovey dating stage, it will hit like a speeding truck later. We readily admit we are not qualified to offer marriage advice for a different faith or moral code than a biblically based standard. If you're a Buddhist, or atheist, you might find some of the advice in this book obnoxious, but aside from moral code differences our handbook is still filled with great advice. If you only gain 10% improvement, that's still improvement!

So what does it take to build a great marriage?

Did you learn anything? Yes / No
Chapter personal benefit appraisal: **HER 1-2-3-4-5   HIM 1-2-3-4-5**
1=not at all, 2=a little, 3=some good stuff, 4=fairly helpful, 5=very helpful

www.u-build.com

36

The Five W's of Building Your Marriage

CHAPTER 7

Where Is Your Plan?

Every house is built using a blueprint or plan of what the house will look like. If you hire a contractor, one of the first things you'll be discussing is the design of the house. Will it be two stories or one, with or without a basement, how many bedrooms, etc. The builder cannot begin any work without the plan.

> *Have you ever heard of the "mad dash?" "I'll love you forever." — "I want a divorce." It's that "dash" in between that every couple should avoid, it comes just before divorce and my observations indicate you either get mad or go mad at that juncture.*

One of the saddest statements ever spoken to me was by a spouse who many years into his marriage said, *"The morning after my honeymoon I knew I had made a mistake."* WOW, can two people, after months of courtship and claiming to be deeply in love, really get married and still not know each other? YES! When a couple is courting one another they only see what the other wants them to see. Best behavior, normal behavior, or worst behavior, which do you think people who are dating show each other? I never passed gas once in front of Paige until "after" we were married. Since then I haven't stopped!

Did you get married with little thought for what might occur in the years after the wedding day? *(This is where you say "yes.")*

What? You got married without a plan for what your marriage was going to look like!!! Tell me it ain't so!

Well then, did your marriage plan include a future date for a divorce? No? But divorce occurs in about half of all marriages, if divorce is not in anyone's plans, why does it occur? Could it be that not planning for the success of the marriage results in divorce?

OK, the truth is no one gets married having created an official plan for the years that will come after their wedding day. Writing out an actual marriage plan is perhaps a bit too anal, but every couple should have solidly discussed their ideas of what they want the marriage to look like as it matures. Yet some couples get married based solely on their feelings with no thought of what comes after the wedding day. They think of the wedding day as the end goal, when it's rather just the beginning.

You've probably heard someone say, *"It feels right, we're in love, and that's all we need."* First off, love is not a feeling, and second it's only one of many components that are needed in a well built marriage. Love is a great and important virtue. But consider that two months after you're married your husband may love fishing more than you.

Frequently, prospective home owners will only have a vague idea or a basic sketch of the custom home they desire. The designer or architect will take the concept and develop it into the final design. A designer helps the couple's ideas take shape while guiding them thru the maze of constraints. The designer or architect will show them what will work and will not, incorporating the requirements of the building codes and making changes as needed. Likewise, when we go to build or remodel our marriage, it is wise to get help in the design phase so the marriage turns out as intended. A lot of people call this "premarital counseling."

Billy Joel did an interview with Chuck Klosterman in 2002, in which Billy expressed deep regret for not being able to sustain a lasting, loving relationship. He summed up his feelings by saying he desired to love and be loved, while noting notoriety and fame provided no comfort. It was a very touching self-appraisal. Billy's feelings are not unique; many people deeply desire the same thing.

A sad fact is some couples will spend hundreds of hours planning their wedding and thousands of dollars for all the trimmings for the ceremony and reception, while having spent no time or money on resources that would help make their marriage a lasting one. Is it wiser to have spent $1,000 on a wedding or on counseling to prepare each spouse for how to be married? Consider that the statistics show one divorce for every two marriages, where does the need appear to be?

Let's talk about a few designs for marriage. The designs we will consider will include some aspects of nonreligious and religious themes. For most Americans, marriage vows occur in a religious ceremony, and typically in a church, synagogue, or temple. According to poll results (details in chapter 20) approximately 92% of Americans say they believe in God or a higher power, and roughly 80% claim adherence to the Christian faith, so it should not seem irrational that we communicate more purposefully to the largest audience of which we are apart. Please bear with us if some portions of the following doesn't apply to you; we respect your beliefs even though they may differ. Take solace in this, we will spank those of us who profess a Christian faith but do not live up to the faith we espouse. We do this because the facts are, people of faith have divorce rates roughly equal to those who profess no faith, and yet the God of the Jewish and Christian faiths clearly does not approve of divorce. The problem is not with the standard, it's with the people pretending to follow it.

Relationships Leading to Marriage

We will begin with a quick review of the relationship options you've passed through, choosing instead to move beyond them and to be married. Being single, dating, going steady and living together are often precursors to marriage. So let's briefly examine each.

Being single—is very likely something you decided was "just not for you." The vast majority of people find they need the company of a life-long companion. You have apparently decided you want to be married or you would not be reading a book on marriage. The neat thing about being single is that you do not have to answer to anyone; the bad part about being single is that you do not have to answer to anyone.

Dating—as a "life-long" relationship endeavor may work for a few playboy types but for the vast majority of us who desire a meaningful relationship, we just don't find this "deep" enough. Dating means no commitment as either party can date other people. There are no bonds or strings demanding that the relationship continue.

Going steady—is often the prelude to marriage. It is a slightly greater commitment than dating. Going steady means you will not date other people, but the relationship still needs to mature to see if a greater commitment is what both parties want. The relationship can still be called off if either party decides they want out. Going steady is like a Post-it, it sticks, but the glue is still very temporary.

Living together—is a form of going steady, but with a sharing of the resources like home, toys, and some finances. Many men like the living together arrangement because it usually includes sex as part of the no-commitment arrangement. Some couples feel living together is a pre-test to see if they can thrive together in a close relationship. Living together is, however, still short of a perpetual and lasting commitment as either party may depart without cause. Some states recognize a couple as married by "common-law" if they have lived together for a specific amount of time.

More often living together is an illusion of commitment.

Engaged—in this arrangement there is a non-binding commitment to get married. It is temporary but with the promise of one day making it official. Engaged couples start showing more of their personal side and become slightly more vulnerable to one another. Being engaged is like duct tape, it offers a pretty strong bond but can still be removed if need be.

> *"It is perhaps a gloomy statistic that 95% of us who live in this world will not achieve great wealth, we do not own a mansion nor a castle, we may never be able to buy a Ferrari, a Lear jet, or a 200' yacht, yet this seemingly disadvantaged group of people have everything needed to obtain the joy that comes with a great marriage. Sadly many choose not to."*

In discussing all of the above relationship dynamics, we find them all lacking the binding and lasting characteristics of commitment and that is where marriage comes into play. Marriage carries contractual and, for people of faith, spiritual requirements. "Marriage," by design is supposed to be an everlasting commitment. But marriage is still not that clear cut, so let's look at some contrasting designs of marriage.

Marriage Designs

(a) You can see your marriage as a partnership.
Partnerships are based on contracts that have rules that are supposed to benefit and protect each person. Although this sounds nice, for most people in partnerships they are thinking about the benefits and not the liabilities. There is this natural tendency to expect all the benefits but not to assume the liabilities. Even in business relationships, partnerships are often troubled, with neither party really content in the arrangement.

Equal partnerships are said to be 50/50 and some marriage counselors have espoused this kind of marriage arrangement. Yet a 50/50 marriage means the two people are still behaving as individuals 50% of the time, and only operating as a partnership the remaining 50% of the time. If we examine this closer, it means that 50% of each spouse can be doing whatever they choose outside of the marriage relationship. A spouse in this type of relationship might respond with a statement such as: "This is my time; I get to do what I want." This arrangement implies that you each have activities or relationships that are personal and off limits to the marriage relationship. It's like each spouse has two worlds they pop in and out of, their married life and their personal life. To see if you're living under a partnership type of marriage you can look for certain signs, i.e., one partner insisting on handling all the money, Friday night out with the guys or girls, keeping your incomes separate, vacationing separately, having separate checking accounts, having separate passwords and user IDs, and so on.

FACTOID – Marriage is not taking two people and bringing them together under a part-time partnership agreement. <u>50/50 will rarely work in a forever marriage. A marriage has to be 100/100.</u>

A 50/50 marriage is unacceptable in our view. It's too easy for the 50% that is outside of the marriage, doing its own thing, to screw things up for the marriage. This means one or both of you will eventually put personal desires or goals ahead of, or equal to, the commitment to your spouse. It's also far too easy for a spouse in a 50/50 marriage to claim they are doing more than their fair share and then to blame the other spouse. A 50/50 marriage is really only a partial commitment. For a marriage to survive both parties must be fully committed to it all of the time.

> *Be tolerant of the human race. Your whole family belongs to it—and some of your spouse's family does too.* Author Unknown

(b) You can get married to fill a void in your life.
How many have heard someone say *"You complete me"*? How about *"I've found my soul mate."* These are very romantic sayings and my wife and I have uttered these same words to each other. We even sign *(converting words into hand gestures)* this to each other in a room with other people. Indeed Paige and I are lovers, we are best friends, and we are confidantes. Over the years that we have been working on our marriage we truly fit like a glove on a hand. Yet, no matter how romantic *"filling a void in your life"* sounds, we both believe that marrying a person to fill an emptiness in your life may be misguided. Why? In examining our own lives, we have determined that there seems to be two relationship voids built into each of us, one spiritual, and one physical/emotional.

The physical/emotional void—It is indeed the void that calls out for a lifelong spouse. This is not lust, but it frequently starts out that way for men. In this void, it is a desire to have a life-long companion who will be with you to share your tears, your joys, and keep you warm on a cold day.

It's someone to come home to. It's to love and be loved, it's not eating alone, and it's sharing movies and more. It doesn't matter whether your beliefs are evolutionary or biblically based the need for a male and female to join in a union fulfills the purpose of procreation.

The spiritual void—It is a void built into us that no man or woman can fill; a yearning to be connected to the spiritual aspect of our existence. For people of faith we will satisfy this in a relationship with God, for those who don't believe in God, they may seek to understand their existence in natural means, but in either case the drive to connect with creation or our Creator is present. From an individual or couple perspective we believe this is a void only a relationship with God can fill. To put a spouse into the spiritual void slot and expect they can fill a void meant for God is an effort in futility. This longing or yearning is persistent and rarely satisfied by other means. Some people try to appease this spiritual yearning in various ways, believing a marriage, a baby, a new home, traveling the world, or some other new venture will satisfy the craving. But it is our experience and that of millions of others that this void cannot be satisfied by any earthly relationship or endeavor.

If I'm building a home and I'm framing up the wall and I ask for more 2x6 studs and someone brings me floor joists, is that going to work? Heck, no! Recognizing which void is lacking is very important to satisfying it. If you're married and you now find yourself with the same lonely feeling that you had before you got married, you might still need to address that spiritual void. Don't blame your spouse because you feel something is still missing. It may not be that you're missing something in your marriage; it may be you're missing something in your soul. Filling that spiritual void is something only you and your Creator can take care of.

FACTOID – Generally, people have two voids that need filling in their life, one is spiritual and calls out for a relationship with God, the other is physical/emotional and cries out for a relationship with a life-long spouse.

This leads us into our next point. Perhaps just as disappointing as looking in the wrong place to fill the soul void is to only give your faith lip service. OK, it's time we add some real clarity. The divorce rate for people who believe in God is roughly the same as people who do not. Roughly one in two marriages will fail whether the couple believes in God or not. The evidence clearly establishes that merely espousing a belief in God makes no difference in the success of a marriage; however, you'll learn in chapters 19 and 20 there is a hugely dramatic improvement in the longevity of the marriage when the couple's dedication to their belief is factored in.

(c) You can get married believing you are good, stable, and caring people and you both are of the same faith and moral code, what could go wrong? But a good portion of these marriages fail because one or both spouses have disregarded the many warnings about outside influences, which we will collectively call "the enemy." Any worthwhile venture has to consider various aspects of "risk management," and marriage is no exception.

Are you naive enough to think there are no outside influences or temptations that would seek to destroy your marriage? We will go into more detail in later chapters, but in basic terms what risk management means is you have to pre-decide and have already determined what your actions will or will not be when faced with certain temptations. Think of it like a great playbook for a football team, the team has already planned its offensive game plan, but it also has a bunch of defensive plays based on whatever the opposing team throws at it. Married couples who fail to understand the need for a strong defense are destined to encounter far more marriage trials and storms.

(d) You can get married and be <u>willing to give up all that you are</u> to create something different. This point seems to fly right over the heads of couples in the vast majority of troubled marriages because many of their difficulties are based on a "self" or "me" marriage mentality. Yes, you were once single, but you are no longer single after you marry, so why hang onto any part of your singleness? Marriage is different and different is what you were seeking, i.e., to no longer to be single. In the Bible it says when the two become married they become "as one." In a nutshell, the goal is to lose yourself in your marriage. "You" as an individual fades away, and "you" as a couple comes into focus.

Using a parable, a marriage should be viewed as the two of you getting into a small boat together and being carried out into the middle of the ocean and left there. The "ocean of life" is vast and filled with uncertainty from one day to the next. There will be calm days, rainy days, sharks swimming around you, and some violent stormy days, but because you have committed to and really need each other, you will both work together to keep your boat (marriage) afloat. In this castaway scenario, both people are always working for the good of each other, both are responsible for the care of each other; it's an "always on" or 100/100 effort.

OK, with all that said, what plan did Paige and I use? It was pretty simple:
- Let's get married and see what happens.
- We wanted to be forever in love, but had no idea how to achieve it.
- However, we did receive some premarital counseling from my wife's pastor. We also jointly agreed to adhere to the same biblically based model and moral code for our marriage. Thus, we always had a reference standard to go back to.

When a builder goes to build the house, he and all of the subcontractors and suppliers focus on the task of building. Are you focused on building your marriage? What is your goal for marriage? Is it to have a great one, or to preserve your own identity? Are you afraid to put all you are into it? Are you prepared to do whatever it takes to get the job done? How committed are you? Are you "united" in effort?

This message is a simple one. **"The two become one."** You both have to make that choice. Becoming one means *"no cutting each other down anymore."* No stabs, no jabs, no condemnation, just encouragement and support. Your marriage should be a reflection of both of you acting as a single unit promoting and caring for the unit over your own desires and needs.

Couple's project—Husbands and wives please take a few minutes to discuss what you want your marriage plan to be. If you have significant differences discuss how you can work thru those differences. Some examples of long-term plans could be to remain married, to feel secure in the marriage, to feel loved and respected. All of these are great goals. As we progress through the handbook we help you understand that whatever your plans are, it will take effort to accomplish them.

For instance, so you want to feel secure in your marriage, how will you accomplish that? What materials, tools, and support are needed to accomplish your plans? Don't set anything in concrete until you get through the entire handbook.

Did you learn anything? Yes / No
Chapter personal benefit appraisal: **HER 1-2-3-4-5   HIM 1-2-3-4-5**
1=not at all, 2=a little, 3=some good stuff, 4=fairly helpful, 5=very helpful

CHAPTER 8

What Materials Are Needed?

A home is built using many differing materials. There is concrete, rebar, nails, wood studs, plywood, sheetrock, carpeting, locks, trim, plumbing, wiring, roofing, and much more. Materials are the substance that makes the house, or in this case the marriage, take shape. They are the things that people see when they look at your home or your marriage, the things they talk about when you're not around.

> The question is this: *What if **you** really did make your spouse and your marriage the priority?*

Whether you're building your home or your marriage you already understand there are good materials and materials of poor quality. In this chapter we'll list the good materials for you to consider building into your marriage. You will notice that many of these are considered "virtues" and thus also establish a person's character.

FACTOID – "We are what we eat," and likewise our marriage is equal to what we put into it, no less and no more.

Good marriage building materials:
- Forgiving
- Moral convictions/standards/religious convictions
- Servant attitude/willing to be helpful
- Generous/unselfish
- Sacrificial
- Healthy self-esteem
- Apologetic
- Good work ethic
- Optimistic/hopeful
- Encourager
- Dependable/reliable
- Satisfied/content
- Healthy
- Friendly
- Occasionally naughty/sexy
- Loving

- Curiosity, the healthy type
- Calm/gentle
- Caring
- Trust builder/trustworthy
- Desire to learn, grow, mature
- Flexible/easygoing
- Humility
- Integrity
- Decisive
- Nurturing/protective/supportive
- Respectful/polite
- Open/straight forward
- Thankful/grateful
- Balanced
- Faithful
- Strong
- Courage/bravery
- Visionary/goals/aspirations
- Loyal
- Self-controlled/self-disciplined
- Reflective
- Ability to listen
- Efficient/not wasteful
- Considerate
- Responsible
- Initiative
- Truthful
- Innocence
- Patient
- Sensitive
- Compassionate
- Honorable
- Humor
- Leadership
- Kindness

Make an effort to build your marriage from the materials in the list you've just reviewed. All of these are good materials; they are high quality, and using these materials will strengthen your marriage. You build these into your marriage by practicing them in your own life and as you relate to each other. The more you use these materials the more visible they become in and outside of your marriage. Just as 2x6 boards frame a house and give it shape and strength, the various materials listed have qualities that give strength to your marriage. Each item builds greater strength and greater function into your marriage.

> While attending a marriage seminar on communication, John and his wife listened to the instructor declare, *"It is essential that husbands and wives know the things that are important to each other."* He addressed the husband: *"Can you describe your wife's favorite flower?"* John leaned over, touching his wife's arm and asked, *"Gold Medal All-Purpose, isn't it?"*   Unknown

Obviously we could go into a lot of detail about each of the materials mentioned, discussing their properties and why they are good personal traits as well as how they benefit the marriage. We believe you, our readers, are smart enough to know these are good materials and, in an effort to reduce the overall length of our handbook, we have decided to let you discuss the benefits of each material between yourselves. We all are lacking in various areas of these materials, but we should make an effort to incorporate them into our lives. These are the good materials to build into a marriage. For instance, if one or both of you is not very forgiving, you can work at being more forgiving and thus build it into your marriage relationship.

Couple's project—Discuss each of the building materials listed on the previous page and relate to each other how important they are in building your marriage. If one or the other spouse feels a material is lacking, then discuss how you can both work at including it in your marriage in the future. You might want to circle the materials you feel you are building into your marriage and then place a star beside the materials you'd like to build more into your marriage.

Did you learn anything? Yes / No
Chapter personal benefit appraisal: **HER 1-2-3-4-5   HIM 1-2-3-4-5**
1=not at all, 2=a little, 3=some good stuff, 4=fairly helpful, 5=very helpful

> *"If you ever said "she drives me crazy" when you were dating, do not be surprised when that continues after you're married."*

CHAPTER 9

Who Is Helping Your Marriage Grow?

Couple's project—We are going to start this lesson with a confession — Turn and say to each other *"I need help."* Husbands, please resist the temptation to say, *"Yea I know!"* after your wife utters those words.

We hope you were able to admit that you need help. We'd be the first to call out anyone who is so prideful as to deny it. They are at best blind to their own failings and at worst, a liar. **WE ALL NEED HELP.** Some more frequently than others, some more intensely, but we all need help. Get over it, it's a good thing. Ever try to take on a football team by yourself? How'd that work out for ya? The concept of a team should not be underestimated when it comes to keeping your marriage healthy and vibrant.

> *"I have a 60 lb. mostly muscle-weight advantage on my wife. I can tame a 1,400 pound horse, push a 6,000 pound car, but my wife can make me act in ways that neither friend nor enemy would have thought possible. Her power over me is intoxicating and she'll use her "wares" to turn me in any direction she wishes."*

To build or remodel a home, a team of supporting people is needed to get the house to completion. We have designers, building inspectors, and sub-contractors consisting of excavation crew, foundation crew, concrete finishers, framers, roofers, siding crew, sheet-rockers, painters, cabinetry crews, plumbers, and electricians. OK, you get the idea. It takes a lot of people to get a home built, or to remodel a home, but when we ask the typical married couple in crisis who is helping them to build or rebuild their relationship the answer is often silence.

At best one or both of them is "whining" with some friend, family member, or coworker about how rotten it is. That's rarely going to help even though it might feel good to snivel about it. We are not saying that "talking" *(rather than whining, gossiping, etc.)* is bad, indeed you should speak with supporting people. That is our point; they should be people who are going to help you, who will challenge your positions and help you repair the things that you can fix. If you're talking to a coworker who has several divorces behind him or her, well that's like asking the fox where to hide the chickens.

9

You'll be getting advice, but it may not be good advice.

FACTOID – If you can name one person who never needed help, you'd have to name a person that didn't have parents, never went to school, never read a book, and never got sick. The logic is self-evident, we all need help.

Let's use a baseball team as an example this time. Pretend you and your spouse are standing on the opposing team's field facing a fired-up lineup who wants to crush you. Wouldn't you, as a wise coach, seek to build up your team with some solid heavy hitters? Wouldn't you bring in some trainers? Wouldn't you seek to fill your side of the stands with people who would cheer you on and support you? This same principle applies to not only good sports teams, but also good companies, good educational institutions, good leaders, good contractors, and good marriages.

And don't make the mistake of assuming that your leadership quality negates needing help. You can be a leader, but every leader still needs lots of help. Wise managers surround themselves with knowledgeable people who have experience and wisdom. Frankly, only a fool will try to go it alone.

I was a fool when it came to raising our daughter; I didn't seek help. While I wasn't the worst father, I was far from a good one. I should have sought the help and experience of those who could have helped me to understand what it really takes to be a good father. I wrongly thought that just having a father in the home (something I did not have) would be enough. I didn't have anyone who would hold me accountable for being a father. My largest mistake was thinking that working long hours to bring home the most amount of money was the best way to help my family.

My second mistake as a father was not spending a good portion of the free time I did have with my child. I was clueless that I had a problem until it was way bigger than it should have been. It's taken years for my daughter to heal from my mistakes and to forgive me. Learn from my mistakes— get help!

(Paige interjects here) While Bob feels he made child-rearing mistakes, I made my fair share. Frequently I did not take the supportive role of a wife and mom by standing next to my man in agreement, but instead allowed Bob to be the "bad guy." I let him take the fall while I remained silent in many of the decisions about raising our daughter.

Fortunately, kids can be resilient and we lucked out as our now adult daughter loves us in spite of our failures as parents.

> *"Men who have a pierced ear are better prepared for marriage. They've experienced pain and bought jewelry."*
>
> Comedian Rita Rudner

So where can you find support to help you build your marriage?

People:
- Close family members or friends who have 20 years or more of a good marriage
- Marriage counselors from your church
- A mentoring couple who has been happily married for more than 20 years
- For hire one-on-one marriage counselors *(Generic yellow page marriage counselors are a hit and miss situation. If you do decide to use one, do not be discouraged if it doesn't work out the first time. Get referrals from people who can recommend them. Stay away from any marriage counselor who has been divorced unless they have at least 25 years in their 2nd marriage.)*

Other:
- Retreats and conferences that focus on marriage relationships
- Books, tapes, and other instructional materials
- Teaching and/or sermons centered around marriage relationships

Let's put this in the form of an example: If you are constantly working too much and rarely home (a workaholic), who can you depend on to help you understand that work must be less important than your marriage? A couple should have some friends or family that will be candid and who can hold them accountable if they are no longer being open and forthright with each other. If you have no one close that you trust then a mentoring couple or third party counselor is warranted. It is important that whomever you trust in this area of support is permitted to speak frankly with you and you will listen and accept their counsel.

Some couples find a truly great support team in an older "mentoring" couple that they can confide in to help them. It's a great no-cost way to get the extra support your relationship may need, especially if you're not able to really be open with each other. Many older couples would love to be a younger couple's mentor and no special training is involved.

9

Marriage and/or relationship counselors bring an independent and third party perspective when dealing with marital issues. As an example, couples often express money problems as a top trouble spot in their marriage. A good marriage counselor will quickly and confidently help the couple understand that money is not the problem, money <u>management</u> is the real culprit. With that revelation, both spouses can be guided to an understanding of how to manage money.

When it comes to child rearing, a good marriage counselor will explain that there is a fairly wide range of child-rearing techniques available to parents. Often couples will become too narrowly focused on the differences between their individual child-rearing styles while completely oblivious to several other options that may be better than either spouse's ideas.

A good builder would never shortchange learning new building techniques, and neither should you avoid getting other informed opinions on how to improve your marriage.

"After Deb and Jim attended a marriage conference dealing with communication Deb commented that she thought their communication could improve. Jim responded by saying that he totally agreed, she should know he is horny all the time and he shouldn't have to ask for it. Deb has not brought it up since."

The Never-Spoken-about Secret

A guy drives into the auto repair shop and says his car is not working right. It doesn't move forward very well, and it has no reverse. The auto mechanic pulls it in the shop and puts it up on the hoist and immediately finds a large wooden stick driven up thru the transmission oil pan and it appears all the oil has gradually leaked out. The mechanic comes back to the owner and tells him the problem. The transmission needs to be removed and rebuilt. The owner tells the mechanic he doesn't think that is it because it's been at least four weeks since he drove the car into the woods, and it worked fine until just this week; he tells the mechanic it must be something else.

If you are thinking the owner of the car is not dealing with reality, you'd be right. But this example is a set-up to something that comes right back to us. We'll share with you what is never said but frequently true regarding the problems people bring to marriage counselors. This is the

54

dilemma counselors spend the most time dealing with. It can be the most frustrating part of working with couples and their troubles. It is not figuring out what is wrong in a marriage as that is often obvious. It is also not knowing how to fix and remedy those problems either. The dilemma for many marriage counselors <u>is getting one or both spouses to admit they have a problem.</u>

Often marriage counselors must spend several sessions or several hours tiptoeing around the obvious trouble to keep one or both spouses from ending the therapy. Even if you've never been to a counselor you may have heard the well-known TV psychologist Dr. Phil McGraw say "You can't fix what you won't acknowledge." That is a clear confession of the frustration Dr. Phil met with when he was practicing his trade. Obviously, he has not forgotten it. Couples could much more quickly, if not also much more easily, repair their relationship in a few sessions if the counselor didn't have to tiptoe around and slowly spoon feed clients into accepting their role in the problem.

So do yourself a favor, when you go to get counseling, or when you ask a friend for a straight up honest opinion of what might be wrong, be willing to embrace the reality of it and immediately work on the needed changes. The sooner you do, the sooner you'll find peace in that area of trouble.

Couple's project—There is no doubt every couple can benefit from extra help, so now we'd like you to discuss if you should entertain getting some marriage counseling

Did you learn anything? Yes / No
Chapter personal benefit appraisal: **HER 1-2-3-4-5   HIM 1-2-3-4-5**
1=not at all, 2=a little, 3=some good stuff, 4=fairly helpful, 5=very helpful

> *"It's not hard to understand why men are confused. Our women want us to buy them roses, which have thorns that cause us to bleed when we handle them and they only last a couple of weeks. Contrast that with our desire for a new crescent wrench, which is adjustable and lasts forever. Can you see why we men think our ideas are better?"*

www.u-build.com

CHAPTER 10

Which Tools Are Needed?

Tools make it possible to build the house. Without tools the very best we can come up with is perhaps a lean-to. It is with tools that the actual work gets done. We take the plan, the materials, the support help, and use the tools to accomplish the tasks. Without tools we would just have a pile of materials. Contractors will use hammers, saws, nail guns, caulk guns, wrenches, measuring tools, levels, paint rollers, etc., to build a house. Likewise, we have tools that help us build our marriages.

Tools are very important to accomplish each task, but not all tools are used all the time. Some are used just for a short while, and some are used on and off. You will find yourself bringing out the tools listed below as often as you need them in building or remodeling your marriage. Using these tools helps build up your marriage, they also help repair your marriage and the best part, these tools help to get the work done faster. Some of these tools blend with the materials mentioned in chapter 8, and are similar to carpenters using some of the building materials to make a scaffold or concrete forms, thus some tools and materials can become interchangeable.

FACTOID – Every job and all work is easier with the right tools. Marriage is easier when the proper tools are used, too, and it's much harder when you avoid using them.

Tool #1 Touch
Affectionate touching can be things like holding hands, kissing on the lips each day, cuddling while watching TV, sitting next to each other when driving, etc. Touch is one of the most basic of human needs. Touch has

been cited in helping to cure depression, helping hospital patients recover quicker, and we all know it comforts those who are grieving. Touch is sometimes far better than words, a gentle touch can bring calm and reassurance.

When a man lovingly holds his woman it conveys to her that *"it's going to be all right."* She feels secure and can rest in his arms and feel calm in the midst of life's uncertainties. When a woman comes to her man and pulls herself close to him and puts her head into his chest, he feels like he is being supported, that he is being honored, that she understands the dragons he slays each day are for her. He relishes her attention and it builds his strength. Touch is a very good tool to use daily.

Tool #2 Respect & Honor

If I give you a million dollar mansion, if I provide great sex, if I make you laugh, if I do all the other things in a good marriage, but I do not respect or honor you, will you be OK with that?

Let's briefly examine these two terms:

> Respect – *granting consideration for ability, wisdom, character, experience, a courtesy, an expression of value. When given, it is a positive affirmation of a person. To hold regard for, to value or show favor, an acknowledgement of acceptance or right.*

> Honor – *to impart a sense of worth or value or merit or rank above others. To honor imparts an importance above the norm, dignity, distinction, honesty, integrity of noble character.*

It's important that spouses set each other in a place of respect and honor that no other earthly person holds. This isn't about a college degree; it's not about solving the world's problems. You can have a degree or be the president, but if you do not have honor or respect it is meaningless. The lowliest farmhand can have more respect or honor than a president. Honoring and respecting your spouse is a tool in building a great marriage and these qualities must be actively applied.

When husbands and wives honor and respect one another, not only in private, but also amongst other family and friends they elevate their spouse to a position that others envy. Honor and respect your spouse in front of others and they will notice; but more important your spouse will know by your words and actions that they are the main thing in your life.

When a person is treated as valuable, they develop a greater sense of purpose and worth, which gives them confidence they would not have otherwise. When you treat a person as if they have nothing to contribute, you'll get nothing back.

Tool #3 Fight Fair

Disagreements are going to occur, that's true for any relationship. By fighting fair, this tool assures that no fight gets out of hand, there will be no cutting down of the other spouse and no "condemnation type weapons" will be used. When a disagreement comes up, the couple will focus on the topic of the discussion rather than fiery emotion. My mom fought emotionally. She got emotional, and sought emotional damage. Sadly, I'm not sure the reasons for the disagreements or resolutions were anywhere as important to her as inflicting emotional damage in those who opposed her. She used her words with ferocity cutting, slicing, and inflicting injury. To be fair, she could also be very loving too.

Focus on the topic or concern by talking it out, describing it, and discussing the resolutions. If you nurture a *"for the benefit of the marriage union"* solution, you will be using the tool correctly. If no agreement can be reached, perhaps counseling is required.

Here's the deal. There is NO, repeat NO marriage issue that is new to your marriage that many thousands, if not millions, of people have successfully worked thru before. The object is not to defeat each other, but to defeat the problem. As someone once said, *"I have seen the problem in the mirror, and the problem is me."* Remember, if you win the argument it means your spouse loses. You love your spouse, so you want your spouse to succeed right? When you have a fight or a disagreement your spouse should never be made to feel "small" or "condemned" or "belittled" during the exchange. The war is not with your spouse; your spouse is a part of you!

We had one spouse say, *"I never raise my voice,"* and *"I never cuss when we fight,"* like that somehow makes everything else they say OK. NOT! Not raising your voice and not cussing is a good thing, but you must not speak to your spouse as if they are the enemy.

Cultural differences lead us to understand that some people interact much more passionately than others. Italians, Jewish, and Irish people all have an ethnic born background of passion. Of course this is an over generalization, but most people would identify with the statement.

59

10 Perhaps you have noticed that in a family environment an Italian family can have some of the most alarming fights, in which you think the whole family is going to kill each other, but they can be found hugging and loving on each other days later. They seem to have an understanding that the passion will erupt, then die down, and all will be well again. While many other cultures might think this is a very chaotic way to live, these families seem to have come to an acceptance of verbal warfare that does not harbor bitterness.

When I worked with my dad in his construction company, we'd fight about a particular issue on any particular day, but the next day was a new day, neither one of us carried baggage from the previous day into the new day. Fight less, but when you do fight, fight fair.

> *"My husband and I have never considered divorce, murder sometimes, but never divorce."* Joyce Brothers

Tool #4 Forgiveness

This tool is so vital in a marriage it cannot be used enough. When you master using forgiveness it liberates love. Forgiveness allows the person who gives it to be free from the weight of bitterness, anger, animosity, resentment, hostility, and hatred. Forgiveness does not erase the scars of wrongs; rather it allows the wounds inflicted to heal. If forgiveness is not applied the wound will grow, become infected, and eventually cause death to the marriage. Some people feel that granting forgiveness is conditional upon the other person asking for forgiveness. If that's true, then your healing might never occur. Forgiveness works in spite of the other person's request. We are not saying the other person should not ask for forgiveness, for we would hope that would occur. Rather, do not let your wound become infected because your spouse did not ask for forgiveness.

I need to tell you a short story about the completeness of forgiveness because it was a light bulb moment for me. An employee of mine got into some trouble and asked for a loan to help him get thru his predicament. I gave him the loan with the understanding he would pay me back within a year. I contacted him several times seeking payments, which occurred a couple of times but fell short of the amount I loaned.

Once I realized that getting my money back was not going to occur, I had to forgive the loan and put it behind me. At once, I moved from feeling wronged and bitter about not being paid, to praying for the guy because I knew his life was heading south for several other reasons. But here is the key: even if he should appear today with the money in hand, I would refuse it because the debt is forgiven, it's gone, there is no debt left to be paid. Even more interesting is I truly have completely forgotten how much he owed me.

This is the kind of forgiveness that spouses must offer to one another; it's a complete forgiveness. Whatever occurred in the past is forgiven, which means it is no longer an issue to be recalled. We are not saying you will forget the wrong that was done to you, but it will be much more possible to forget if you are not harboring any bitterness over it.

Tool #5 Unity or Oneness
Working as a single unit cannot be overstated. No sports team is going to win or succeed if they do not work as a single unit. It is highly important that a couple line themselves up as a single force so that all who see or think about them know they are "one." Some express this condition of unity as "oneness." Just remember, it's not you and him or her, it's "us." You act like and are viewed as a forever married couple. You represent oneness, unity, acting as one, no one attacks your spouse without attacking you, you have your spouse's back, and they have yours. This communicates to others you are a single unit. More detail on this in chapter 21.

Tool #6 Check & Balance
Couples only move when in agreement. Paige and I only move forward on medium to larger decisions if we are in agreement. Neither one of us would sign a contract without discussion and the other's agreement. We would not take out a credit card, or make a purchase costing several hundred dollars without agreement. Vacations, trips, large gifts, etc., all require agreement. And most importantly, we do not hold it against the spouse who says "no" and shuts down the pursuit of whatever was desired. *(Well except for that time Paige wouldn't let me buy a helicopter!)* We need to view our spouse saying "no" or "let's wait" not as a bad thing, but as a potentially good thing. It's the check and balance that we all need. When you view your spouse's role in your marriage relationship correctly, you understand that when your spouse does not agree it can be a very good thing.

Tool #7 Confess
Buck up, own up: I hate it when I do wrong. I hate it worse, much worse,

10

when I have to admit my mistake. I'm not sure if it's harder for me than other people, but it's hard. Confession says, *"I'm not going to hide this, I blew it."* It's a naked no-excuses confession. I don't think I'll ever forget the times in my life when I really blew it, but owning it and confessing it was paramount to regaining my self-respect and my spouse's trust. No whining, no sulking, just true repenting confession. It's very liberating and not doing it leads to greater deceptions down the road. If you sin, if you hurt, if you did things you shouldn't have, own it, confess it, accept the consequence, and move on.

Tool #8 Never Give Up

At what point in the Super Bowl game does the team that's either winning or losing give up? How about the teams in the NBA finals? They never give up! A business manager might say, *"It's time to cut the losses and quit."* Great, that might be good for a business profit/loss scenario but it's very likely not a good decision for a marriage. Statistics have shown that the majority of people who divorce wish they would have tried harder to make it work. What is really interesting is these divorcees are offering a self-assessment: *"I should have worked at it more."* We will discuss instances where divorce might be a real consideration in chapter 17, but for now your attitude is supposed to be one that endures and says: *"I'm in this until the end and I'm going to work at keeping the boat floating."*

There was a real life chronicle about a Chinese sailor who survived over four months alone lost at sea after the ship he was on was sunk by a German U-Boat. This sailor still holds the record for lone survival in a raft at sea. When interviewed he told reporters he caught rainwater to drink and fashioned makeshift hooks to catch fish. His ordeal gained him enough notoriety that he was eventually granted American citizenship. Faced with seemingly insurmountable odds, he chose not to give up. Yet another story tells the tale of several Mexican fishermen who reportedly survived for nearly 10 months at sea. They too had determined to not give up. In the midst of adversity, all of these survivors came out on the other side being better off than they were before. If your marriage is drifting in the sea of uncertainty, send out an SOS and get rescued. Let it be your legacy that you made every effort to not only keep your marriage intact, but did everything possible to make it flourish. Let them say you never gave up.

Tool #9 Get Off the Throne

[For you toilet readers, its OK, continue] We cannot tell you the times we have had disagreements settled by climbing down from the "kingy" or "queeny" thrones. Very often marriage disagreements occur because one or both spouses independently decide that they "rule." Some spouses are content to let a more dominant spouse run things, and it is certainly a very common condition to have one spouse with a dominant personality. But that doesn't mean being a dictator. Good leaders are servants. We practice a simple reality check in our marriage. The Big Guy is always right—no, we don't mean the man in the marriage, we mean God. As a couple of faith, we believe God is our Creator, thus He knows what's best, what works and what doesn't work. As such, we firmly have established in our minds that God is the sole person on the throne, which leaves no place for either of us. In other words, the throne is already taken!

Tool #10 Prayer
For couples of faith, always pray during or after any family trial or shaking. In our home, one of us will initiate this activity in a period of disagreement or a trial. It is very hard to be mad at a spouse while you're talking out loud to God in your spouse's presence. God knows our thoughts, He knows if we are faking it, embellishing it, milking it, or flat-out lying. Prayer has a way of humbling us and bringing some peace to the situation. And better yet, it brings the Big Guy into the picture.

Love requires cultivating. Did you know love is not a feeling? It's often described this way, but it's because many have never taken the time to think about "how" they love. The fact is, we "choose" whom we will love and when and how we will express our love. We make very deliberate actions to show our love. Unlike how it is portrayed in the soaps, love doesn't instantly flood over you and take you captive. That might be described as lust. Rather, we must cultivate love and then it grows within us. If you do not cultivate love, it will certainly fade away. It sounds a lot like work doesn't it? But it's really not. Not as much as you'd think anyway. There'll be periods with some hard work to be sure, but most days are average, some are effortlessly easy. Work causes muscles to grow stronger, so by committing yourself to work in your marriage it will grow stronger too.

The Tale of Two Farmers

One farmer likes to take the easy road; he plants a peach tree seed in his yard. Thru the course of time the tree grows in spite of some periods of little rain. The farmer doesn't waste his time watering the tree, nor does he fertilize the soil. The tree begins to produce some fruit which initially seems quite good. However, he also neglects to prune the branches. Pretty

63

soon the tree has so many buds that it's producing many hundreds of peaches; however, the tree already lacks the food and water it needs to produce good fruit. The farmer neglects to cover the tree with netting to protect the fruit from birds and insects that ruin much of the crop. So while this first farmer did indeed plant a seed, and it looks like a peach tree, it has damaged peaches with poor taste and poor quality.

The other farmer also plants a seed. However, he first tills the hard ground; he adds mulch to the soil, then he plants the seed. He waters the soil when periods of no rain occur; he fertilizes the soil so the peach tree will have all the nutrients it needs. As the tree grows he covers the tree with netting to protect the fruit. Each year he prunes the branches so the tree does not produce too much fruit, so what it will produce is very good quality.

The moral is why do marriage at all if you're not going to do it right? It is certainly worth doing right. Cultivate the love of your spouse; help them love you by showing them your love. Do you want to produce withered, poor-tasting fruit or luscious, sweet fruit? Both tree planters are farmers in the technical sense of the word, but only one will be known as a good farmer. You are married, so are other people; will your marriage be known as a good marriage? Then act like it, do the work to get you that reputation.

Time for another participation exercise. We'd like you to agree together that you will review the instruction you've received up to this point and discuss how you will apply what you've learned over the next few months. Each of you can hold the other accountable in reminding the other to use these tools. Perhaps you'll agree to make a change of one kind or another every few weeks. Please now agree to remind each other. Do not be offended when being reminded; because making changes will indeed be mechanical for a while. You may have spent years doing it the wrong way so it's going to take some time to reprogram your actions. Remember this is a **SAFE TIME**.

Tools make everything easier; tools require that we pick them up and use them; tools also make the job faster. Don't forget the tools you've just been taught when building your marriage, and if you have other tools that work for your marriage, by all means use them.

Did you learn anything? Yes / No
Chapter personal benefit appraisal: **HER 1-2-3-4-5   HIM 1-2-3-4-5**
1=not at all, 2=a little, 3=some good stuff, 4=fairly helpful, 5=very helpful

CHAPTER 11

When? The Order of Things Married

When a builder starts to build the house he cannot build the roof before he constructs the foundation and the walls. He cannot paint the sheetrock before he hangs, tapes, and textures it. The key to being a good builder is really based on the understanding of how (the proper order) a house is built. While there is some flexibility with some tasks, many tasks must occur in a certain order. If the order is not followed, delays and rework will be required. Good contractors are generally masters at organizing the timing of all the tasks in completing a project.

> *"I think marriages and funerals should have a lot in common because if a marriage begins correctly, both spouses will have died to self on the wedding day."*

Again, we have a similar concept with marriage. When putting the emphasis on the wrong things at the wrong times, we will encounter trouble. If we rush to complete something that we should actually spend purposeful time on, we can also run into difficulties.

FACTOID – When you get the cart in front of the horse, the only direction the horse can go is backward.

Order Hypocrisy

Let us give you a few easy examples of order hypocrisy in a marriage. One would be the NASCAR driver who spends nearly every waking hour working on his car. He is rarely home and tells his wife, *"Hey, you knew the life you were marrying into."* Yet at the track he gathers for prayer asking God to bless and protect him during the race. A second would be the executive who spends 60 hours per week climbing the corporate ladder, ignoring the greater worth of his wife and children to gain a higher title and pay scale. He goes to church on Sunday, when he doesn't have a golf date with the other executives, and believes he is a "good family man" doing all this for his family. Or how about the schoolteacher totally wrapped up in her schoolwork and school activities? How about the housewife who spends every waking hour serving the needs of the children, but lets her husband fend for himself?

11 You know how long those trophies and professional titles are going to last? It ain't the money because about 60% of it is going to go away in the divorce. Ignoring our spouse and/or family is a poor—no, it is a VERY BAD investment. As men we are often guiltier of abandoning our wives. We think, "I'll get married then I'll pour myself into my job, so that later I can retire and then give my woman the attention she deserves." Yet our wives sometimes think the greater role is being the mother believing, "I'll get married and have kids. I'll pour all my energy into raising my kids, and then after they are raised I'll spend some quality time with my husband." These are clear examples of building a marriage in the wrong order. In these examples <u>no</u> marriage building was actually taking place, both spouses were building elsewhere. As you'll read below, we are not telling you to ignore your children or your career, rather to keep them in the proper order of devotion.

The Proper Order of Devotion

Your spouse – On this earth your spouse should be the most important person you relate to. You'll read later in another chapter that your spouse comes even before "you." A person who has this in proper context is supporting, building, encouraging, and helping their spouse become all the man or woman they can be. It is your tender attention to your spouse that causes them to flourish and grow and quite naturally makes your marriage flourish too.

Children – If your children still live at home, they should come next. In every area the best thing a parent can do to love their children is to love their spouse and show their kids that their spouse comes before them. Children must understand that they cannot cause a division between their parents and if they try, they will feel the consequences. If you are remarried and have kids from the first marriage, those kids <u>must take a back seat to your current spouse</u> in the family pecking order.

Faith – And for those of us who profess a belief in God our devotion or trust in God should be foremost. As a Christian, every moral principle, everything we do in life is or should be based in the moral concepts that God has handed us. Our moral compass is based in the instruction book God wrote and we first need to be true to our belief and trust in our Creator and Lord. By making God number one in our life, this submission helps establish all of our moral standards and related actions. If we are professing an adherence to Christ, that we've been adopted into God's family, we will honor God with our service, devotion, and love.

We are following His will, setting aside our own.

Other priorities – Many priorities will shift positions within your lifetime. Things like your job, your friends, other family members, periods of helping neighbors, special projects, perhaps some hobby or sport, personal goals or aspirations, education, etc. Occasionally, a spouse will have to devote a significant amount of time to something that demands much of their physical, mental, and/or emotional energy. Examples might be a week of intense studying for a final exam, a few weeks caring for a very sick family member, or a job requirement that forces a spouse away, such as in the case of a serviceman or woman when ordered overseas. Obviously, longer term stressors will come up and we discuss a few of those in a later chapter. Make every effort to keep any top three priority disturbances as short term as possible.

In every marriage where we've witnessed the proper order being followed, the marriage thrives. We are not saying your marriage will fail if you do not follow this order. We are saying whenever we didn't follow it, we had troubles. But we are 'not right in the head' unlike the rest of you!

While we are asking each of us to live up to our moral code, it's time to kick some butt once again. We have known several couples including pastors who got the order wrong, placing a higher weight on church than their families. Putting our devotion to God first doesn't mean church or ministry takes all your time from your spouse or family. It means the relationship with your Creator, your morals, ideals, prayers, meditation, and guidance holds the primary slot in how you will live your life. While it is certainly a noble desire to save the world, if your marriage fails while trying, it appears you had the balance and priorities wrong.

> *"Bob's driver's license says he's well over 50; however, I say he is closer to 11 or 12 with some occasional spikes up to 15 or16."*

I heard a story about a man who was a senior executive at a big company. He had a lot of demands on his time, but anytime his wife or a child called, he always stopped whatever he was doing and took the call, even if he was in a meeting. His wife and kids knew they mattered more than the job. This executive had his priorities in the right order!

11 | The Order of Things Less Important

Other less important priorities pertain to "material things," "money," or "fame." There should never, repeat <u>never,</u> be a time when any of these things get into your top list of most important things. If you think putting money or fame before your spouse and kids is the better way, then perhaps you should ask some of the Hollywood movie stars or high-end sports athletes if they think the trade was worth it. These famous and very wealthy people may have whole buildings filled with cars, huge yachts, private jets, but very often they have failures in marriage and great insecurities in relationships. Your possessions may be smaller but just as alluring with regard to stealing your time and energy. We are saying there is no real happiness in "stuff" and for most of us the stress of payments will far outweigh any fleeting sense of joy. They are simply not worth acquiring if any part of your marriage might suffer.

It's amazing that so many Americans have so many toys: so many they do not have the space to keep them. Drive by a couple of storage unit facilities and see how many boats, motor homes, and other toys are parked there for months on end. Some of them don't look like they've been moved in years.

Should a young newly married couple buy a new car? Should a couple go into debt to buy a second home? Buy a boat on credit? Should you change jobs? Should you rent or buy a home? Should you have or adopt a child? Those are all real life questions that couples consider every day. We cannot answer these questions; these are for you as a couple to answer. Timing could be a real consideration in all of these decisions, but the decision rests jointly with you as a couple.

> *"The idea of united oneness in a marriage is so important that I think every newly married couple should be put in a small boat and set into the middle of the ocean. Out there in that vast ocean they would learn to become dependent on one another for their joint survival. They would discover the strength in each other's words of encouragement, and dread the thought of losing the other to such a degree that when they've returned to land they could never be separated by man or beast."*

The choices are not restricted to *"yes"* and *"no."* A third choice is *"wait or not now."* None of us likes to hear the "no" answer, but "no" is often warranted. I really, really wanted to buy a helicopter. I've been a pilot for over 29 years, and love to fly more than about anything else, but it has to wait, and it is still waiting. Why? We are not at a place where I can outright buy a helicopter, and I'm not willing to put the extra stress on my marriage by buying one on credit. Add to that an economy that is very shaky now. Am I missing a dream? Sure, but it's a dream of far less importance than my marriage. The answer is "no" for now, but it's also a "maybe" for later. I could actually buy the helicopter on credit, but that would mean working more hours away from home to pay for it, and also being at home less while I'm off flying the helicopter. It would put greater stress on our finances. When I talk it out, the answer is clearly no. Some people tell you to live your dream; we do not disagree, we have several dreams, but the most important is to have a great marriage. Making sure we keep marriage at the forefront means we might have to set other dreams aside for a while.

If you are not self-disciplined enough to save up and pay cash for something, then perhaps you should not buy it. Even if you have the cash, is it really something you need and will it benefit or hurt your marriage? The lack of self-discipline in finances is just as true for doctors and lawyers as it is for blue collar households. I don't recall the publication, but it cited a study of upper middle class people like doctors and lawyers and it found that many of these well-to-do people living in fancy houses who drove fancy cars were very close to financial disaster. The article found that in an effort to assume the level of affluence society or peers expected, these professionals wasted their salaries on trying to keep up and were basically living from paycheck to paycheck. *"Discipline, Grasshopper, it's all about self-discipline."*

Don't just mouth it, be determined to LIVE it. Keep the proper order of things, teach your kids by example on how to have a joyful marriage. If you let your job, schooling, friends, sports, toys, kids, or other family members come between you and your spouse, you're in the wrong. Man up, or woman up and get it back on track!

Couple's project—spend some time talking about your individual order of devotion, what it is and what you as a couple would like it to be.

> *"Let's pretend for a minute that it's your spouse who is responsible to make you happy, Good, now that that's over, you can get back to taking care of it yourself."*

11	Did you learn anything? Yes / No

Chapter personal benefit appraisal: HER 1-2-3-4-5   HIM 1-2-3-4-5
1=not at all, 2=a little, 3=some good stuff, 4=fairly helpful, 5=very helpful

www.u-build.com

Home Improvement: Determining What Needs Repair/Maintenance

CHAPTER 12

Maintaining Your Home—Routine Maintenance

Woman says…
"If a marriage is meant to be, then you will not have to work at it!"
Idiot!

Man says…
"We've been married all this time and I've not had to do anything."
Moron!

A man or woman who utters those statements ignores a law that is pervasive for the entire universe; it is referred to as the 2nd Law of Thermodynamics. This law is less commonly known as the Law of Increased Entropy and means that the quality of matter and energy deteriorates gradually over time. In layman's terms it means: "Everything that exists will move to a greater degree of decay." In our backyard Idaho way of looking at things, it means *stuff will always fall apart or breakdown!*

A cloth will wear out, a car will eventually rust away, a home will fall apart, etc., <u>unless</u> energy or effort is put forth to keep or restore them in good condition. On its own; everything falls apart. In maintaining our homes we have to: replace decking, repaint, remove rotten or termite infested wood, re-carpet, and on and on. This same principle can be applied to marriages. A marriage takes some effort to maintain; it requires tune-ups, and it requires repairs, adjustments, and care.

> *"I love it when my woman gets up, grabs my hand, and leads me into the bedroom. However, I am quickly sobered up when she occasionally spins around, walks out, closing the door behind her while telling me not to come out until I've thought about the way I've recently spoken to her or treated her. Talk about a gear-changer. I get the feeling she's talked with my 6th grade teacher!"*

If all that sounds like work, well it is certainly some work, but the more tools, materials, support, and knowledge a couple has, the less effort has to be put into it. Why? Because serious damage is headed off before it occurs. OK, let's boil this down to man talk, why do you check and change the oil in your truck, replace the brakes, tune the truck up, or even add gas? To "keep it in running condition." *(Silence here ladies, let the gears turn; a light bulb will come on, just wait a bit.)*

Is it better to check and change the oil and oil filter or let the engine seize up? Which is more work and more costly? One more point, performing maintenance not only avoids seizing up the engine, it makes the car more dependable. Do you or your spouse waver between giving it another try and divorcing? Why not perform the work required to make your marriage something you can depend on?

FACTOID – Therapists indicate that approximately 65% of couples who seek counseling waited until after infidelity had damaged their relationship.

Hopefully, we now have both the men and the women agreeing that a marriage takes some effort and that a little bit of regular maintenance can prevent bigger problems later.

Men, we have to grasp that it's the little things *(routine maintenance)* that add up and really mean a lot to yer woman. But just so we don't get all lopsided here, women need to understand that the male also needs some lovin' and attention to keep the engine running smooth too.

> *"After my husband and I 'won' each other's heart, we then began the work of becoming 'one.'"*

So we want you both to agree, just maintaining the marriage will take work and if you want a <u>great</u> marriage, it will take a tad more effort than simply maintaining it. The same principle applies to your home and in an effort to help my fellow male Homo sapiens understand this let me explain. You can just maintain your car but you can also add a *"nitrous super charger,"* and it will perform far above other cars anywhere. How about not just maintaining your woman, but loving on her to such a degree, she comes at you like a super-charged, tricked-out NASCAR rig? I'm telling ya men, when you honor and cherish your woman; she cranks it up for you too!

We are going to list some simple things here that husbands and wives can do to kindle each other's love and respect. Go thru the list, place checks near the things you'd like your spouse to do for you. Then each spouse can pick thru them over the next few months and apply them. These little acts of affection and caring are the glue that holds and grows a marriage.

Some of these reflect the trying times we are in and they *won't cost you anything to use.* Even if your marriage has suffered thru an affair, these points are <u>musts</u> for rebuilding.

Things a woman can do for her hubby:

1. It's absolutely imperative that our wives "respect" us. Our wife's words should build us up and encourage us to go slay those dragons every day. If we've broken your trust, we agree it will take time to rebuild it, and as we do, please acknowledge that we're going in the right direction.

2. Tell hubby with some frequency that you "admire" him. If he has been providing for the family, thank him regularly for doing so.

3. If your hubby is out of work or stricken with some prolonged sickness, let him know you're in this together no matter what. In this day and age it's vital to have a woman supporting a husband who has lost his job. Helpful ideas in getting a new job can be good, but not if handled in a way that says he's not looking hard enough. For many of us men, it's quite easy for us to feel like a failure on our own, it's an internal thing. Sometimes we teeter on giving up, but a wife's support helps us live higher than we feel.

4. Ask what you can do to "turn him on." While some men like negligee garments, others will prefer having their woman clad in just a plain white dress shirt. Contrary to popular belief, it's not all about "sex" for married men even though we always seem to be seeking sex. Sexual intimacy is very reaffirming as it conveys we are still <u>your</u> man. It's OK that you act sexy and feminine with your hubby, he loves that you act like a "woman"!

5. Clutch your man when you are in public. When you grab his belt, when you hang on to his arm, he will feel you are conveying a message to all the other guys, that this is <u>your</u> man. Your husband will walk a little taller because you're showing this affection in public. Dr. Phil walks taller when he leaves the set of his TV show because his wife, Robin, is on his arm when he exits.

6. Occasionally as you lay in bed together, when you cuddle, don't be afraid to explore the "family jewels" or run your hands across his chest. You may elicit a response in your husband, but your gentle hand caressing him is far more than a turn on, it lets him know that you find him desirable too. Your touch affirms your attraction to him.

7. Embrace those "hints" he tosses your way for sexual intimacy. Don't always wait for him to move, drag him into the bedroom, seduce him, and use your wares to say "I want you."

8. Help him understand what he can do to make your intimacy more enjoyable. Pleasing you is actually something he really wants to be good at.
9. Ask him: What are the three most important things you can do to affirm him?
10. Other _____

Things a man can do for his wife:

1. It's absolutely imperative that a woman feel secure with her man in general and while in his arms. Men if you've ever lashed out at your wife, you've broken down that trust and it must never happen again. Regularly let your woman know you are going to stay with her, thru thick and thin, but just as important, she must feel like you will protect her and never hurt her.
2. Show her every day, not just when you have time, that she is the most important thing to you: above kids, work, sports, whatever. Let her know when she needs you, you'll be there for her. In this way you honor her. She might be the weaker vessel physically, but you show her honor when she is put ahead of others.
3. Help her with raising the kids. Not only do the kids really need you to be a part of their lives, but your wife really needs your help. Read a book to them at night, play a game with them, go walking, help with schoolwork, etc. Hug those kids every chance you get so it's a normal function, even as they grow up into teenagers.
4. Help her with chores when she's overwhelmed. I never used to do laundry or dishes. I hated it and never wanted to let my wife get me where I was delegated this portion of the chores. However, after my business activity fell off, my wife was the only one working. I knew I had to step up. Now I do most all the chores except for her laundry, which she tells me "not to touch!"
5. Here is a list (A to Z) of little things that will score big points and reaffirm your devotion to your wife:
   a. Have her sit in front of you at the couch and comb her hair with her favorite brush.
   b. Give her a foot message.
   c. Give her a hand message.
   d. Borrow some biker clothes, or some cowgirl clothes and take pictures of her dressed up. If you want to score really big, have her bring friends over to do it with her. Girls like to dress up, and if you are the one taking the dress up pictures of her as a cowgirl, biker chick, princess, etc., she gets to enjoy a good time with you.

This can be a great project for couples too, where both husband and wife take pictures of themselves dressed in some theme.

e. Get her a spa treatment package every once in a while.

f. If she works, have flowers delivered to her work (in front of her coworkers) once every few months or on birthdays, Valentine's Day, and/or anniversary. *(And guys, I gotta tell ya, to this day I do not know what the heck a "valentine" is! Not important—she does.)*

g. Open the car and house door for her—makes her feel honored.

h. Surprise her with an inside or outside picnic. Make it simple things like her favorite cheese, crackers, chunks of meat, some wine or sparkling cider.

i. Give her a hot towel treatment. Here are the instructions: you have her lie naked on the bed with a big beach towel under her. The beach towel keeps the bed from getting wet. Make sure the room is not cold. With two more large heavy towels, take one and put it in the sink or bath and wet it with very hot water, as hot as your hands can stand. Then wring out most of the water, take it over to your wife, and spread it out over the top of her. *(It will feel very hot to her.)* While that towel is on her, get the next towel ready, and then swap it with the one that's on her. Do this about four to six times. Then cover her up with the bed covers, she's likely going to fall off to sleep.

j. If she works, put a love note in her lunch that says, *"You're hot!"*

k. Put some Post-its on the mirror and little love notes in the fridge or anywhere you know she'll look. When she sees these, she knows you're thinking about her.

l. Call her on her phone, but when she answers, do not say anything. Have the music of a good love song turned up on your end of the phone, after about 20 seconds of the music, turn it down and tell her she is special to you.

m. Take her window shopping to the mall. Even if she buys nothing, just walk with her *(hold her hand if she likes that)* as she looks at clothes and smells perfumes. Tell her what you like or do not like. Encourage her to buy something if the budget allows.

n. If you really want to score big, write down the size of her pants, dress, shoes, shirt, ring size, and favorite perfume. *(I wrote my wife's on the back of a business card I keep in my wallet.)* Then every once in a while go to a women's store, and buy her something you think she might like. It doesn't matter that she may not like what you bought, the fact you did it is what matters. Save the receipt so she can return it if necessary.

o. Make her favorite coffee or drink in the morning and have it waiting for her when she gets up. Or get her a gift card to a corner espresso shack.

p. Give her a full body massage. Use oil if she's OK with that—spend about 10–30 min. Don't make it sexual; concentrate on deep muscle massage.

q. Fill the bathtub with HOT water, maybe add some bath crystals if she has some, light a few candles, next roll up a towel she can lay her head on in the tub, turn off the lights, and set a small glass of wine beside the tub. Let her enjoy the hot bath, drink, and the total peace. NO KIDS!

r. If she has her own car, wash, wax, and vacuum it for her. Put Post-its on the dash saying she's one hot babe! If the car heater or air conditioner is broken or the car needs the oil changed, take care of that for her. As much as you can afford to, make the car dependable for her.

s. Encourage her to get together with her other women friends and spur her on to do this at least once a month—not to go to bars, but maybe to eat out or get out with other girls. Meanwhile you get to have some quality time with the kids.

t. If she's been paying the bills (writing the checks) ask her if you can help or even take over that task. Relieve her of the anxiety of paying the bills, but do not freak-out when you finally realize it's hard to balance the budget.

u. Take the lead in seeing to it that you and the family attend church, read the Bible, and pray. Many women really want their husbands to take the lead in spiritual matters.

v. When she is in front of other women, be attentive to her, give her big smiles, run your hand up and down her back so she and the other girls know it's all about her. Show your affection openly for her.

w. Spice her life up occasionally, especially if she is generally stuck home with kids. Go for a boat ride, horseback riding, rollercoaster ride, or a motorbike ride. Most women have a so called wild side—they *(with the safety of their man)* wanna act out of character once in a while, to cut loose if you will. Likely your wife has an idea or two she can give you.

x. When she is waking up in the morning or going to sleep at night, just run your fingers along her face as you gaze at her. Move to her neck and shoulders. If it's warm enough, you can uncover her and gently run your fingers across her body. Stay away from erogenous zones, this is just softly running your hands of admiration across her form, appreciating every little curve and bump.

y.	When watching a movie, grab a blanket and cuddle up together on the couch. Just enjoy cuddling together, being in each other's arms and being close.

z.	And this is far from the least: make sure you kiss her gently on the lips with regular frequency. That kind of kiss where your lips kinda engulf hers…it's slow, deliberate, and passionate. Perhaps a few kisses on the neck, with a couple of hot breaths.

6.	You plan a family event where you handle ALL of the details. Like a trip to the zoo, a camping trip, trip to the beach, or something similar.

7.	Make sure you back your wife in disciplining the children or getting them to do their chores. Neither spouse should be their kid's best friend; they must first be their parents. Once the kids are grown and responsible, then you can be friends.

8.	Ask your wife which holiday she would like you to remember above all others, the one that makes her feel special when you remember. Then make every effort to remember that day and make it special for her. My wife has three that she requested I remember; the rest I can ignore. Her birthday, our anniversary, and Valentine's Day. I want to inject something here speaking for other men. We can be greatly intimidated with trying to buy our women something. For real, I never feel as inadequate as when I'm trying to buy something for my wife. After 30 years, it still causes me anxiety. I feel each gift has to be better than the last one, and I'm always at a loss for what she really wants. Women, ask your man if he feels like I do, then help him feel better about it.

9.	Other _____
	_____

Things you do together:

1.	Have a date night with regular frequency, just the two of you. Go out, stay home, bowling, a movie, walk the mall, whatever, but try to get by yourselves at least once every couple of months. I have to admit, I'm slothful in doing this but when possible we should make the effort.

2.	Sit down as a couple and try to figure out how to lighten the load. Moms and dads really need to simplify their lives; we cram so much into life it's exhausting us, so much so we are spent and often have little to give anyone else. Work to simplify and downsize your life so you can enjoy the time you do have.

3.	Clear the house, or just your bedroom. Set up your boom box or CD/DVD player, put on a CD with rich sounding music. Turn it up (don't tick off the neighbors if you're in an apartment) and just be mellow in the music. We like Celtic music, or the theme from *Last of the Mohicans* and similar kinds of music.

4. Discuss where you've come from and where you want to go as a couple. If you've been married one or more years, discuss the good things about those years. Bring up the high points, discuss your dreams for the future.

5. While we all want to put our kids thru college and/or give them a lavish wedding, you may not be in a position to afford it. Let your kids know that money is tight; do not be ashamed to tell them they will have to go without or earn it themselves. Kids are very resilient, they get over it. The best thing you can do is focus on keeping your marriage in top shape with no extra financial burdens added. We had a main financial goal of paying off our home before much of any extra spending was allowed. If your home is paid for it really frees up the rest of your life.

6. Every few months discuss with each other in a **SAFE TIME** things you'd like to see improved. Only when our spouse feels they can be honest about something and not get retribution are they willing to say what's on their mind. Recently my wife told me she wants me to dress a little better *(I wear clothes until they are rags, literally!)* and it's something I have to work on.

7. Discuss how to live within your means, how to get some savings going.

8. Discuss the spiritual aspects of your marriage—going to church, reading the Bible, and/or praying together.

9. Make an effort to spend at least 30 minutes of every day having one-on-one meaningful communication. Talk about whatever you desire, but spend at least 30 minutes of quality time talking to each other.

10. Use the tools in chapter 10 more often.

11. Other _____

_____

Undoubtedly, you both have a few more things you could add to this list, things you would like your spouse to do for you or things you can do together. So we encourage you to bring them up and write them down. There are a few blank pages at the beginning and end of this handbook, use them for your notes. Sometimes you may have to remind each other to look at the list or even ask for something from the list. While it may start off somewhat mechanical, it will become more natural over time. To get the ball moving, go over the lists you just reviewed and point to one of the items and ask your honey to do it for you.

FACTOID – Every couple that employs communication techniques such as SAFE TIME is being proactive in avoiding major conflicts in the future. It's like changing the oil in your car, making it last longer and more dependable.

12

> *"Our modern American society has pre-programmed many couples into believing that marriage is a game of chance similar to the game show "Let's Make a Deal." They casually make a spousal selection figuring once the box is opened if he/she is not the "prize" they really wanted, they can readily trade him/her away for another. They never seem satisfied enough to leave the game show and keep the original gift."*

Every home is going to require maintenance. And it's a fact that <u>every couple</u>, repeat, <u>every couple</u> is also going to have issues to deal with in their home. Financial strains, challenges raising and disciplining kids, working too much or too little, anger or self-esteem issues, emotional outbursts, sicknesses, intimacy issues, hurt feelings, and on and on. So what separates those who survive from those who don't? Doing the maintenance to keep the little problems from growing into big ones and properly dealing with the issues that come up. Be proactive instead of reactive; fight **for** your marriage, rather than fighting **in** your marriage. Care for your marriage, foster everything needed to have a great marriage. Do not leave issues unresolved because that is like planting termites in the structure supporting your marriage.

A note on balance here: some of you are "beaver" types, and you are going to go after improving your marriage with gusto, with the goal of having the most beautiful marriage on the block. Well, we have two words for you, STOP IT! Everything in balance…you do not need to read 100 books, attend five marriage conferences a year, and go to three couples' retreats every summer to have a great marriage. If you have a passion like we do to help others, that's a good thing, but don't burden yourselves with another obligation or activity so much so that it is out of balance. Contrary to popular belief, too much of a good thing can be "too much." It is a very natural desire to want your marriage to be transformed overnight, but please do not go overboard, give it some time. We all want a passionate relationship with our spouse, but keep in mind if you try to heat up a stew using high heat, you'll burn it and it will be popping and splashing all over the place. It's best to turn up the heat gradually till things start to simmer and then you can maintain that heat.

12

We do not want to force you to do something you really are not convinced you should do. However, take this opportunity to cement in your mind what you know is good for your marriage. Remember we said we'd be pushing you some. So in keeping with this book's theme of having readers actively involved in building your marriage, we would like you and your spouse to turn to each other and repeat something like the following statement.

Couple's project—*"Honey, I apologize for not giving our marriage the attention it deserves. I promise with your help to make a better effort at maintaining our marriage. Let's keep reminding each other to do it better."*

Couple's project—Pick an item from the list and do it for the other today or tomorrow. Begin to do these for each other with regular frequency.

Wife visits a marriage counselor for the first time, sits down, and begins: *"All my husband wants is sex, sex, sex."* Counselor responds, *"Bless you child, many other husbands want their wives to also cook, clean, raise the kids, and give up the channel changer! What can I do for you today?"*

Did you learn anything? Yes / No
Chapter personal benefit appraisal: **HER 1-2-3-4-5   HIM 1-2-3-4-5**
1=not at all, 2=a little, 3=some good stuff, 4=fairly helpful, 5=very helpful

www.u-build.com

CHAPTER 13

Do You Need to Perform a Major Remodel?

There comes a time when the owners of a house decide it's time to give it a facelift and bring back its luster. At other times repairs are immediately needed because the house is no longer useful as designed. The same is true for many marriages. Occasionally, a major remodel is less of a choice and more of a necessity, as the home (marriage) becomes no longer functional in one or more areas.

> *"We went to one marriage seminar where the speaker said over and over that a little spice is all that's needed to get a marriage revved up again, but it hasn't worked for our marriage. My wife has thrown dozens of spice bottles at me and the only thing it's given me is bruises."*

A couple should seriously consider a major marriage remodel if they have not been diligent in performing regular maintenance in their marriage and symptoms are showing up that suggest the marriage is in distress.

If you regularly have been working on your "stuff" as a couple, each growing and maturing into being a better spouse, seeking the advice and counsel of others, reading books, growing spiritually together, talking with each other in deep and meaningful ways, then it's likely a major remodel is not needed.

Let's clear the air about a couple of things, time to man up here.

Being "bad" is easy; hell, it's really easy. All a person has to do is spread around an attitude and be self-centered. "Bad" is just wearing a costume with an attitude. People who wear the badass costume are trying to hide some weakness they do not want others to see. Yet, you have to be far more of a man or woman to live up to your responsibilities than to push others around. I use to wear this attitude to keep everyone out, but it doesn't work at all in a marriage.

Conversely, doing nothing, otherwise described as apathy or indifference, is another easy road for the person choosing to do nothing. Some spouses are apathetic to avoid making a mistake. They figure if they do nothing, they can do nothing wrong. Others do nothing because they are lazy. People who wear the apathy costume are hoping no one knows it's them hiding behind the mask, avoiding all of life's trials. If you've been <u>good for nothing</u>, it's <u>time you were good at something.</u> We're asking you to be good at your marriage!

Both men and women are equally capable of putting on the *"bad costume"* or the *"apathy costume."* So let's grow up, get past these two obstacles, and work at having a great marriage. Let's get serious about doing a major remodel if we need one. The goal is to have a really great marriage. To achieve that, we have to refocus our minds and emotions and zero in on <u>repair</u> and not blame.

Couple's project—Right now please say this to one another: *"Honey, I apologize to you for I have often fought seeking to blame you over myself. I see now that this is the wrong attitude, it is not about blame and I am sorry for behaving so poorly, for indeed I love you."*

FACTOID – All marriages face storms and trials. A key difference in how long the storm lasts is whether a couple runs into the bottom of the ship hiding from the storm or grabs the controls and steers out of it. Don't fear the storm, fear doing nothing while you're in it!

When a remodel is required it is often revealed during or after a storm or trial. Have you ever lived in a house when a storm hit? You quickly knew the roof leaked because you had three or four pans scattered around to catch the dripping water. The storm revealed the areas that need repair.

Storms & Trials

There is a misconception that when you get married you'll experience fewer troubles. The truth is that you inherit more and different troubles, but you also gain many beneficial features too. Some of the storms *(stressors)* can be sickness, pregnancy, money issues, infertility, sexual dysfunction, raising kids, loss of job, depression, despair, fire, abuse, loss of loved one, adultery, fear, shame, moving, changing jobs, debt, family interference, addictions/compulsions, boredom, and many others.

What you gain in marriage is someone to go thru the trials with, even though they may have been wholly or partly to blame for causing the trouble. While we should expect a certain amount of storms and trials, that doesn't mean we accept everything that comes our way without trying to deal with it.

Remember, it's far less about blame and far more about repairing the damage and setting up new boundaries to protect your marriage.

For instance, if one of the spouses has been sexually abused in the past, that needs to be dealt with, it cannot be ignored. Addiction to drugs, alcohol, pornography, spending, gambling, food, etc., are all storms that require a remodel. A major remodel will entail spouse-to-spouse discussions, very likely professional counseling, changes in behavior, rebuilding damaged areas, erecting protective boundaries, sometimes a change of setting (moving), and changes in priorities or other dynamics of the relationship. We will touch more on some of these topics in chapter 16.

Some marriage gurus will tell you that the above listed stressors or storms are not the real problem. They say all the marital strife boils down to communication, or values, or criticism, or some other component of human psychology. Listen, we will not disagree, some of these "professionals" are backed by thousands of subject observations. Yet for most people it is not an intuitive task to know what's going on inside another person's head. If we wrote a book and said all of your problems will boil down to "defensiveness"—just be less defensive or just communicate better—not many married couples would read it, and for sure not many men would be able to relate to the message. However, both of those human interaction activities are worth understanding. The point is, these storms come, and we need to survive these storms and we need to mature while going thru them. But the reality is some couples will indeed suffer damage going thru the storm and the damage will require either a major or minor remodel.

Doing nothing promotes even more decay. Damage ignored will often result in the total collapse of the marriage. Think about it this way, you're about to climb into a ship that will cruise to Alaska, but the captain tells you they've found some damage they didn't know about. There is a good amount of water leaking into the hull, but the bilge pumps seem to be keeping up. Do you still want to go on the voyage? Do you trust the ship to stay floating? OK, point made; do not ignore issues in your marriage, resolve them.

> A question to those living in a troubled marriage: *"If you cannot get along with the one you love, how can we expect you to get along with those you don't?"* Yet we ask this not of divorced people, for they have already answered.

Storms ain't all bad. Let's stick with our watery ocean theme a while longer. In an earlier chapter we talked about being in a boat in the middle of the ocean and facing the sharks and storms while drifting for months on end. It is during the storms that our inner strengths or the lack of them are revealed. It's also in storms that we, as married folks, learn we are not alone. If storms cause one of you to become unglued or emotionally unstable, that's no cause to give up, take each opportunity to grow in learning how to deal with these storms. It should be obvious, when you cannot escape the storm you have to deal with it. You may be able to leave your spouse, but you'll never be able to get away from life's storms. Fears, all kinds of fears, cause us to act out in ways that are emotionally poor. Obtaining a secure feeling can be very calming even in a storm. Take charge over your feelings. Someone asked, "Did worrying change anything other than your otherwise previously good disposition?" Many people find great peace by trusting God for the outcome during any trial.

Storms are going to come and go, and at various times each of you will actually be the cause of a few. Your spouse is going to cause some, your children will cause some, some will come regardless of either of you, so these are facts we should accept. Storms give us growth, maturity, and experience, and teach us many valuable lessons we can pass on to our children. You can get pissed, you can get depressed, you can hide in a glass of alcohol—but we are suggesting that what you need to do is <u>focus on getting thru it.</u> We sincerely suggest doing a remodel before you decide to tear down your marriage.

FACTOID – What all good sailors do when they encounter a storm is to protect the ship by trying to minimize damage as all hands work to get the ship out of the storm. Great advice for married couples!

Other Warning Signs

Relationship test—one clue that a person or couple is having relationship troubles is when they switch to having a "close" relationship with an animal over their spouse. Animals are a bit handicapped because they do not talk back; usually they are smaller and more controllable, they cannot voice criticism, and they will come back to you time and time again without the need to "work things out." Whenever we see a spouse giving more attention to a critter than their spouse, we know the marriage relationship is likely troubled.

If you haul around a dog, cat, or bird everywhere you go, you've very likely got "people" relationship issues. If you have inside pets, are they more fulfilling than the weaker relationship you have with your spouse? Do you hold and caress your dog or cat rather than your husband or wife? We are not saying that animals are bad, nor are we saying you are a bad person; not at all. We have two dogs and two cats and at one point we had five horses, too. Animals can be very good for the aged, sick people, and those living alone. However, we are saying they should <u>never become a substitute or a larger priority than relationships with people.</u> Maintaining people relationships can be hard. Today it is even harder as most people's love seems to be growing cold for one another. It's rare that someone (even friends) is willing to take the time to invest in fostering the relationship.

How long has it been since you've <u>enjoyed</u> sexual intimacy together?
Do you usually eat separately?
Do you and/or your spouse practice the silent treatment on each other with some frequency?
Do you vacation separately?
Do you argue frequently?
Do you often feel you're walking around on pins and needles trying to avoid the next fight?
How fragile is your marriage?

These are marriage relationship questions. They are important questions because most couples who divorce later wish they had made a better effort to repair the marriage relationship. I think there is some confusion about what "tolerance" really is. In this day and age of sensitivity training and diversity gurus, even married people are being indoctrinated that they shouldn't bring up character flaws of their spouse even though it may be interfering with their marriage relationship. Out of fear of being judgmental, the relationship is allowed to degenerate. A couple may have issues with each other but they don't bring them up and they grow further apart as a result. It's better not to offend them, r-i-g-h-t?

That's crap! If you believe something is offensive and hurting your relationship, then by all means bring it up! Marriage REQUIRES you to be open and honest. Don't bury problems, address them. The flip side is not to let every little thing grate on you. It's going to be an emotional rollercoaster if one or both of you are super sensitive to every little thing. So we are asking you to be real with each other. Do not be afraid to bring up issues that are stressing your marriage relationship, but also be aware one remedy is that you may have to readjust your thoughts so that the stressor is no longer an issue.

Escalate or Harmony?

If someone steps on your toe, do you respond by breaking his leg? Are you justified in inflicting a much more severe injury upon him? No! Yet many couples fight by escalating attacks on each other, seeking greater and greater injury. When your spouse says, "Mom is being evicted, she might need to move in with us for a few weeks," do you escalate the situation by responding in anger that you are going to seek a divorce? That is no way to respond.

We must "learn" to work on the problem not escalate it into a bigger one. Couples have to get a handle on not escalating topics into heated disagreements. Refocus and begin to talk about the issue or problem. If your spouse comes to you with a problem, in this case, Mom is about to become homeless, how can you help your spouse solve the problem they just presented to you rather than escalate it into an argument?

FACTOID – Two choices in any difficulty: If you want to make the problem bigger, you will. Conversely, if you seek to solve the problem, you will.

In the days before the recent earthquake in Haiti people were milling around, troubled by traffic lights, overdue bills, car troubles, in-laws, kids, and some were likely in the midst of a disagreement with their spouse. However, in less than one hour all those aggravations melted away—they no longer mattered. You see how things can change in a person's mind in just one hour. Americans are for the most part spoiled, lazy, self-centered, and far too opinionated. We've been super-sensitized to everything; we no longer have calluses on our hands to show we've worked thru difficult times. We are going to make a very simplistic statement that can have a profound affect on your marital harmony and bliss if you choose to embrace it. Many will choose to deny it, but its truth is plainly evident. *The very moment you decide in your mind that you have a good marriage, you will have it!* Remember, experiencing troubles and trials is normal and present in good and bad marriages. Much of the battle is in your head, not in your circumstances.

We've often shared with couples facing marital troubles that we all have a tendency to blow things up into proportions they were never meant to be. We'll give you an example of putting something under the microscope and blowing it up way out of proportion. Everyone sleeps in a bed, but in the overactive mind of a clean freak, they can get so focused on the "dust mites" *(little critters who live in our mattress and eat our dead skin)* that they are unwilling to sleep in the bed. To most of us they are invisible mostly harmless little creatures. But a few people put them under a microscope (in their mind) and they begin to look larger than life. By comparison, one spouse is yelling and carrying on about a giant problem that's invisible to the other. No wonder we sometimes look at each other and say, *"What the heck are you talking about?"* Bob and I have said that to each other many times!

Conversely, there is a balance—it is good to have some compassion. Here is an example of not being understanding: Your wife is pregnant, you tell her, *"Women everywhere for thousands of years have had babies; it's not a big deal."*

It's this kind of insensitivity that made one inventor rich by making a "full upper body snap-on simulated pregnancy device." It allowed men to experience just a little of what a woman has to carry around 24 hours a day. Hopefully, many of us men are quick learners and we will indeed be more perceptive in that area.

Remodeling requires tearing down some things that are not functional, not working, or otherwise subtracting from the value of your house (marriage) and rebuilding that area with new, better materials.

For young couples, we can only say it is gonna take some time (likely years) to mature into more caring and understanding husbands and wives. Yet, if we are honest, it appears a portion of men and women will never mature. The good news is you are reading this marriage handbook, which means you desire to mature in your marriage relationship.

13 **Couple's project**—Using the bull's-eye targets that follow, consider your "inner self" at the target center. Next place an X where you feel your spouse is, in relation to how close they are to your innermost self. Assume each black ring is a defensive layer that protects you from harm. The closer someone is to your inner circle or heart, the more they can harm you; however, the greater the love and bond between you will be. If you are totally vulnerable and have nothing you keep from your spouse, then you may have allowed them into your inner most being.

[Paige comment] I just noticed these two targets together look like Bob's eyes when I tell him, "We need to talk".

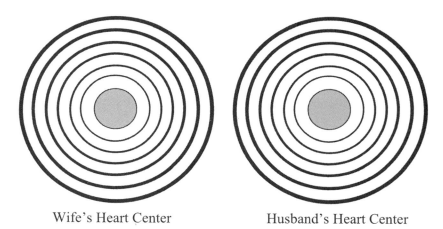

Wife's Heart Center   Husband's Heart Center

Did you keep your spouse out of your center bull's-eye zone to protect yourself? Maybe you needed to because of past abuse, but it's important for both spouses to recognize that the goal is to be inside the very center of each other's core. You cannot achieve marital oneness until you are willing to be one, which means no barriers between you and your spouse.

We believe your marriage is not where it should be until you can place your spouse in the bull's-eye with your inner self. Yes, you're totally vulnerable, but totally immersed in each other too. When this occurs it means nothing can come between you. We admit being fully vulnerable is scary, but being fully vulnerable is what fosters the deepest intimacy. If you could not place your spouse inside your very core that means some fear or fears is keeping up the defensive walls and those are areas that need to be dealt with.

When a soldier serves with a group of men, they very often develop a deep bond, they know each other's weaknesses and strengths, they have each other's back, and they depend on each other. Your marriage deserves at least that much compassion and caring. If you cheated on your spouse and are finding it hard to understand why something like a one-night fling that didn't really matter to you has hurt your spouse so much, you need to understand the difference has a lot to do with how close your spouse had you in his or her inner circle. Infidelity really, really hurts because you were likely the only one who was allowed to be close enough to do a lot of emotional damage.

I have protective barriers between myself and other folks outside my center core, but my wife is in the center with me; she alone has the ability to sneak up on me and devastate my world. We have to allow this complete inner core vulnerability to have a great marriage, for only then is the intimacy at its highest and best.

Do you remember the 14 test questions you took in chapter 2? Those questions were to help you determine where your marriage was at that point in time, to reveal if it was showing weakness. Now it's up to you to determine where you want it to be. Do you desire deep intimacy? How will you get from where you are in your relationship to where you want to be?

> *In an effort to help me feel more secure in our marriage, Bob tells me over and over that he's "committed." The last time he told me that I responded, "That's enough, go check in already!"*

There have been times when we have intervened with a couple when it was apparent we cared more for their marriage than they did. Sometimes one or both spouses will be so beat up or have lost all hope that their marriage could amount to something, they just give up caring or trying. While a few have gone on to divorce, others were saved and went thru the remodel process to come out in the end with a great marriage. We are convinced every marriage can be a great one, why not really apply yourselves and see what happens?

And if you have a great marriage, don't be afraid to reach out to friends and family who do not. Give them books, pay their way to a marriage retreat, become a mentoring couple, and help them restore their marriage. We've made new and lasting friends by reaching out to strangers we barely knew when they let it slip their marriage was falling apart. When

13 someone says "my marriage sucks" that's your cue to help them. Get an address, and send them a couple of marriage books.

Do you need a major or minor remodel?

If so, work at cutting out the stuff that's damaged; work at replacing it with new and better materials. Use the "tools" when you rebuild, get "help" to accomplish the work. As a general contractor I never did a remodel that wasn't messy, I never did one that wasn't more time consuming than I estimated, I never did one that went as planned, but the finished product was always, repeat, ALWAYS far better than what was there before. Let the remodeling begin!

Couple's project—At the end of the handbook are a couple of blank pages. We'd like you to write out a list of items that you feel could be troubling issues in your relationship. Keep the list to less than 10 items. It is not important that you agree on each item. Writing them down will bring clarity and attention to them. A contractor would be making a similar list if he was inspecting a house for areas that need a remodel. These are what you will work on (remodel) in the coming months. If need be, you can tear out the list and bring it to your first marriage therapy session, which will jump start the process.

Did you learn anything? Yes / No
Chapter personal benefit appraisal: **HER 1-2-3-4-5   HIM 1-2-3-4-5**
1=not at all, 2=a little, 3=some good stuff, 4=fairly helpful, 5=very helpful

www.u-build.com

CHAPTER 14

What Not to Bring to Your Marriage Ceremony, and Other Relationship Killers

In the previous chapter we talked about a few reasons to consider a marriage remodel, be it major or minor. Remodeling is an "after the fact, or after it's been built" activity. In this chapter we will address what an engaged or newlywed couple should make every effort not to build into their new home. At our website we will soon be offering a great tool for engaged couples to truly prepare for their marriage union, so look forward to that. However, not to ignore our already married couples, the items listed in the following pages can be like termites, they may have been ignored and been brought into the marriage by one spouse or the other and have since been secretly chewing away at the structure of the marriage. While it is now after the fact, they will likewise need to be addressed.

> *"Most people settle for a fuzzy image of a marriage while lying 12 inches away from them is the real deal. A "great" marriage is not a wedding day photograph on your dresser; it's the person sleeping next to you in your bed. A marriage should be alive, breathing and vibrant. Don't hold the picture and smile, hold your spouse and smile!"*

A requirement is that as a couple you should be at a place where you can talk about relationship killers as this subject material can bring out passionate feelings. If your relationship is somewhat unstable or you have a concern about talking over these points without a 3rd party present, then it is prudent to go to a marriage counselor who will help you work thru them. Not all of these may kill a marriage, but without a doubt they will put additional stress on your marriage. Consider this a **SAFE TIME** as you discuss these.

It's important to understand, WE ALL HAVE ISSUES. None of us is perfect, but in an established marriage union we should be seeking the higher ground, seeking the mature aspects of adulthood, and always moving toward bettering the marriage union.

As we mentioned in a prior chapter, some people reach various levels of maturity quicker than others, while some people never seem to mature. Some individuals mature in a few areas of their life, but don't in others.

14 Some of us weave in and out of being mature and immature. Indeed, even in a mature marriage we sometimes fail and do an immature act. But we should always pick ourselves up and try to be better.

So here is the deal: if you cut out some of the "crap," you'll experience fewer storms. If you mature in your relationship, the storms you go thru will cause less damage. So by talking about these relationship killers now, you'll be on your way to having an understanding of how your spouse feels about them, instead of learning about them in the middle of a big fight.

> *"I'm truly sorry, but if there is a fire in a building where my wife is present, I'm going to pass over all of you to get her out first. It's not that I have an aversion to you, I just have a great love for her. In my eyes, your worth has yet to be determined; my wife's worth has already been established."*

Most people will not be honest in admitting they have a compulsion or addiction. Hey, who wants to say *"I'm weak in this area," "I fail at maintaining a high standard,"* or *"This addiction controls me."* But you are not alone; many of us will have trouble with some compulsion to a varying degree. Let's agree to be honest and with that honesty your spouse must be willing to hear this stuff and not "freak," but agree to help get you over these weaknesses.

Couple's project—As a couple you should go thru the list, with grace, and in love. Check the items that you may have to deal with as a couple. *Remember the two of you are working on oneness.* Mark the things you want to have less of in your marriage. Again, remember, this is a **SAFE TIME**; neither spouse cuts the other down while we work thru these.

Because we know some of you are not going to be honest, we have already worked out a compromise. We want each spouse to select at least the top three items from the list below that are issues you are or have struggled with, and either place a mark by them or talk about them. If you're really mature, go for the whole enchilada, otherwise pick at least three.

FACTOID – Termites are critters that work beneath the surface, mostly hidden from view, and chew at the structure of your home to weaken it. Most marriages have termites too, but they can be eradicated.

Addictions/Dependencies/Compulsions

- Prescription drug abuse (generally along the lines of painkillers, narcotics, tranquilizers, etc.)
- Illegal drug abuse or use
- Alcoholism
- Pornography/sexual addictions
- Lying/dishonesty
- Infidelity
- Spending/materialism
- Hording
- Gambling
- Parental dependency
- Food/overeating
- Workaholic
- Neat or germ freak
- Preoccupation with sports or other social events
- Preoccupation with TV, Internet, chat rooms, blogs
- Perfectionist
- Condemning or belittling character
- Other? Write yours in here:

Emotional Factors

- Anger/rage especially that leads to verbal or physical abuse
- Jealousy (unfounded, controlling)
- Excessive bond to a group, gang, or club that would interfere with the marriage unit
- Overemotional, huge and/or frequent mood swings
- Apathy/indifference/complacency
- Critical tongue, never complimenting, negative
- Degrading/condescending tongue
- Non-compromising; "my way is the only way"
- Controlling personality, i.e., military type atmosphere in the home
- Manipulative, scheming to get your way
- Retreating to within, not engaging
- Unfounded fears
- Non-touching or little touching
- Prideful/cocky/egotistical/arrogant
- Wicked/evil actions or intentions
- Demanding
- Impatient

- Being a doormat to others
- Secretive, i.e., *"This doesn't concern my spouse, it's 'my thing.'"*
- Stingy
- Careless
- Nagging/coarse/disrespectful/overly critical
- Immaturity, foolishness
- Grouchy/grumpy
- Negativity
- Cowardly
- Messy
- Foolish
- Prejudice
- Overly anxious
- Self-righteousness
- Procrastinator/unreliable/not living up to promises
- Shame, holding or hiding it, a disgraceful part of our life we try to hide
- Very low self-esteem
- Bitterness/un-forgiveness
- Other? Write in here:

> *I can make my husband shudder anytime I want by using my "wares". He does the same for me when he not only drives to, but turns into the mall. Life is good!*

The above list of relationship killers is meant to spur discussion in these and other areas. If yours was not mentioned, bring it up. You'll learn in chapter 22 about personality types, that we all have a mixture of good and bad properties. We are purposely bringing them out in the open, but just with your spouse for now. However, individually or collectively you should seek professional help if you need help. And getting counseling is OK—remember, we all need a team to help us build or rebuild a home. Compulsions drive you to do things you do not want to do; getting help to get over them is a very wise and necessary activity.

Every one of the items in the list above can be healed, solved, or treated to remove the threat to the marriage. We call these relationship killers because they, like termites, cause hidden damage. Dealing with them before marriage is best, but the truth is many of us fail to get rid of them, and bring them into the marriage union. After awhile, the structure weakens and it becomes evident to all that termites are eating away at our home. Owning up to our "issues" is the first step in conquering them. If we never own up, healing and repair will never come.

One key to a lasting marriage is to never allow issues beyond the *"concerns & struggles"* stage without seeking resolution. After using this "resolution remodel" a few times, you'll get good at it, and it will come naturally. *"Hey honey I'm starting to feel bitter about this. I want to discuss this during a SAFE TIME and not let it blow up into a storm later."*

So which is the worst of all the relationship killers listed? Frankly we don't have an opinion on that, every one of them is capable of destroying an otherwise healthy marriage. While infidelity is a huge trust breaker, it can occur haphazardly with no emotional tie. So while infidelity is certainly very serious, it may have been a meaningless one-time event that came with deep regret and repentance. Is a non-caring apathetic spouse any better? Is living with a person addicted to drugs any better? All of these can be destructive depending on the intensity. That is why they should be dealt with and guarded against.

The goal is not to injure or damage you or your spouse when working thru this chapter. The goal is to improve the conditions that will allow the relationship to flourish. You're looking for damage-causing factors and seeking to eliminate those areas. The enemy is those pesky termites, not your spouse. Even when dealing with severe relationship killers such as infidelity, there is little to be gained by seeking to destroy the offending spouse. The focus for any marital issue should be, *Is there true repentance and can it be resolved (nearly every trouble can be), and if it can be, how?* What changes need to be made to not only rebuild the relationship, but to make it stronger?

The Power of Our Words

We'd like you to understand the power in words, the power we hold on our lips and tongue. While we spew forth words and accusations when defending our turf, perhaps we've not really thought about how we subconsciously or consciously exploit this power.

If your discussions turn into arguments or become heated and/or become condemning, then that aspect needs to change. Words such as *"you never"* or *"you always"* are rarely true, so while they are injurious, they are also likely exaggerations. Words are powerful! They can tear you down or build you up, and some people are masters at using words to destroy. All too often, words do have the desired effect and tear down the intended target.

Conversely, our words of encouragement build up people. Encouraging words work for little Johnny who is about to play in his first baseball game and is scared to death, as well as 40-year-old Sara who is about to give a speech before several hundred people and is also frightened. When we encourage people, that encouragement does something magical to give them the confidence to go forward. When we cut them down, it can have a devastating effect on their feelings, which has nothing to do with working out a solution.

FACTOID – Our words carry the power to build up or tear down. Our words can solve problems or create more. In a marriage we must train ourselves so our words build up and solve problems.

Maybe you're one of those who think you're so tough that you can ignore condemnation. Perhaps you think because it's just your way of venting, your spouse should be able to handle it. We've got a little experiment if you care to try, but I can tell you, you will be adversely affected because this aspect is an integral part of human psychology.

At the next hockey or basketball event, ask if you can go stand alone in the center of the court with a few thousand people looking on. Ask the announcer to have the spectators boo at you for several minutes as you stand there. You'll walk away emotionally shaken and troubled even though you know they were just booing you as an experiment. Harsh words kill, even when done in jest, and more so when done in anger.

As emotional creatures, we do not like being put down, even when done jokingly as it inflicts serious damage to our inner psyche. A spouse who cuts down their spouse either purposely or jokingly does harm. Each and every time they do it, it adds up to greater and greater damage. It's a termite type of damage that will one day cause the structure of the marriage to fail. We are not supposed to damage our spouses; we are supposed to build them up. So look for marriage termites, and work to repair the damage before it gets too bad.

We have a friend who cut down his wife frequently both in public and in private. Frankly, it was embarrassing to be around him when he did this. His marriage failed, which was very predictable. In the end, even with a change of heart, he couldn't regain what he had destroyed in the relationship. He fostered termites of resentment every time he cut down his wife. We all can learn from his failure.

The concept of building in a marriage is not guaranteed to be beneficial just because building activity is taking place. The question needs to be asked, what are you building? Very often couples will build walls between themselves. These relationship-blocking walls are built from unresolved issues and problems in the marriage. One unresolved issue after another gradually builds up the wall so that one day both spouses find they are operating independently of the other with hardly any emotional bonding. Always work issues to resolution; don't let a wall build up between you and your spouse. It's too easy after you've made one or two emotional blocks to just keep adding more.

Some marriage counselors will guide couples to prioritize problems. The top severity problems are described as being in one of the following categories: immoral, illegal, unethical, or uncaring. So it stands to reason you should desire to settle these kinds of issues more purposefully than other types of issues such as how you raise your children, how you handle the finances, etc.

Your Home a Breeding Farm?

Yes, it's true. Regardless of where or what kind of home you live in, your home is a breeding farm. Yes, most of you are breeding kids (hi five!) but 95% of us are also breeding other things too. You are breeding unity or division, harmony or bitterness, love or anger, respect or disrespect, and more. You see, the principle is we reap what we sow, so if we sow good relationship seeds, we will get a crop of good relationship fruit; however, if we plant bad relationship seeds, we will reap a bad relationship crop. When one spouse begins to act negatively it will often cause the other spouse to respond in a negative manner. This atmosphere can begin to feed on itself until the whole house is filled with negative emotions, bad feelings, and a broken relationship. It is therefore imperative that each spouse stop negative emotions and responses as soon as possible and seek or plant seeds of harmony.

Understanding Escalating Emotions

Many passionate people have never really considered the expressional steps they move between in an escalating conflict but it is worth examining them. I am a passionate person and I found myself wondering why I can be so caring for weeks only to act like Attila the Hun when something hits me the wrong way. I was confused about it until I realized that that same passion can work both ways. When I'm on your side, I will work hard with you to succeed, but like many Lion types, that same passion to care and provide gets exaggerated when I feel disrespected. By examining the negative passion, I found ways to break its cycle.

> *"When you reach the end of your rope, tie a knot in it and hang on."*
> Thomas Jefferson

Escalating intensities of negative passion may start with discontent of one type or another. We feel wronged, or disrespected, or ignored. It might begin with the rolling of our eyes, or a facial expression of discontent, then move to finger pointing or other outward body expressions such as the crossing of arms, followed by strong or forceful talk and an elevated voice. If allowed to escalate unrestrained, perhaps swearing and/or yelling will occur next.

Disagreements on the subject material then moves from the topic at hand to personal attacks on the person and typically broad exaggerations. If left unchecked, and at its worse, it can escalate to physical abuse.

One key to understanding how to "disagree in harmony" for a person of passion is to know where unchecked passionate anger leads and to select "getting off points" well below what you may have escalated to in the past. We've just showed you the steps of ever increasing anger. Now that you know how you get there, start choosing to step down or off the ladder to a much more respectful way to work out a disagreement.

It's very important to confess your faults, expose the termites, and then as a couple work to eradicate them. Marriage is about working out solutions for the troubles of life that you would otherwise be going thru by yourself. Just keep this in mind, it's not about blame it's about finding solutions together. We cannot emphasize enough how liberating confession can be.

Did you learn anything? Yes / No
Chapter personal benefit appraisal: **HER 1-2-3-4-5   HIM 1-2-3-4-5**
1=not at all, 2=a little, 3=some good stuff, 4=fairly helpful, 5=very helpful

Who Is the Enemy?

Is fighting all the time working for you? Is the silent treatment working for you? When is the last time you and your spouse had a good laugh together? Do you find your spouse repulsive? Do you tiptoe around issues because your home seems to go from one storm to the next? Do you feel you are living with the enemy? If so, is this what you call marriage? Is this what you wanted in your marriage?

The above certainly occurs in the homes of married couples, but these are not the signs of a healthy marriage. We are going to work thru four main points in this chapter; it's going to be very important that you get these. We believe there is a concept that needs to be so well understood that it needed its own chapter, so let's get going.

> *"People have said that famous sports athletes and movie stars have a greater pressure and difficulty on their marriages because of their fame and being in the public eye. We disagree; the only difficulty was letting anything at all compete for their attention over their spouse. Saying "no" to outside influences might not make you a lot of money, but it's part of the equation in ensuring you have a long-lasting and great marriage. Every couple has to make these same choices every day."*

Point #1

The most important point is who the enemy is not—**the enemy is <u>not</u> your spouse!**

15 | **Couple's project**—We'd like you to turn to each other and say—*"You are not the enemy."*

In our first few years of marriage we made the same mistake many couples do and that was fighting like the enemy was each other. When a fight breaks out, any kind of fight, we are programmed so that there is a winner and there is a loser and that we should strive to be the winner. <u>That's the wrong concept for a marital disagreement.</u> If you win, it means your spouse loses; yet your spouse is someone you love. However, they are not losers and it's pretty dimwitted if you make them a loser. RIGHT? *(Bob is whistling here while the light bulbs come on for each spouse.)*

It's remarkable that the person we married, loved, and wanted to spend the rest of our life with magically becomes (in our mind) the enemy. Even if your marriage was to fail, you should never see your spouse as an enemy, for you loved them, they loved you, and somewhere you both messed up. Many marriage failures can be traced back to malfunctions of one sort or another, but failing to work out issues or mistakes is not a just cause to make your spouse your enemy.

If we look at our human body we see it as a single unit, yet it is made up of many parts. Let's check out a pair of legs taking a hike down a mountain trail where one leg stumbles, breaking the other leg. Does the injured leg say to the other leg, *"Hey, I wouldn't have gotten this banged up if you would have been more careful not to slip"*? Not at all! I have actually taped conversations between several pairs of legs! *(I didn't say I'm right in the head.)* What actually is said is something like this: *"I'm sorry for stumbling."* To which the other leg typically responds: *"No, it's my fault. I knew that we were on some shaky ground, yet I also went along with the risks when I shouldn't have. I should have supported you more."* The healthy leg says: *"I'll hop us outta here and get us to a place of safety."* Afterward they usually state that they are glad they both made it out and then begin apologizing to each other all the more regardless of who may have caused the stumble.

> *"I'd certainly agree with you that terrorists are the enemy, I might even agree with you that criminals are our enemies, but I'm going to find it hard to believe your spouse is too."*

You see the goal was never to place blame, but to get to safety and get the healing process going and to remain ONE.

102

If your own legs will carry each other out of danger to a place of safety, why not apply the same principle in your marriage?

"**Condemnation**" is a tool of the enemy. If you can get around blame, then the enemy has one less arrow with which to destroy your marriage. The enemy loses and you both win! Later in this chapter we are going to discuss the following in more detail, but given that the majority of Americans are Christian, most of you will likewise have a biblical understanding that the enemy is Satan who opposes God and those who seek to follow after God. As such, we can tell the difference between both because each has different attributes. Condemnation is not an attribute of God, however, it is of Satan.

God will use "**conviction**" not "condemnation" to move people who are in a relationship with Him. Conviction can be a heavy ordeal; it forces us to look at ourselves in the correct light, it understands God knows everything in our hearts and thoughts and we cannot lie to God. Conviction moves us to correct the wrongs we have done, and then to seek and ask for forgiveness. Conviction doesn't make us small like condemnation; rather it lets us determine our own guilt or innocence.

Some storms come indiscriminately and do not originate with either spouse, i.e., accidents happen. We are with each other to serve each other, to protect each other, to love each other, to care for each other. It's less about blame and more about healing. You have to make a choice. Is it more important that you win and that your spouse is blamed, or that healing occurs for the marriage union? Do you want to be right more than you want a strong marriage?

Couple's project—OK, time for a confession. Turn to your spouse and one at a time make this confession: *"Honey, I have wrongly sought to win arguments and make you the loser. Who was right or wrong is less important than finding answers. I have behaved in a manner that I now know is wrong. I'm sorry, truly sorry, and I ask your forgiveness and help in improving our relationship."*

The power of our words is important, not only in solving problems, but also in confessing and forgiving.

FACTOID – You have to know your enemy; when you don't, you'll be caught unaware. Consider that it was just a chunk of frozen water (a large ice cube) that sunk the *Titanic*.

15 | Point #2

Remember the saying *"I looked in the mirror and saw the enemy was me."* This is often the case; we are our own worst enemy and we are certainly part of the problem in a troubled marriage.

> *The road to divorce has many signposts along the way but these signs are carelessly ignored. "Concerns or struggles," if left unresolved, lead to "disillusionment" that if left untreated will lead to "withdrawal and isolation" that if left untreated will fester into "anger or bitterness" that if left untreated will lead to "misery and very likely divorce." Why travel this road? Why would a couple willingly ignore all the signs?*

When a plant in our garden dies, who is responsible for its death? Where does the buck stop? Yep, with us. It's our job to tend to the plant because it's in "OUR" garden, and likewise it's our job to tend to our marriage. When issues creep in between us and our spouse and we do not deal with them before they turn into a major crisis, whose fault is it? Yes, it's ours! We are not saying that whatever the other spouse did was OK, or that they are blameless. What we are saying is when <u>you</u> are not doing what <u>you</u> can to foster a great marriage, when you are not dealing with the issues in a timely fashion, the outcome is pretty predictable. One spouse or the other is going to fail in some manner, and at that point it is up to the other spouse to step up and lead the marriage to the place of safety. You must admit you are part of the problem even though you didn't initiate the infraction. And this is not a percent share thing; it is rather a yes or no question: "Are you any part of the problem?" The answer will be yes 99% of the time, even when it is infidelity by the other spouse.

Couple's project—Turn again to your spouse and one at a time speak the following statement to each other: *"Honey, I'm part of the problem in this marriage, please forgive me if I've never said this before."*

Point #3

The enemy is everywhere and it's not just one enemy, there are many of them. In every large company there is a department called "risk management." The sole task of this department is to manage risk, to keep the company from doing things that may harm the company down the road. Married couples need a risk management plan and it's most important to start this plan in the early years of the marriage.

A home has many enemies; it can be damaged by rodents, insects, pets, wild animals, children, vandals, rainstorms, ice storms, wind, falling trees & branches, flooding, earthquakes, foundation settling, etc.

Building a fence around your marriage is indeed required if you are to keep out predatory marriage killers. Fences are built to keep things in and keep other things out and they also signify ownership. With this understanding, isn't a fence a good thing to have around your marriage relationship? A fence means there are things you'll not let in to your property. For Paige and me a fence isn't strong enough, we like having a wall, something very strong.

Understand it may appear greener on the other side of the fence. But Astroturf, while greener, is none the less fake. It appears perfect, but it's not the real thing. No one who is carelessly willing to have an affair with a married person is virtuous enough to trust, so why go through the pain of divorce to get hooked up with someone who already has shown no respect for a marriage union?

How does risk manifest itself? By temptation, by opportunity, by "flirting" with danger, by seeking a thrill, by satisfying unmet needs, by looking over the fence and coveting something you feel you do not have.

> As a guard against even the appearance of wrongdoing, Billy Graham had a policy that he would never be alone with any other woman than his wife, Ruth. It became known as the Billy Graham Rule.

As we can see, Billy Graham had an understanding of risk management. Often threats and risks come at us innocently. Infidelity rarely just happens. It usually begins with subtle contacts that blossom into an affair. Many adulterers report they didn't go looking for sex or an affair, it *"just kinda grew into a relationship."* How does a casual relationship mushroom into an affair? It happens because little or no barriers or risk management have been set up. We have to build walls and decide ahead of time we are not going to look over those walls, and if we do we will not venture outside our yard.

When Bob and I got married one of the first things we decided to do was set up some risk management fences, not because we were taught that, but because we knew we both needed them. We quit going to bars, we got rid of all our old boyfriend/girlfriend pictures, we quit contact with old boyfriends/girlfriends, we quit getting drunk *(actually stopped drinking altogether for many years)*, we didn't go out dancing with other couples, and more. Prudes? No, we selectively removed a bunch of situations that often lead to temptations and high risk opportunities. Even with these fences we found we had new risks that we had to manage after we both found ourselves flirting in Internet chat rooms. Fortunately, we realized the new danger and then built a fence to keep that influence out too. Some of you might say we cut out all the fun! We would respond we made sure we had an <u>enduring fun</u> rather than misery by cutting out the things that came with a poor risk versus reward ratio.

Danger signs—Do you look forward to going to a store, office, or a home because of someone of the opposite sex? Do you frequent chat rooms, blogs, etc., because someone of the opposite sex flirts with you? Do you exchange cell phone text messages with anyone that either crosses the line or is heading that way? Are you sending and receiving some flirty email messages? Do you like giving and receiving touch, hugs/kisses, etc., from someone that is not your spouse? Does your mind wander into a land of "what if" about someone of the opposite sex? How about a friend of your spouse you are attracted to? Are there secret things in your personal life that you keep from your spouse and would be embarrassed or ashamed if they found out? If so, the enemy is testing your boundaries to see if he can destroy your marriage.

We've already told you there are no perfect marriages; we do not have a perfect marriage but we have a great one. It would be a misunderstanding on your part if you think we've not experienced threatening events that rocked our marriage, for we have. Even with boundaries and an awareness of risk management, we've stumbled and had to perform remodel work and put up new fences.

Remember, we've had to learn what a good marriage is as we had never seen one before, thus we've made mistakes just like many couples do, but we've headed off many as well. Besides chat rooms, we've also wandered into romance novels, and erotica. And we did these things while we still loved each other. For most of you reading this handbook, you have to admit you have strayed too. We are sharing with the whole world our mistakes; we are only asking you to share your weaknesses with each other, and if need be, a marriage counselor.

FACTOID – X-rays are used to detect unseen damage in the human body, in metal welds, and in all kinds of structural applications. Unseen weakness must be revealed and repaired; to do otherwise is to willingly let a future failure occur.

When weaknesses are found in our defenses, we seek to make them stronger. For instance, we heard that a pastor instructs couples to bring up to each other any event or outside relationship that could be threatening to the marriage union. His theory is if a couple openly shares any vulnerability it takes the previously undisclosed (thus secret) weakness and puts it out into the open.

It works like this: Let's say a woman at the office seems to be getting a little flirty and maybe even suggestively teases you. While the attention is something we all desire, it's a doorway to infidelity. Having previously agreed that either spouse may bring up a "potential" threat, the husband informs his wife and thus exposes the flirtatious activity. By doing so he invites his wife to quiz him about it, and his wife is now aware of the potential hazard. She is also free to question her husband's motives when he appears to lower a protective wall between the coworker and himself. Practicing this technique is an admission that we can be weak and fail on our own, so we involve our spouses to help us in our resolve to resist temptations. It is imperative that when your spouse shares a threat with you, and the name of a person they are trying to resist, that you be supportive rather than condemning. Bringing you into the situation is supposed to help not hurt; you must be there for each other. If you blow up into a fit of jealousy and anger, who will your spouse confide in?

We have occasionally gotten into arguments that instead of being settled that same day went on for days. During one of the darker periods in our marriage we were emotionally distant from each other for weeks. We had both hardened our hearts not only to each other, but to God's prompting to apologize and seek forgiveness. We'd hidden things from each other; we'd shared things with others that we didn't share between us. We've had periods when we were bitter, unforgiving, angry, and stubborn. Some of these detachments occurred simultaneously with trials we were going thru. We've had two miscarriages and delivered our little boy, Matthew, dead. We both suffered with medical diseases we are still being treated for. We both had periods where we sank into deep despair/depression. We've had financial troubles and even had a bankruptcy. You see, our married life has been filled with things we are ashamed of, trials, tribulations, etc., but we worked thru them, and so can you. Life can be tough and many threats can come at us, but for most of us, we believe it is far better going thru life with a life-long partner than going it alone. We have to pick ourselves up and go at it again no matter how many times something in life knocks us down.

Point #4

Not everyone can fight calmly without needing to vent their passion. Thus, it can be effective to put a face to who your enemy really is. A face allows the internal hostility to be expressed and outwardly directed. However, you should not make that face an actual person. The enemy is those pesky termites, not your spouse, or you can use the technique Paige and I use. It's based on the Scripture, *"We wrestle not against flesh and blood but against principalities and wickedness in high places."*

We always see Satan as our enemy. After we accept our own role in any matter, we join together to fight this biblically identified troublemaker. The Scriptures have a lot to say about Satan and describe Satan as our real enemy, so we are correctly fighting the one who should be fought; in effect we are aligning ourselves with God's word on the matter.

Even if you do not believe in any religious or spiritual entities, we're sure you can see the marital benefit that comes from focusing your anger at something other than your spouse.

| *"If you're going through hell, keep going."* | Winston Churchill |

We understand you may feel like your spouse is the enemy, we understand you both may frequently injure the other with words and body language. You may have lived the last 10 years with a spouse you are convinced is the enemy, but that is not marriage even if you have remained married.

Your spouse is not the enemy, but indeed there are enemies out there. We want to caution you that you cannot be too vigilant when it comes to protecting your marriage. It is really important not to allow a weak point in your defense wall. When you find one, shore it up and repair it as quickly as possible.

Couple's project—Discuss what this chapter means to you and how you can apply it in your marriage.

Love your spouse, love your spouse, love your spouse…
Love him with kind words, love her with kind words…
Love her with actions, love him with actions…

Did you learn anything? Yes / No
Chapter personal benefit appraisal: **HER 1-2-3-4-5   HIM 1-2-3-4-5**
1=not at all, 2=a little, 3=some good stuff, 4=fairly helpful, 5=very helpful

www.u-build.com

CHAPTER 16

Physical, Emotional & Mental Abuse, Adultery & Trust Issues

Physical Issues

We always ask couples to consider that some medical aspect could be causing or exacerbating marital difficulties. This area should always be considered as we have personally encountered this in our own marriage. All the counseling in the world will be ineffective when one or both spouses are suffering from some undiagnosed medical condition. If a marriage distress alarm is lack of intimacy, could it be due to a low testosterone level in the wife or husband? It is important to use symptoms as a guide to finding root causes as too many people try to treat the symptom rather than the underlying cause.

> *"I was married by a judge, I should have asked for a jury."*
> Groucho Marx

Some studies indicate that a significant portion of the population has undiagnosed hormonal imbalances and/or disease. Do your emotions seem to run away? Are you troubled by anxiety, fears, anger outbursts, or other emotions that just seem to sweep over you? If either of you suspect that an undiagnosed medical condition could be affecting your personality or emotions then please seek the required medical attention to answer that suspicion.

FACTOID – No amount of counseling is going to heal a broken leg. Don't go to a counselor when you need to see a physician.

I had been diagnosed with hyperthyroidism but only after Bob took me to the Mayo Clinic. Prior to that, I was diagnosed as having "anxiety" by our family doctor. I indeed was demonstrating a form of anxiety, but it was being caused by an overactive thyroid gland, something our family doctor ignorantly failed to diagnose for a period of two years. A second-rate doctor will fail to see a symptom as an indicator and incorrectly treat the symptom rather than the cause. My then family doctor wanted to treat me with anxiety medications believing that anxiety was my root ailment.

But the correct treatment for my condition was to destroy the overactive thyroid gland and then supplement with synthetic thyroid for the remainder of my life.

Finding the root cause was a big relief, and you'd think that this would have settled the matter. However, without a thyroid, I require a very exacting amount of medication to replace the missing hormones. Failure in achieving the exact dose has occasionally caused emotional mood swings lasting many weeks because the medication can be hard to balance in some people. At one point about 12 years into our marriage my lab test results were wrongly calculated and my doctor raised my medication when it should have been reduced. This resulted in a very dramatic change to my personality; I acted like someone Bob didn't know and wasn't sure he wanted to know. We had a very difficult time until we figured out the meds had been the cause of the problem. Now later in life I am going thru menopause and again I find myself with another hormone-related condition and once again require medications to restore balance to my emotional health.

As noted above, some prescription medications can induce strange behavior. Bob has battled a couple of diseases in which the treatment regimen required that he take a drug called prednisone. Prednisone is a corticosteroid that along with many other negative side effects brings out a short-fused anger in most people. He had to take this medication for about three years. Getting off that medication became a focal point to restore our marriage into a healthier condition.

In many of our experiences, the emotional mood swings, anger, and anxiety were due either to a medical condition or prescription medications. Thyroid issues, hormonal imbalances, estrogen, testosterone, the so called "midlife crisis" hormonal changes, etc., can all be corrected by various means; however, those remedies are likely based in pharmaceuticals not interpersonal counseling.

The point we want to make here is that for a significant portion of the couples in marital distress, a spouse's irrational behavior can be related to a genuine medical condition. Thus, we want you both to seriously consider that there could be a real physical condition that needs to be diagnosed and dealt with if you are experiencing a loss of marital harmony. We do not place an excessive amount of faith in doctors, nor drugs, but they do in fact play a vital role in healing various maladies in the human body. While seeking treatment remember that medicine and pharmaceutical remedies should be used only when required and no more than required. It does little good for a marriage if one spouse becomes addicted to the numbing effects of painkillers or tranquilizers.

Emotional/Mental

There are also emotional or mental disorders that while not physical in nature are like a computer virus; they attack the operating system in our mind and corrupt its ability to function. Some of these disorders are: post-traumatic stress disorder, panic attacks, depression, phobias, addictions, compulsions, etc., all of which bring a different dynamic into a marriage. Any difficulty in the marriage relationship usually exacerbates these kinds of conditions, which can further injure the marriage. Unfortunately, these can feed on one another creating a vicious spiral. We are not trained to counsel in these areas; however, there are many resources that can help a couple work thru them.

Very often these types of maladies require working with a medical professional such as a psychologist or psychiatrist. These medically trained professionals will also be aware that something physical could be out of balance causing the emotional disorder. Medical science has found that certain chemical balances must occur in our brain for our mind to function properly; without them unusual behavior can occur. At one point in my life over 20 years ago, I experienced a panic attack that was due to stress. I was working very long hours while running my own business, which had me operating on adrenaline most of the time. The cure was to sell the business and take up another line of work.

Trust Issues

There are several types of trust issues that are frequently to blame for marital troubles. One type has to do with previous sexual and/or physical abuse, another infidelity, and still another can be found in blended (previously divorced parents with kids) families.

FACTOID – There is no relationship of any value or worth where trust is not one of the most important ingredients.

These trust distresses are only related because they adversely affect a relationship, otherwise the manner in which the trust is damaged is quite different. Each of these issues carries impacts for how, when, or if trust can be built or rebuilt between you and your spouse.

113

16 Blended families—In a blended family situation trust has to be earned by each new parent, but building trust can be unfairly subjected to the whims of children who can easily corrupt the environment leading to trust. While it is natural for a parent bringing kids from a prior marriage into a new marriage to be protective of their kids over the kids of their new spouse, the marriage will be severely impacted if both spouses do not act as one. The parents must show <u>all</u> the children that they are still children and subject to the authority and oversight from either the natural or the stepparent. However, it is really the responsibility of the natural parent to enforce all rules within the house until the children have accepted the stepparent as someone they can trust. The natural parent is likewise seeking to gain confidence in their new spouse, to determine if they can be trusted with their children. Blended families require additional marriage and parenting skills beyond the scope of our book, but many books have been written on the subject.

Abuse—When one or both spouses have been subject to abuse either as a child or in a previous relationship, letting down protective barriers is very difficult. It can take years before they feel they "know" their spouse well enough to make themselves vulnerable again. This topic is also beyond the scope of our book, but there are many resources available to help couples work themselves above and beyond the senseless actions of an abuser. If you are currently being abused, please seek the help of your local law enforcement agency and/or health and human services department.

> *My wife recently took advantage of one of our SAFE TALK times to request that I work on being more presentable or "debinare," I told her it's my practice not to try to be something I can't correctly pronounce or spell. I thought it was settled, but for my birthday she gave me a dictionary.*

Adultery Issues

Everyone would agree with regard to adultery that trust has been lost and must be rebuilt for the marriage to be salvaged. Consider the plight of the spouses of famous personalities who were caught in adultery in 2010. It is not enough for them to suffer thru the betrayal of their spouse, but they had to be dragged thru the weekly humiliation from the media. Affairs are bad enough on a private level; it must have felt like being run over by a truck that kept going back and forth as the media continued to replay the events.

It is much harder to restore trust when others outside the marriage are working hard to make sure the event is never forgotten.

There is something very repulsive to most of us if we are forced to picture our trusted, lifelong companion being intimately entertained in the arms of another. How is a loving, devoted spouse supposed to process infidelity—it doesn't make sense on so many levels. There are no good excuses for infidelity regardless if it is the husband or wife who strays. In most of the publicized 2010 infidelities the famous marriages tragically ended. It saddens us that these otherwise nice people didn't have the marriage survival tools they needed to build their marriage and remodel it when damage was found.

Even when there is an attempt for reconciliation couples will typically use the infidelity event to regurgitate all kinds of unresolved hostility from the past. If that were not enough there will be two separate internal battles going on while relationship repairs are being explored. One battle will be with the spouse who was violated, he or she will have erected all kinds of emotional fences for self-protection while at the same time knowing the fences will have to come down at some point if the relationship is ever to be restored. And another battle will be raging inside the spouse who was unfaithful with regard to desiring that intimate activity be restored as soon as possible for that will be the sign that the marriage and trust has a chance. On top of all that, both spouses will be dealing with emotional and perhaps professional shame.

Sexual intimacy might be the hardest part of healing a relationship damaged by infidelity. In working to repair the damage and save the marriage the adulterer is faced with months of gaining their spouse's trust back. At the same time the offended spouse has no desire to climb back into the sack as the wound will take time to heal to a point where they will be ready for intimacy. To the wounded spouse of an adulterous affair, reengaging in sexual intimacy makes them feel like their cheating spouse can expect them to ignore what they did to them. The very act of intimacy may cause the injured spouse to revisit the pain of the infidelity every time intimacy occurs. And while all this drama is going on, the male testosterone level is raging at the same pace it did when the affair occurred. Many men will fold and give up on the marriage because they feel they cannot control the urge to wait for intimacy to be restored with no expectation of when or if intimacy will again occur.

In such circumstances, trust has to be established and restored as quickly as "reasonably" possible while at the same time admitting that trust takes time to rebuild. This means getting it all out in the open, it means being bathed in the issues standing in the way of trust, it means putting into action all of the tools, support, materials, etc., to provide healing so trust can be reset solidly in its place of honor. New risk management boundaries will have to be put in place to guard the couple's relationship from future damage. We believe that a couple who has experienced infidelity <u>must</u> invite the help of a good marriage counselor into their marriage restoration plan. The spouse who wandered will have to agree to be held accountable in every area of their life while the relationship is being rebuilt. If marriage is work, then a marriage that has suffered from infidelity will take ten times more effort.

Except for the most obstinate, when a man or woman wrongly strays, they know it; there is very likely deep regret. It is hard to imagine that any spouse guilty of adultery can seriously think destroying a family is a good exchange for a few hours of sex, but it happens all the time. We previously discussed the need for a good risk management plan to guard your marriage from the temptation opportunities that come upon us all. In today's world, both sexes are bombarded with television programming that seems to glorify if not numb us to the act of infidelity.

Whether or not you decide to reveal one or more acts of infidelity that your spouse may not know about is up to you. Some marriage counselors advise against it, others insist on it and for this reason we advise you to seek professional help when tackling this area. Every one of us is different; we have to know our own limits, what we can handle and what we cannot. I'm the kind of person who would want to know if my wife had an affair, but Paige says she would prefer not to know. She feels unsure if she could recover from that information, I feel I could.

What we do recommend is that in any instance where adultery has occurred, if the third party is still in the area where you live or work, or if others who are aware of event will continue bringing it up, that you as a couple consider moving out of that area. But only consider moving after you have discussed this with your marriage counseling professional. Moving is another stressor in a marriage, it does nothing to help repair a marriage; it rather removes the chance that either spouse has to face the involved third party of the infidelity.

There are several great resources for couples dealing with these areas and we highly recommend that couples invest in obtaining whatever resources are required. We list a couple of great book resources in chapter 30 at the end of our handbook.

Couple's project—Discuss if one or both of you should get a physical check-up or if perhaps you should both seek professional counseling to provide for healing in any damaged area. Don't be too proud to fight for your marriage.

16

Did you learn anything? Yes / No
Chapter personal benefit appraisal: **HER 1-2-3-4-5   HIM 1-2-3-4-5**
1=not at all, 2=a little, 3=some good stuff, 4=fairly helpful, 5=very helpful

www.u-build.com

CHAPTER 17

When to Burn It Down and Start Over (divorce)

Given that the majority of those who divorce say incompatibility was the reason for their divorce that would mean about 50–70% of those who are out there looking are already "acknowledged incompatibles." Chances are very good they will hook up with another incompatible person. Chances are it will be someone who was also so incompatible that their last spouse could not live with them either. Do you like those odds?

The fact is a few of you have flipped ahead to this chapter. You're the spouse that is leaning toward getting out because that seems easier than dealing with this stuff. You've flipped forward hoping we will license you to get the divorce. You find the work and mess of a marriage remodel very objectionable and want approval to bail. You'll read later in the statistics chapter that the chances for each successive marriage lasting after the first are worse and worse. Why? It seems neither "ex" has considered that they need to learn how to work thru issues. They continue to remarry expecting they might finally marry the "right one" and when they finally find the right one, there will no longer be any issues. This is an exceptionally wrong assumption. Only when you learn to work thru the issues can your marriage survive. For most of our readers, divorce is not the remedy, and the sooner you begin working on your marriage, the sooner you'll find the happiness you desire.

What to make of it. One couple had a pastor who only had a couple of hours to perform the wedding; he had a funeral before the wedding and one after. He didn't have to change clothes for any and started each event with "We are gathered here today".

17 However, sometimes a contractor will come upon a building in which the damage is so extensive, it must be torn down. For some homes, there are life and safety issues that make repairing the damage in the house just too astronomical and it will be better to level it and start over. This is true for some marriages; they for one reason or another cannot be fixed, so ending the marriage is deemed the appropriate course of action. This should be a rare event and yet it is far too common today. We are being sucked into the drain of throwaway marriages and kids at such a rate some couples now consider a divorce a normal function that follows marriage.

We do not recommend divorce for the following reasons:
- Lack of love or falling out of love
- Lack of intimacy
- Irreconcilable differences

If we were court judges and you came looking for divorce approval from us for any of the above reasons, we would not grant it. Why? Because the reasons above are temporary conditions that can be solved with proper counseling, teaching, and tools. These issues can be overcome and a great marriage can be born out of it.

So when can a marriage be terminated instead of getting a major remodel? This is our "A list":

- **Abandonment** – if your spouse leaves you for an extended length of time, does not communicate with you, and truly has abandoned you, divorce may be an option.
- **Abuse** – if your spouse is physically abusive to either you or your children then halting the abuse is most important. A variety of solutions are available but if ineffective, divorce is warranted.
- **Adultery** – if your spouse has left you for another and there appears no way to reconcile then divorce may be an option.

Before you consider divorce ask yourself these questions:

- Have you done everything in your power to save the marriage?
- Has your spouse refused not only your attempts to reconcile, but also attempts to seek help from a disinterested 3rd party, friends and/or family?
- Aside from your spouse's motives, are <u>your</u> motives less than pure in seeking this divorce?
- Have you engaged in one-on-one sessions of marital counseling?

FACTOID – You're not the best looking person, you're far from the most intelligent, you're not especially talented, you have some emotional issues and hang-ups, and a lot of people make more money than you. What I'm saying is, you and your spouse have more in common than perhaps you thought.

Even a supposedly dead marriage can be brought back to life. Have you tried everything? Is there a spark of life? Would CPR and a defibrillator bring it back?

Do you really want to be in the dating mode again? Do you really want to come home to an empty house or apartment? If you were once willing to fight for your marriage, but now are not willing, what has changed in you?

Growing up I taught my daughter that her attitude was all in her head, she can choose to be happy and content, or mad and upset. I'd tell her the difference between being happy or mad is the amount of time it takes to change your face from a frown to a smile. No matter how far gone you think your marriage may be all that lies between you and your spouse having a good marriage may be the changing of your thoughts. Do your part; if the only thing between a weak marriage and a good marriage is your attitude, then change it!

> *"Vulnerability is at the core of a marriage. No enemy stands a chance of inflicting the kind of damage my wife can. She alone holds the key that can start a nuclear meltdown within me. Yet I give this key willingly to her and she to me, for a marriage becomes more exciting when you put your complete trust in another. To never be fully vulnerable is to never have been fully married."*

I'm sure you've heard of "AAA" also known as "Triple A." You can use this memory key to remember the three reasons that "may" make divorce acceptable. Abandonment, Adultery, Abuse.

When any of the 3 A's is involved, healing is possible and should be sought above other options, but it will often entail really hard work. These types of marriage damages are tougher to resolve. However, restoration is possible and marriages can come out at the other end being far better than those that have not been tested with similar trials.

17 Separation

Another important consideration prior to filing for a divorce is to consider a separation followed by a rebuilding of the marriage from the ground up. We highly recommend a separation of several months before a couple proceeds with a divorce. Ideally you'll both be participating in weekly counseling sessions during the separation. Separation that does not include counseling may toggle some change in one or both spouses, but the changes will likely be shallow and short-lived. Professionals work with couples until issues are fully resolved. If you repair the porch, but the roof is caving in, you still have unresolved issues needing attention. At the very least you should be seeing a mentoring couple several times a week while separated. We discourage being separated longer than six months or so as the statistics indicate that being separated for over a year greatly increases the possibility of divorce. If you separate, seek help while you are separated.

Let's return to our house building theme to get an understanding of why a separation might be useful. When homesteading began in the American West, many settlers improvised by building something akin to a lean-to or a shack. They may have desired a nice home but lacked the resources to build one. Other settlers were so enamored with having a place to call their own they made efforts to build a home without the knowledge and understanding of where and/or how to correctly build a home. They had a great vision, but no real knowledge of how to accomplish it. Some of these homes would hold no heat at all, some were built in places that flooded during spring rains, and others were built with too little or too much sun exposure. Some used the wrong types of wood and materials, and still others found out that the rain or varmints could easily get in. And to top it off, many others found that they built too far away from a source of year-round drinking water. Some shacks simply blew over when a strong wind came.

> *"I have great sympathy for those who have been thru a divorce because divorce is one activity that is always painful. Yet the divorce didn't happen by accident. Every marriage begins as a fantastic voyage, but many couples wrongly assume they were passengers on the ship, rather than the crew. Thus no one was steering or tending to the marriage ship and it drifted into one fierce storm after another. Such tragedy need not have occurred as the marriage ship did not have to drift; it came with an engine and rudder that apparently was never used."*

These well-meaning early settlers had a worthy vision but didn't build their home correctly. After a few months or a few years they came to realize that vision without knowledge is a recipe for pain. Sometimes most of what they built had to be torn down and rebuilt using a better plan. Having learned from their previous mistakes, they sought guidance, materials, help, and other resources as needed to "get it right" the next time.

We hope you see the connection here. Some people get married in the same way. They have a vision to have a great marriage but due to a lack of knowledge on how to build a great marriage, they build it based on flawed concepts. We all hate to feel foolish about our actions and may even reject that we have put X number of years into this, only to find we had built it wrong. It should be comforting to know that this type of marriage situation can *(sometimes easily)* be rebuilt rather than burnt down. I have a motto in my business: *"An attitude of continuous learning and improvement."* When we learn more, we get better and better.

OK, what if you examined your marriage and determined it's in very poor shape? Ending it is one choice, another is to rebuild it the correct way, and the sooner you start the sooner you can enjoy the finished product.

Every couple's vision for their marriage is like a very nice home but after a few years some couples feel like they've ended up with a shack. We want you to know that a great marriage home is very achievable. Fortunately, having a great marriage has nothing to do with income, intelligence, money, or power. It's entirely based on each spouse's desire to work together and to obtain the help and resources to get it done.

To further help you understand this concept, we will next give you an example of a modern marriage that is built using a flawed building plan and yet has a very good chance of becoming a great marriage.

FACTOID – You are as screwed up as the rest of us, unless you don't know it, then you're more screwed up!

Of the 3 A's let's call out "abuse" as the one we use for our example. Abuse is a very serious family issue. If one or both spouses were raised in an abusive home, they stand a good chance of applying similar abusive practices in their marriage. For clarity, abuse is wrong; it's a type of torment that all too often is ignored by family, friends, and neighbors. It demoralizes the person at the receiving end (be it mental or physical

123

abuse) and only accomplishes its goal by intimidation and fear. A marriage that has abuse in it is one that indeed needs to be rebuilt. If it's never dealt with, it will continue to wreck relationships, not only with your spouse but your children as well. When abuse is not corrected in the current generation, statistics strongly indicate the children and grandchildren will also employ similar tactics.

Let's say you're an abusive person, are we saying all the problems are due to you? No, and I'll take you back to an earlier chapter where we told you that testing reveals more than a person's knowledge. Testing also shows us there may be something flawed with the teaching methods, information given, or the teacher. A spouse that is abusive in a relationship has been taught the absolute wrong way to work out differences. Rather than continue building a marriage the wrong way, we learn that what we've been doing is just not right and we set about fixing it. While it was wrong that you were taught the wrong interpersonal relationship skills, it is more wrong to continue to abuse those whom you love. Nobody, not our spouse, family, or friends, admire an abusive person. This is often one of those "secret" areas in our life we hope others outside our family never know about. We believe many abusers do not want to be abusers, they want to fix it, but just do not know how. Own your issue, seek help, work to fix it and let the people marvel at the new marriage you built rather than talk about the mess you currently live in.

We need to clear up a misunderstanding about abuse; abuse is not "correction" and it is not "punishment" as most abusers have been wrongly taught. We correct and/or punish our children when they do wrong, *(immediately followed by a loving embrace and reassuring words)*, we punish people who break the law, we punish animals that misbehave, but we do not "abuse" any of these. Abuse is not to be tolerated, but sadly many people who have come from an abusive home end up practicing the same wrong they experienced.

> *"Love is grand; divorce can be a hundred grand or more."*
> Anonymous

For clarity, punishment is not something to be used as a tool in marital conflict. It's fine (when used appropriately) for our children and animals, but not our spouses. Do you withhold sex to punish your spouse? Do you stay out all night to correct your spouse? Again, you may have been taught wrong; a loving couple interacts differently. While one or the other may need to change, spouses do not correct one another using punishment. Also we've said this before, never inflict condemnation. Conviction is the path to true change, inner thoughts that measure ourselves against the model are what cause us to want to make the changes required.

Like many children of broken families, Paige and I were emotionally wounded by parents who divorced. In counting the cost of divorce, you as parents must own the responsibility that comes with having kids. You will read in the statistics chapter that the odds fall heavily against the children of divorced parents. You must weigh the emotional damage to your children in considering the cost of divorce. We are not saying you should stay miserably married for the sake of the kids, we are saying you should be happily married for the sake of the kids. You really have to ask yourselves what stands in the way of being happily married to your current spouse. Is there anyway, anything, that can be done to improve the marriage? One improvement often leads to another.

If you're able, we'd like you to discuss with your spouse how you feel about divorce. Ideally, you'll desire to say to each other that divorce is something you'll never consider, that your efforts will be to always work thru issues and find solutions.

Couple's project—Take a few minutes and talk about this subject. Refrain from saying, *"If you ever cheat I'll divorce you."* Rather, it's better to say, *"What can I do to help you keep the fires burning for me alone? Or what can we do to strengthen our marriage?"*

"When you were single you alone were responsible for the direction of your boat in the vast ocean of life. You had many choices to make that determined how successful your voyage would be. Your parents taught you that if you were diligent and worked hard, you would be successful and the storms of life would not swallow you up. When you get married you trade in your boat for a ship. The ship is more complex but far more capable of handling rough seas, provided the couple is steering the ship rather than sunning themselves on the deck."

Did you learn anything? Yes / No
Chapter personal benefit appraisal: **HER 1-2-3-4-5   HIM 1-2-3-4-5**
1=not at all, 2=a little, 3=some good stuff, 4=fairly helpful, 5=very helpful

Marriage Front and Center

CHAPTER 18

Putting the Special Back in Marriage

As we contemplated the subject matter to put into a handbook about marriage, we naturally found ourselves meditating about the different aspects of our marriage union. While Paige and I view our marriage as special, other couples seem to give little thought about theirs. To each their own, but we'd like to take you to a few places our thoughts traveled.

> *"Being in a long marriage is a little bit like that nice cup of coffee every morning—I might have it every day, but I still enjoy it."*
> Stephen Gaines, documentary filmmaker

Throwaway Mentality

In our current American culture we are taught that everything is a throwaway item. We toss out billions of dollars' worth of items that other cultures would keep. For those of you old enough to remember we use to repair things rather than replace them. However, today with no thought of repair we toss out good shoes, TVs, furniture, clothing, and anything that is old or out of style. It goes further, we are indoctrinated that it is simply not enough to have this or that, it must be the "best" this or that. How many people do you know who have a simple style cell phone, let alone a plain old landline telephone? You might have a washer and dryer but you're deluged daily with commercials that say you need the newer better model. We've been bombarded with a form of materialism that says anything old, worn, or out of date should be replaced. We toss out billions of dollars of food every year because it's a little stale or old. We're afraid this has permeated our thoughts so dramatically that we now have the same regard for marriage and perhaps even our children.

What are your thoughts about this throwaway mentality that has crept over our society and perhaps into many modern marriages?

Humanity without Marriage

Next our thoughts wondered to how our modern society would be without marriage. Would it be a good thing to do away with marriage? Would people choose to remain together, would families disappear without a parental unit forming the base for the family? Would women even desire to bring forth children? Would all moral boundaries fall away and an "anything goes with anybody, any time" mentality rise to the top? Would there be any lasting relationships? Would there be more trust or less? What do you think would happen?

FACTOID – Nothing is really special—unless it's special to you.

Are Married People Different?

Contemplating further we considered those we knew who were married, those who were divorced, and those who were single. We have a lot of great friends, and we've never thought of them as more or less better or worse than others regardless of their marital status, sex, race, or any other particular attribute. Indeed our friends are who make up our life experiences. Of those we call friends we see no difference, but our thoughts moved to dreaming up a scenario that challenged our feelings. Go with us on the following mental journey and see where it leads you.

Take yourself back about 200 years in time; imagine yourself as a general in an army on the front lines of a war between three great nations. The Grand Poobah of your nation is going to send a delegation of four leaders to meet a delegation of equal number from each of the other two nations. As the general you are aware that all three nations have battle lines drawn in the shape of a triangle with a large open grass field between each. You are not aware of what the dispute is about that has brought you to the battlefield this day. The terms of the meeting are based on all three sides sending four leaders who will represent their nation in peace talks. If the talks do not succeed, it will result in the start of a bloody war the following day.

The three nations were formed when a moral divide occurred; people separated based on three relationship dynamics. One nation was formed based on their marital status and a belief that they would never get divorced. The second nation was made up of those who were divorced. The third nation was made up of those who never married.

In one hour these 12 leaders from three separate nations will be coming together to discuss the terms that might avoid war. As a general, you do not personally know the individuals selected to represent any of the three nations other than the basis for each nation's existence as a separate nation.

What are your thoughts about the three delegations who will be coming together to discuss terms of peace in an effort to avoid war?

Your opinion on such philosophical topics would be as valid as ours, yet we have to admit we believed the delegation of the two committed married couples had to be better at negotiating peace; after all, the fact they were still married and were determined to remain married demonstrated they had negotiated many peaceful resolutions already. They have a proven track record to end disagreements and settle conflicts. At the end of this mental journey, we found ourselves trusting the married delegates more than the other two groups in being able to reach a peace accord. We understood the marriage unit should be viewed as something very special, for those in a lasting marriage have demonstrated their ability to not only love each other, but live with each other too.

An old man got on a bus one February 14th, carrying a dozen roses. He sat beside a young man. The young man looked at the roses and said, "Somebody's going to get a beautiful Valentine's Day gift." "Yes," said the old man.

A few minutes went by and the old man noticed that his young companion was staring at the roses. "Do you have a girlfriend?" the old man asked. "I do," said the young man. "I'm going to see her right now, and I'm going to give her this Valentine's Day card."

They rode in silence for another 10 minutes, and then the old man got up to get off the bus. As he stepped out into the aisle, he suddenly placed the roses on the young man's lap and said, "I think my wife would want you to have these. I'll tell her that I gave them to you."

He left the bus quickly. As the bus pulled away, the young man turned to see the old man walking thru the entry gates of the cemetery.

Unknown

Marriage Is Special

Special – *distinguished by some unusual quality, held in esteem over the norm, not typical of others.*

Valuable – *having worth, characteristics, or qualities that are unique, esteemed, desirable.*

Unity – *acting as one, combined harmony, single purpose by more than one entity.*

18 I tease my wife and daughter that I could get millions if I decided to sell either of them. *(Yes, I'm a sick puppy.)* It's my way of telling them they are very valuable. Truly they are very valuable and each has qualities that make her extra special.

From beginning to end, a couple coming together <u>to act as one</u> and <u>be one</u> seems magical and illogical. A committed couple who willingly agrees to set aside self-interests for <u>common</u> interests and to ensure the relationship will prevail over their individual selves, is remarkable and it appears somewhat rare.

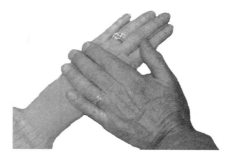

We've all heard of heroic actions when a soldier sacrificed his own life for the survival of his fellow soldiers, and we know how Christ offered himself for the salvation of humanity. The giving of one's life for another is indeed heroic and the ultimate sacrifice. While less dramatic but nearly as impressive, we think couples need to valiantly <u>live for one another</u> and thus be truly committed to marital unity and personal sacrifice in their marriage.

Another thing special about marriage, if it didn't exist before, is that at the very instant we get married we have added new "purpose" to our life, because we are now not just living for ourselves, but also another person. Certainly the kids we produce from marriage also expand our purpose. Purpose is especially important to men. We want to feel we are accomplishing something, that we are needed, that we are useful, and from that perspective there is nothing more valuable than building your relationship with your spouse.

"People are often enamored with my Super Bowl ring. But it's my wedding ring that I'm most proud of. And having a good marriage takes even more work than winning a Super Bowl."
Trent Dilfer, Seattle Seahawks quarterback

Then there is the whole intimacy bond, which is really special. Not "sex," but real intimacy, it's the super glue in a relationship. Dedication to walk where the other spouse walks, to bear each other's burdens, to care for each other, to nurture, honor, cherish, and love. It's the sticky glue kinda bond that is very difficult to break. We become defenders and protectors of one another, never giving up, fighting off any enemy that dares to attack. It forms a kind of bond that is present even when one spouse is not. We could be alone somewhere but friends will still see us as a couple, not as individuals. It's that kind of unity that does not escape people's notice; it is never set aside and is evident to all who enter your house.

FACTOID – When something is really valuable to a person, their actions will indicate its worth.

Marriage should be celebrated and held in high esteem for it is truly phenomenal in its form. People who succeed in an enduring marriage may not be special in the world's view, but they have demonstrated an ability and willingness to change, to adapt, to foster unity, to foster love, to work out differences, to work on their own issues and help their spouse overcome theirs. They have built a relationship of trust. They have certainly worked thru many challenges, but rather than being destroyed by those challenges, they have come out the other side stronger than when they went in.

A marriage of oneness is exceptional in that it forever misses a deceased spouse; it's a bond that even death can't break. The surviving spouse longs to be with the missing hubby or wife. It yearns, it pines to be restored in oneness.

If you're married or getting married, please respect what you have, honor it, foster it, build upon it, and lose yourself in it. Marriage is an honorable institution. If you're not going to give it the place it deserves then you have missed the point and have little understanding about it.

> *"I'm at that age where I can get discounts for being old. It occurred to me while that is a respectful gesture, wouldn't society be better off if we honored enduring marriages in the same way? Imagine sitting in the Waffle House and the waitress says, 'Hey folks, Mr. & Mrs. Smith have been married 30 years—they get a free cinnamon mocha.' Wouldn't that atmosphere of celebration propagate and encourage long-lasting marriages? After all, growing old is nice, but growing old with somebody— now that's something to celebrate."*

18 Remember the early days when you thought of your spouse as your "soul mate," as a "gift" from God? In a traditional marriage the father walks down the aisle with his daughter on his arm and indeed he willingly presents his daughter as a gift to the groom. In many wedding ceremonies the priest or pastor will ask, *"Who gives this woman to be married to this man."* The father typically responds, *"Her mother and I."* This idea of the bride being a valuable gift carried much weight in older times. If a couple keeps the thought that they are each a "valuable gift" then it's hard to imagine they will mistreat the gift.

If you've been divorced this chapter is not meant to injure you. It's meant to move you past drifting or wishing for a great marriage, to moving you toward putting on your carpenter's belt and getting to the task of building a great marriage. Be this your 2nd or 3rd marriage, make this one your last. Settle it in your head, melt it into your heart, and live it out each day.

Marriage is special; if no one ever told you it was, consider yourself told. It's valuable and it gets more valuable with time.

We wanted to add a short tribute here: As we were writing this very chapter we were notified that a couple very dear to us died in a motorcycle accident. After a stressful time in their marriage, Angie and David went to a marriage seminar we recommended and it revitalized their relationship. While we are going to miss them, they died together very much in love and doing something they enjoyed. We hope to go in a similar way. Angie and David, we'll see you on the other side. ((Hugs))

Let the accident above be a reminder to us all, in one hour our life or our love could be gone.

Couple's project—Turn to your spouse and one at a time say to each other: *"Honey, I'd like your help in reminding me to keep our marriage special, to value it and to foster it."*

Couple's project—Discuss with each other how special you want your marriage to be.

Did you learn anything? Yes / No
Chapter personal benefit appraisal: **HER 1-2-3-4-5   HIM 1-2-3-4-5**
1=not at all, 2=a little, 3=some good stuff, 4=fairly helpful, 5=very helpful

www.u-build.com

134

CHAPTER 19

Biblical References on Marriage, Love, Devotion, Divorce

PART 1

If you regularly attend church, you are accustomed to the pastor beginning with prayer before he expounds on the biblical text. If you like, take a moment and pray to God, asking Him to open your eyes and ears to what you are about to read and to prepare your heart to receive it.

Why Have a Chapter Devoted to Biblical Christian Concepts in Marriage?

Polls show that the overwhelming majority of citizens in America (greater than 90%) profess a belief or devotion to God. Roughly 85% call ourselves "Christian." Still another section of the U.S. population is Jewish and thus shares a common devotion to the same God and the Old Testament portion of our Christian Bible. Given these statistics and that the marriage ceremony has its roots in religious traditions, it seems more than appropriate to devote a chapter to the biblical model for marriage and likewise God's instructions relating to it. Aside from all that information, we can tell you our marriage would have failed early on except for our very purposeful effort in trying to follow the biblical directions for marriage.

This is one of our favorite chapters but it also can be one of the most painful. Why? Because in this chapter we will measure our actions (or the lack thereof) against our own moral code for our marriage. We established the need for a moral code in chapter 6. For a few, they will find themselves following the standard, for many more of us we will find ourselves falling short in many areas. In Part 1, we reveal the standards as described in the Bible. In Part 2, we will apply the passion of an NFL coach or perhaps a boot camp drill sergeant to motivate us all to follow our beliefs. If you are an atheist or practice another religion, all we can ask is that you be humored while we address the insincerity in our own faith. Some of you who are not regularly reading the Bible may be shocked to learn what God has to say about marriage and divorce. Hang on, it's going to be somewhat brutal. In all this, remember that God is a loving, compassionate, caring, and forgiving God. If we own up to our failures, He is quick to forgive. God is not surprised at our sin, our apathy, or even our rebellion, but He does ask that we own up to our actions and admit our failures.

> When asked the secret of his long marriage, Billy replied, *"Ruth and I are happily incompatible."*   Billy Graham

For a Christian, we can consider God our architect and building code official of marriage rolled into one. God not only has a design for how the marriage should be built, but also maintained. The Bible might be thought of as the building code; we compare ourselves and our marriage to the building code and make adjustments to ensure we are following the code. When we don't measure up to the code, it's like a "notice of violation" and we need to make the required changes to comply with the code. Perhaps one oddity in this parable is that the worldly standards will often conflict with the Biblical standards. We will thus find ourselves in one or more areas struggling with this tension. Obviously we have to make the choice, which standard will we follow?

The Bible makes it pretty clear for us; we are all sinners on this round ball called earth. Not one of us is or can be sinless, not one of us seeks after God and His righteousness with our whole heart. While seeking to be faithful and true to God, we live in a body of flesh that seeks its own desires. That is the war within us, our flesh nature is self-serving, and our spirit nature desires to please God. While there is a red and blue state type of politics in America, there should be no such aspect to our Christian faith, we are all the same. Christ died for all sinners, He is (or should be) Lord to all who accept Him. We escape God's wrath by Christ's righteousness not our own, He paid our debt, and our guilt could in no other way be removed. As such, not only are we no better than our neighbor, we are no better than our spouse.

> *"If you live to be a hundred, I want to live to be a hundred minus one day, so I never have to live without you."*   Winnie the Pooh

Christian Aspects of Marriage

A Christian marriage contains not only civil (based in state law) aspects but foremost has a divine purpose. Christians should not be getting married solely to get a license from the state, but to follow God's will with respect to the male-female bond. We read in Genesis 2:18–24 (text of this Scripture in the pages that follow) that God's design for mankind was very purposeful in that man and woman were to join together and produce offspring, which thus forms the base for two of the most important units in all civilizations, that being the marriage union and the family unit. Creation of man was the beginning point to many social orders that would follow. After God created Adam, he created Eve, and Eve was called Adam's "wife," and thus the first "marriage" institution was created. From this union children were produced, creating the institution of family. From families were born tribes, communities, cities, and nations. Our social laws defining marriage did not come before the religious purpose of marriage, for indeed the divine purpose came first.

While civil marriage unions performed at a courthouse are merely a matter of two people agreeing to become a couple, the Christian marriage ceremony contains marriage vows that usually require devotion, love, honor, etc., and are often expressed as follows: *"And do you [name] take this woman to be your wife, to love her, comfort her, honor her, for better or for worse, and keep her in sickness and health, and to forsake all others, to keep her with you as long as you both shall live?"* The Christian marriage ceremony "binds" the couple together and demands the faithfulness of the man and the woman to the marriage union. The vows contain the words *"as long as you both shall live"* to denote this union is supposed to be a life-long commitment while the civil ceremony contains no such requirement.

It is in marriage and the resulting family that individuals begin to set up and practice a mini-form of government that is by the couple and for the couple. They alone decide the structure and function of their family unit and how it will be governed. This is why marriage and the family structure must be preserved, for the family unit forms the basic building block for all of society's structures that follow after it. A marriage is the smallest building block of any nation and a family is the next. In a marriage loyalty and devotion are practiced; if a couple in love cannot see the value in being devoted to each other, how can they be expected to be devoted to a nation of people they do not love?

The marriage ceremony takes what would otherwise be secret random sexual acts with perhaps many partners during the darkness of night and pushes it into the daylight with many witnesses and proclaims devotion and fidelity to just one. The vows are not only to each other, they are vows made to God. While civil regulations may expand what a marriage union is, the Christian or biblical marriage ceremony can never be distorted from the original God-intended union of one man and one woman. The marriage of Christians to one another is above and beyond earthly laws and we are thus compelled to comply with God's regulations, not our own.

A civil union has no requirement of a wedding band; however, a Christian marriage requires wedding rings to be exchanged. The ring once given and received is supposed to always be worn to serve as a constant reminder that the wearer's love is pledged to their spouse. This is why those who fall into infidelity will remove their ring prior to the affair; the ring would be a reminder of broken vows and devotion not kept. A short note, rings do not have to be expensive, Bob's wedding band cost $12 and Paige's original wedding band cost less than $200. The rings are symbols of commitment, NOT wealth! The point is, the value of your rings is not an expression of your love.

The Christian marriage ceremony is completed when the invocation is made: "You may now kiss the bride." The marriage contract is not sealed with a handshake, it is "sealed with a kiss," which denotes a greater bond when the spouses' lips come together.

There is another act of the marriage union that has divine symbolism, and that is the creation of life. Generally the couple will give birth to children; in this manner God has granted the couple the ability to bring about life and thus symbolically mimic God in creating life. Married couples become life givers when they have children as God was the original life giver.

Often the Christian ceremony will contain a statement such as *"What God hath joined together let no man separate."* Marriage has divinely appointed aspects, it is an institution created by God, and it is spiritual, physical, and civil. It is a sacred institution in which God places a high value.

Does Marriage Enslave?

Yes! There are a few who claim that marriage is a horrible institution which subjugates a woman. These folks have no understanding of the biblical context of the marriage relationship. This parable is offered to put the marriage relationship in its proper light:

"For the woman was taken not from the head of the man to rule over him, not from his feet to be trampled by him, but from his side to be his companion and equal, from under his arm to be protected and cherished, from his rib, which is closest to man's heart."

It is a perversion of the marriage union to say that a woman becomes the man's property. The perversion is not that the statement is false, for it is true; the perversion is failing to include a line that says the man is also the woman's property. Each becomes the property of the other and both are to serve each other and to serve God.

The fact that a man is usually physically much stronger than a woman means a greater requirement for service while married. Using the extra strength he has been given not against his wife, but to further the relationship in earning a living, doing the heavier chores, defending the family and being the protector. In its ultimate form, the strength element of the man defends and provides for the woman. She is endowed with a nurturing element that fosters the family. While the wife may be weak and defenseless during her pregnancy, she is not alone. The man's duty is to protect her, she is thus not defenseless but has someone even stronger than herself to defend her. He may be somewhat rugged, she is perhaps tender, he uses force, she is the motive for the use of force, he will smell of sweat and she will have a fragrant scent, in all areas the husband and wife contrast and complement one another.

Ladies, I have always liked that Bob steers our family life and is generally the head in our home. Yet on several occasions he has felt overwhelmed with the various aspects of that responsibility and asked me if I wanted to take over. To his disappointment, I have and always will reply "no." It makes me feel secure with Bob being in front, guiding our household through life. I still felt this way when Bob came down with the disease Sarcoidosis and at the same time his business activity evaporated. He felt he was not providing as he should be, but I still felt he was providing me the security I needed. The more I understand about leadership, the more I realize that it is a servant-based job title. My husband takes that responsibility seriously, believing that when anything is going wrong in the home, the buck stops with him. Bob is a natural born lion leader type, but sometimes that burden is more than he cares to bear. He knows God holds him accountable for our family unit.

19 | Biblically-Based Relationships

The Bible is called the instruction book from God. In it we learn that God loves His creation and seeks a relationship with us. He is Spirit and we are flesh, but we are created in His image. The Bible informs the reader there is this life and an afterlife, and for those who have chosen to follow God's will in this life, they will be united with Him in the next. For this period of time when the spiritual world is separated from the physical world, God instructs us to seek Him out, to receive His love and to foster a relationship with Him. God isn't seeking a cursory acknowledgment that He is real, He desires we sincerely seek Him, love Him and desire Him. He describes Himself as a loving Father and greatly desires our love and affection.

A marriage is foremost a relationship, a relationship of devotion, a relationship of love, a relationship that requires effort to maintain. It is a not unlike the kind of relationship that a Christian is supposed to foster with God.

Marriage compels its participants by providing an additional purpose for each spouse to fight for the survival of their marriage union. Likewise we become willing to fight for the children of our marriage union. The family is a miniature nation in which survival, prosperity, unity, joy, and love are all furthered.

Tribes, nations, and governments have risen and fallen over time, but the institution that endures is the marriage institution. It alone is the smallest but most important building block in any society, and only the most perverse of governments seek to extinguish marriages or family units.

God ordains we build our marriage, then our family, then our community, then our nation. God also desires that we invite Him to be part of all these activities and to receive His blessings until that day when He calls us home to be with Him. Hopefully, prior to that day we will have demonstrated our devotion to Him and our spouse.

Over the years we have met many couples both married and divorced. Some of the married couples were on their second or third marriage, while others were still holding onto their first. In general observations we have found no significant differences of marital strife or marital happiness between those who believe in God versus those who do not. However, we have observed that those who daily practice biblical submission to God's authority and who truly endeavor to live their Christian faith, rarely, if ever, end up in divorce court. Their homes are not free of disagreements, but they are generally free of bitterness and contempt. These folks really try to *"walk the talk"* as it's said. They have made their faith a priority and thus their marriages and families a priority. These folks seem to have their ducks in a row; they have established boundaries, and have an attitude of submission and feel that God's eyes are always upon them. They understand that nothing of their thoughts is hidden from God.

> *"Being a Christian is more than just an instantaneous conversion; it is like a daily process whereby you grow to be more and more like Christ."* Billy Graham

As a Christian couple, you each have decisions to make; will the instructions and guidance of God apply to your marriage? Have you been living them? Will you begin in earnest to live them going forward?

OK, let's see what our moral code and God's instruction book has to say about marriage relationships.

Scriptural References

Indeed our God has authored many Scriptures that discuss the marriage union, divorce, love, and related guidance. Below is a small sampling of these. The references will be in either *New International Version Bible (NIV)* or *New American Standard Bible (NASB)* translations.
The emphasis has been added.

We are created in the image of God, as male and female, God "blessed" the union.

Genesis 1:26–28 Then God said, *"Let Us make man in Our image, according to Our likeness; and let them rule over the fish of the sea and over the birds of the sky and over the cattle and over all the earth, and over every creeping thing that creeps on the earth."* God created man in His own image, in the image of God He created him; male and female He created them. God blessed them; and God said to them, *"Be fruitful and multiply, and fill the earth, and subdue it; and rule over the fish of the sea and over the birds of the sky and over every living thing that moves on the earth."* NASB

The marriage union was created by God; He wanted man and woman to be together.

19 **Genesis 2:18–24** Then the LORD God said, *"It is not good for the man to be alone; I will make him a helper suitable for him."* …The LORD God fashioned into a woman the rib which He had taken from the man, and brought her to the man. The man said, *"This is now bone of my bones, And flesh of my flesh; She shall be called Woman, Because she was taken out of Man."* For this reason a man shall leave his father and his mother, and <u>be joined to his wife</u>; <u>and they shall become one flesh.</u> NASB

God makes it very clear He hates divorce. He commands husbands to remain faithful to their wives, that they become one when married and He says we should "guard" ourselves.

Malachi 2:13–16 Another thing you do: You flood the LORD's altar with tears. You weep and wail because he no longer pays attention to your offerings or accepts them with pleasure from your hands. You ask, "Why?" <u>It is because the LORD is acting as the witness between you and the wife of your youth, because you have broken faith with her, though she is your partner, the wife of your marriage covenant. Has not the LORD made them one</u>? In flesh and spirit they are his. And why one? Because he was seeking godly offspring. So <u>guard yourself</u> in your spirit, and do not break faith with the wife of your youth. "<u>I hate divorce</u>," says the LORD God of Israel. NIV

Paul instructs spouses not to withhold sexual intimacy from one another: divorce is strongly disallowed.

I Corinthians 7:2–16 But since there is so much immorality, <u>each man should have his own wife, and each woman her own husband. The husband should fulfill his marital duty to his wife, and likewise the wife to her husband</u>. The wife's body does not belong to her alone but also to her husband. In the same way, the husband's body does not belong to him alone but also to his wife. <u>Do not deprive each other</u> except by mutual consent and for a time, so that you may devote yourselves to prayer. Then come together again <u>so that Satan will not tempt you because of your lack of self-control</u> ….
Now to the unmarried and the widows I say: It is good for them to stay unmarried, as I am. But if they cannot control themselves, they should marry, for <u>it is better to marry than to burn with passion</u>. To the married I give this command (not I, but the Lord): <u>A wife must not separate from her husband</u>. But if she does, she must remain unmarried or else be reconciled to her husband. <u>And a husband must not divorce his wife.</u>

To the rest I say this (I, not the Lord): If any brother [*Christian*] has a wife who is not a believer and she is willing to live with him, <u>he must not divorce her</u>. And if a woman has a husband who is not a believer and he is willing to live with her, <u>she must not divorce him</u>. For the unbelieving husband has been sanctified through his wife, and the unbelieving wife has been sanctified through her believing husband. Otherwise your children would be unclean, but as it is, they are holy.

But if the unbeliever leaves, let him do so. A believing man or woman is not bound in such circumstances; God has called us to live in peace. How do you know, wife, whether you will save your husband? Or, how do you know, husband, whether you will save your wife? NIV

I Corinthians 7:27–28 <u>Are you married? Do not seek a divorce</u>. Are you unmarried? Do not look for a wife. <u>But if you do marry, you have not sinned</u>; and if a virgin marries, she has not sinned. <u>But those who marry will face many troubles in this life,</u> and I want to spare you this. NIV

Jesus makes things clear to those who might question where God's heart is on the matter of divorce, while at the same time emphasizing that the two become one in God's eyes. Jesus doesn't sugarcoat the reason for divorce, and sums it up as "hardened hearts."

Matthew 19:3–8 Some Pharisees came to him to test him. They asked, "Is it lawful for a man to divorce his wife for any and every reason?" "Haven't you read," he replied, "that at the beginning the Creator 'made them male and female,' and said, '<u>For this reason a man will leave his father and mother and be united to his wife, and the two will become one flesh'? So they are no longer two, but one. Therefore what God has joined together, let man not separate</u>."
"Why then," they asked," did Moses command that a man give his wife a certificate of divorce and send her away?" Jesus replied, "Moses permitted you to divorce your wives <u>because your hearts were hard. But it was not this way from the beginning</u>." NIV

We are warned that getting drunk gets us into trouble; we are to "submit" to one another.

Ephesians 5:15–33 "Be very careful, then, how you live—not as unwise but as wise, making the most of every opportunity, because the days are evil. Therefore do not be foolish, but understand what the Lord's will is. <u>Do not get drunk on wine, which leads to debauchery</u>....

143

19 Submit to one another out of reverence for Christ. Wives, submit to your husbands as to the Lord. For the husband is the head of the wife as Christ is the head of the church, his body, of which he is the Savior. Now as the church submits to Christ, so also wives should submit to their husbands in everything. Husbands, love your wives, just as Christ loved the church and gave himself up for her to make her holy, cleansing her by the washing with water through the word, and to present her to himself as a radiant church, without stain or wrinkle or any other blemish, but holy and blameless. In this same way, husbands ought to love their wives as their own bodies. He who loves his wife loves himself. After all, no one ever hated his own body, but he feeds and cares for it, just as Christ does the church— for we are members of his body. For this reason a man will leave his father and mother and be united to his wife, and the two will become one flesh. This is a profound mystery—but I am talking about Christ and the church. However, each one of you also must love his wife as he loves himself, and the wife must respect her husband. NIV

The Bible clearly describes marriage as an honorable act, with firm warnings to honor that vow, and directs all of us to be content with what we have. That is hard for Americans who are bombarded over and over with commercials pushing us to greater discontentment.

Hebrews 13:4–5 Marriage should be honored by all, and the marriage bed kept pure, for God will judge the adulterer and all the sexually immoral. Keep your lives free from the love of money and be content with what you have. NIV

Proverbs 18:22 He who finds a wife finds what is good and receives favor from the LORD. NIV

Proverbs 19:14 Houses and wealth are inherited from parents, but a prudent wife is from the LORD. NIV

Proverbs 31:10–12 An excellent wife, who can find? For her worth is far above jewels. The heart of her husband trusts in her, And he will have no lack of gain. She does him good and not evil all the days of her life. NASB

Proverbs 31:25–31 Strength and dignity are her clothing, And she smiles at the future. She opens her mouth in wisdom, And the teaching of kindness is on her tongue. She looks well to the ways of her household, And does not eat the bread of idleness. <u>Her children rise</u> <u>up and bless her; Her husband also, and he praises her, saying:</u> <u>"Many daughters have done nobly, But you excel them all."</u> Charm is deceitful and beauty is vain, <u>But a woman who fears the LORD,</u> <u>she shall be praised</u>. Give her the product of her hands, And let her works praise her in the gates. NASB

Love is not lust, love is not a feeling; love is a conscious action of our will. We do not fall out of love; we let it die because we apathetically do nothing to foster its growth. In the following Scriptures we learn about love as God designed it.

I Corinthians 13:4–8 <u>Love is patient, love is kind</u>. <u>It does not envy, it</u> <u>does not boast, it is not proud. It is not rude, it is not self-seeking, it</u> <u>is not easily angered, it keeps no record of wrongs. Love does not</u> <u>delight in evil but rejoices with the truth. It always protects, always</u> <u>trusts, always hopes, always perseveres</u>. Love never fails. NIV

1 John 3:16 This is how we know what love is: Jesus Christ laid down his life for us. <u>And we ought to lay down our lives for our brothers</u> (each other). NIV

1 John 4:7–16 Beloved,<u> let us love one another, for love is from God;</u> and everyone who loves is born of God and knows God. The one who does not love does not know God, <u>for God is love</u>. By this the love of God was manifested in us, that God has sent His only begotten Son into the world so that we might live through Him. In this is love, not that we loved God, but that He loved us and sent His Son to be the propitiation for our sins. Beloved, <u>if God so loved us, we</u> <u>also ought to love one another.</u> No one has seen God at any time; <u>if</u> <u>we love one another, God abides in us, and His love is perfected in</u> <u>us.</u> By this we know that we abide in Him and He in us, because He has given us of His Spirit. We have seen and testify that the Father has sent the Son to be the Savior of the world. Whoever confesses that Jesus is the Son of God, God abides in him, and he in God. We have come to know and have believed the love which God has for us. <u>God is love</u>, and the one who abides in love abides in God. NASB

Relationships are a key theme in the Bible; our relationship to God, our spouse, fellow believers, non-believers, and more. How we treat one another is a key theme in God's instructions to His people.

19 **Proverbs 12:18** <u>Reckless words pierce like a sword</u>, but the <u>tongue of the wise brings healing</u>. NIV

Romans 14:19 So then we pursue the things which <u>make for peace</u> and <u>the building up of one another</u>. NASB

Galatians 5:15 But if you bite and devour one another, take care that you are not consumed by one another. NASB

James 1:19 Everyone should be quick to listen, slow to speak and slow to become angry. NIV

Hebrews 13:4 <u>Marriage *is to be held* in honor</u> among all, and the *marriage* bed *is to be* undefiled; for fornicators and adulterers God will judge. NASB

We've included a few Scriptures about Satan to give you an understanding that he is real and he is against you. He is against your marriage and seeks to stop what God is trying to work in your life. Satan is your enemy, not your spouse.

Revelations 12:9 And the great dragon was thrown down, the serpent of old who is called the devil and Satan, who deceives the whole world; <u>he was thrown down to the earth, and his angels were thrown down with him.</u> NASB (*Yep, according to Scripture, Satan is alive and well here on earth!*)

Mark 1:13 And He [Jesus] was in the wilderness forty days <u>being tempted by Satan</u>; and He was with the wild beasts, and the angels were ministering to Him. NASB (*We should not be surprised when we are tempted, Satan tempted Jesus too!*)

1 Peter 5:8–9 Be of sober *spirit,* be on the alert. <u>Your adversary, the devil, prowls around like a roaring lion, seeking someone to devour. But resist him, firm in *your* faith</u>, knowing that the same experiences of suffering are being accomplished by your brethren who are in the world. NASB (*God is clearly letting us know that Satan is here and he's actively seeking to destroy us.*)

1 Timothy 5:15 "…for some have already turned aside to follow Satan." NASB (*Sadly, some people not only do not follow God, they've joined up to follow Satan.*)

FACTOID – The most dangerous of people (Hitler, Stalin, Mao Tse-tung) are the individuals who did not follow a moral code. Civilized people live by some form of moral code that guides them in the way they should live and interact with each other. | **19**

Couple's project—Discus the biblical defined framework for marriage, asking yourselves if this is the moral code model you desire to follow. Review your past and current understanding of God's design for marriage.

PART 2

When a recruit joins the military, he/she is sent to what is termed "basic training." Sounds harmless enough doesn't it? But anyone who has gone thru basic training quickly learns that a very zealous drill sergeant will be in your face intensely motivating every recruit to excel at levels they never thought possible. They are broken down and rebuilt stronger, wiser, more determined, and more disciplined. While basic training is very hard, it is very necessary. Yet every recruit who has gone thru basic, is very proud of his/her accomplishment. Likewise this section will be hard for all of us to swallow; these words apply to Paige and me, as well as anyone calling themselves a Christian.

As we stated in the beginning of this chapter, God is a loving and merciful God. But He speaks very strongly in many portions of the Bible seeking to motivate His followers out of rebellion and apathy by requiring that we apply ourselves with intensity. Throughout the New Testament the very loving Jesus came down very hard on those people who were not conforming to God's design and rather had adopted their own way of living life. We won't change what we do not acknowledge, so we are going to wear the drill sergeant hat for the remainder of the chapter. We are talking to the entire Christian community and we will get painfully real in the hopes we, as well as you, will open our eyes and seek to live more like God desires. We need to hear this as much as you for we frequently fail in living up to the standard and we have also been indifferent to being true to God. But we confess our failures, pick ourselves up, dust off, and go again. In the end either God's word is honored as the truth, or truth is whatever we each decide to call it.

Man up, Woman up!

So this is the deal: If we are going to join this club called "Christianity," we must make every effort not only to wear the colors of the club, but to follow the rules and regulations of the club. It's time to pee or get off the pot. We should get rid of the cross if wearing it is all that distinguishes us from people who do not believe in God. *"Don't remain a poser!"* Someone once asked, *"If a trial were held today with the accusation that you were a Christian, would there be enough evidence to convict you?"*

We know this is hard stuff; yet it applies to each of us. The Scriptures require that we not be ignorant about our faith; we must begin to study the Bible so that we know it and pattern our life after it. Only by reading it can it become a part of our daily life. I occasionally *(OK, frequently!)* disappoint myself in not living up to what I believe, but that doesn't excuse me to ignore it or fake my way thru it, it means I need to try all the harder. We need to really submit to God's authority and embrace His forgiveness and love when we do not.

FACTOID – If you're not living as God instructs, you are either testifying that you believe God is wrong, or you're going to have to admit you are wrong. Which is it?

God holds marriage in such very high esteem that His Son and our Savior, Jesus Christ, will be married to the church after He returns to earth. Of all the ceremonies, all the honors, all the riches God has at His disposal, God chose to culminate the end of the age triumph over evil, in a marriage. *(Rev 19:7–9)* Pretty cool, huh!

Yet a problem for many of us professing to be Christians is we seem to have excluded God from our marriage and do not hold our faith in God, nor our marriage, in a special place. Seemingly we have put God into a box we only bring out on Sunday or other special occasion. God didn't ask us for two hours in a week of devotion, he asks for 24 hours a day, 365 days a year. We are not supposed to turn on and off our Christian nature, rather to wear it all of the time. We personally believe the chances of any worthwhile venture succeeding, including marriage, are greatly magnified when we bring the procedures and concepts God set up, into them. God is perfect, we are imperfect, thus it's wise to want and need Him in our marriage relationship. But the divorce rate is the same for Christians as it is for non-Christians. Why is there no difference?

The stats will come later in chapter 20, but the lack of contrast in Christian marriage success seems to be based on a large populous of Christians not actually following God's plan for marriage. As Christians, we have to face that we are the problem; our divorce rate is roughly the same as non-Christians because we are failing, not God.

There is a saying that circulates amongst some in the Christian circle. It goes like this: ***"Faith, Family, and Friends"*** and is a little quip to help our minds focus on the correct order of things.

Let's do a reality check; there is no wedding gift we receive on our wedding day that will have any real lasting value. If value means money to you, then perhaps you'll say: *"We have all these gifts and these expensive rings."* All we can say to that is, if the marriage doesn't survive what good is any of that? Whatever it is, gifts, rings, money, it will decay and pass away. At some point sooner or later, we will also pass on. We can take nothing with us when we die; the only thing that will survive to the other side will be our relationship with God and Jesus Christ if it existed at all prior to our passing. Thus a Christian will put faith at the top of his list; he/she will foster the relationship with God above others.

The next relationship will be family, with the spouse being the primary relationship followed by the children, then other family members and friends. It is a Christian principle that if you get these priorities correct and keep them correct, you'll be well on your way to keeping the important things important.

As we stated in the introduction, we are not qualified to comment on other moral codes, but we feel we have every right to speak about ours; we can critique our own Christian behavior because we have solidly joined ourselves to this group. We personally believe Christianity when practiced, not only blesses us in this life, but provides the only path to eternity with God.

> A couple asked, what is the secret to being married for 25 years? After a minute of mental math I answered, *"The secret was to remain married each day for 9,131 days in a row without interruption."*

It is true that a very large number of people profess that they believe in God and have accepted Jesus Christ as their Savior, and at the same time never <u>practice</u> what the Bible tells them to do, or have never really entered into a relationship with God. Belief is not enough however.

James 2:19 says "You believe that there is one God. Good! Even the demons believe that—and shudder. NIV

Many people recognize and believe "God is God," but never relate to Him as "Father." Some profess an understanding of the Father's plan in sending Jesus Christ down to the earth to redeem, and call Jesus their Savior, but they forget He has also earned the title "Lord." Jesus Christ is our **"<u>Lord</u>"** and "Savior." At the point of confession, repentance, and proclamation of our acceptance of Jesus Christ, the Bible says we are adopted into the family of God and are deemed "born again." The person begins a walk that changes them, "if" <u>they are willing.</u> God does not force change; He does not force us to love Him. We have to make those choices and make the effort all on our own.

Believing in God is simply not enough according to the Bible.

Though it is true that a Christian marriage will be blessed, it is also true according to Scripture that *"Satan is a roaring lion, seeking whom he may devour."* Even Christ was tempted by Satan. Christ as our perfect model rejected the temptations. As we read in Part 1, *Satan was cast down to the earth,* but he has not yet been cast into hell. We know that Satan *(with the brief time he has remaining)* seeks to destroy anything and everybody that seeks a relationship with God. We are warned over and over to be aware, to watch, to know who our enemy is, and yet many Christians act like the devil is nowhere around.

It is a sad truth that ignorance is bliss, but ignorance frequently leads to failure. Let's clearly put it into words: *"If you are a believing Christian, Satan will come at you often seeking a way in to destroy your relationship with God, your spouse, your children, and other believers."* Any time we turn on the TV or log on to the Internet we are bombarded with adultery and failed moral standards. Being a Christian doesn't mean easy street and it doesn't mean we are immune to temptations, but in studying the Bible and having a relationship with the Father; you'll know how to keep yourself out of trouble and know how to respond when trouble tries to set in. Just calling yourself a Christian is no guarantee of a loving and lasting marriage; you have to "live" Christianity too! And we must live it not by our own plan, but by God's plan.

Does any of this sound familiar? It should if you are a devoted Christian and regularly read/study your Bible. If we let God in, He begins to fill that spiritual void; a true relationship with God develops and as it does, God changes us from being self-centered to God-centered. When we become less self-centered, we become better spouses because we are meeting our spouse's needs at a level at least equal to our own. And yet this is a process that takes time and many of us will still wander back into the self-centered mode from time to time.

With that understanding, a new adopted follower and child of God enters into a relationship with God the Father and His son, Jesus Christ. How is a relationship defined? It should entail seeking God's direction by reading the Bible daily, praying daily, attending church, tithing of our income, growing in an understanding of God, etc. By contrast a "casual" Christian may have the correct belief, but does nothing to cultivate the relationship, thus the "soul void" still finds itself unsatisfied and in need. It's akin to trying to bake a cake without the main ingredients; it will never turn out until we add what's missing.

19 Some people will say the relationship is just one sided, they talk to God, but He doesn't communicate back to them. Well that's not a true statement. God has certainly spoken to you and me. God wrote a very long love letter (the Bible), so long that in your lifetime you will not be able to comprehend all of the wisdom and knowledge contained in it no matter how many times you read it.

Digging Deeper, Casual Christianity

We examined the biblical framework for marriage in Part 1 of this chapter, and we began to explore the contrasts of various aspects of Christian life at the beginning of Part 2. Other observers have examined these contrasts and looked deeper at those of us in the Christian community and found a pretty clear line separating two camps of Christians. To differentiate two classes of Christians, a term was coined for one group; they were termed the "casual" Christians.

Indeed we can corroborate this divide in the marriage/divorce statistics in chapter 20. When we dig deeper into the statistics, we find there is indeed evidence of a divide within Christian marriage achievement. We find one group of devoted and practicing Christians who enjoy a monumental gain in marriage success over another group of Christians, who are identified as casual in the application of their faith.

OK, so you believe in God, but is God really <u>relevant</u> in your life?

Relevant – *Significant, important, having an important bearing in matters, pertinent, included not excluded from the process.*

This seems to be the dividing question that separates the casual Christians from those who truly make a dedicated effort to practice what they believe. Yet, that is indeed the choice we each have to make, if we claim to be a believer and/or follower of God we have two choices, align with God's plan, or ignore God's plan and follow our own plan. Has your life been self-centered or God-centered? Could you be a casual Christian?

Can you imagine a "casual" NFL football team? There is no doubt in anyone's mind that this team is going to lose every single game. A casual pro football team is laughable because there is no reasonable expectation that this team could succeed. By definition, it must fail. Yet that is indeed the way many Christians approach their faith, and sadly also their marriage. It's pretty much just lip service with no dedication, no self-examination, no adherence to the God-ordained play plans, and no team effort. Which team would you bet on, the "casual" NFL football team or the "dedicated" NFL football team? This is not a handbook about casual Christianity, however, it is a handbook on marriage and what it takes to build an enduring and happy marriage. We would be complacent if we did not help our readers understand and remedy what appears to be the clear reason for the failures in Christian marriages.

In May 2009 a George Barna article described the following regarding casual Christians.

Barna: "Casual Christianity is faith in moderation. It allows them to feel religious without having to prioritize their faith. Christianity is a low-risk, predictable proposition for this tribe, providing a faith perspective that is not demanding. A Casual Christian can be all the things that they esteem: a nice human being, a family person, religious, an exemplary citizen, a reliable employee—and never have to publicly defend or represent difficult moral or social positions or even lose much sleep over their private choices as long as they mean well and generally do their best. From their perspective, their brand of faith practice is genuine, realistic and practical. To them, Casual Christianity is the best of all worlds; it encourages them to be a better person than if they had been irreligious, yet it is not a faith into which they feel compelled to heavily invest themselves." http://www.barna.org/barna-update/article/13-culture/268-casual-christians-and-the-future-of-america

In September 2010 while were in the editing process of our handbook new information from the Pew Research Center found that Christians knew less about religion than atheists and agnostics. While embarrassing, the findings are not surprising to those who are neighbors to the casual Christians in America. Here is the link to the report: http://pewforum.org/Other-Beliefs-and-Practices/U-S-Religious-Knowledge-Survey.aspx

To put this in context, a person can claim to be a student at a university and nevertheless not be recognized as a student. If the student is not attending classes he will not be acknowledged as either a student or a graduate. The most flattering reply the dean can report is that the person did enroll, but failed to show up. The casual Christian is likewise claiming they are a student of Christianity, but a student who refuses to show up. An actual student of the Christian faith will be maturing in their knowledge and in their relationship to our heavenly Father. If you claim

153

to be a Christian, you should be on a journey that is changing you day by day into a more Christ-like follower of God. As an actual student of God, you should be praying every day, reading the Bible every day, gathering together with other believers to study the Bible, tithing to your church, and helping in the ministry of the church in some fashion.

Using other examples, is a person an auto mechanic if he knows little about automobiles? Is a doctor a doctor if she knows little about human anatomy? If I claim to be a Christian, should I be educated in what I claim to be? Summing up the casual Christian, they make the claim of being a follower of Christ but in very few aspects of their life are Christ's teachings applied or relevant. With little or no study of what the Bible teaches the casual followers fail in being able to apply its wisdom.

Sometimes the causal Christian will take their nearly nonexistent understanding of small portions of the Bible and modify it by mixing in new age philosophy while claiming it as their version Christianity. For some unknown reason they believe they have a better plan than God does. In effect, they declare by their words and actions they know better than God and worse they may believe God approves of their modifications.

A casual Christian has set their faith on the shelf. Somewhere in the house sets an unopened Bible that was handed down when grandma died. Should I feel bad if I know more about the statistics of football teams than the Bible? Should I be concerned if I know more about how to mix drinks or bake cakes than what the Bible has to say about how I should live? Do I read more romance novels or porn than the Bible? Am I justified when I make my own rules?

Dang this is hard stuff, isn't it?

We previously discussed that a ship's captain will frequently compare the actual course and direction of the ship to the desired course. That's the essence of this chapter, when we compare ourselves to the written word of God, do we find ourselves on the desired course?

In summary, we must look at our beliefs and actions to see if we are on the right course, but we are not going to stop there. The next step is, would our spouse, family and friends say we are true to our beliefs? Do they have the right to correct us if we are not?

Christians Are to Judge One Another

19

Judgment is often portrayed in very negative terms by sayings such as "Who made you the judge?" and "Don't judge me!" But we really need others to take notice of our actions and words and provide feedback on how we are doing. Indeed everyone who reads our book will make a judgment as to its content and effectiveness. Judgment when offered properly and truthfully should be viewed as a very good thing. We are going to expound on this because your desire is to have a great and lasting marriage, and we need to help you understand that if your faith is based in Christianity, then you should not only expect, but welcome the critique of those around you.

There are a number of passages in the Bible that inform the community of believers who take the name "Christian" to love, help, encourage, teach, pray for, and to judge one another. The judgment aspect is the topic we will briefly discuss here and it has to do with correcting or calling out each other if our words or actions do not line up with the Scriptures.

1 Peter 4:17 *For it is time for judgment to begin with the family* [Christians] *of God*... NIV

John 7:24 *Stop judging by mere appearances, and make the right judgment,* NIV

1 Cor. 5:11–13 *But now I am writing you that you must not associate with anyone who calls himself a brother* [Christian] *but is sexually immoral or greedy, an idolater or a slanderer, a drunkard or a swindler. With such a man do not even eat. What business is it of mine to judge those outside the church? Are you not to judge those inside? God will judge those outside. Expel the wicked man from among you.* NIV

1 Cor. 11:31 *But if we judged ourselves rightly, we would not be judged. But when we are judged, we are disciplined by the Lord so that we will not be condemned along with the world.* NASB

1 Tim. 5:20 *Those who continue in sin, rebuke in the presence of all, so that the rest also will be fearful of sinning.* NASB

Judge – *to form an opinion about, evaluate, deliberate facts and evidence, to rule a verdict of compliance or noncompliance.*

Thus we see from the biblical passages we are indeed to judge ourselves and those in the Christian body of believers. We are to compare our own activity against the instructions found in the Bible. When we do not line

155

up with the Bible we need to make changes so that we do. If we choose to continue down the wrong path, then other believers need to tell us and remind us we need to repent and realign ourselves with God's instructions.

For a Christian, the Bible is our moral code; it is the book we say we will follow. Ideally we are reading the Bible frequently, studying it, and aligning ourselves to it. When we don't, we should be able to count on our spouses and our fellow brothers and sisters in the church to remind us that we are in error. For instance, when it comes to marriage topics like infidelity, abuse, divorce, etc., the Bible is very clear that we as Christians should guard against these. If the person that is caught up in such activity will not correct him or herself, then someone else near to him or her should. Often, the first person to judge our actions will be our spouse.

In our marriage we practice this biblically authorized form of judgment on each other and occasionally with other believers. We likewise have been approached by fellow Christians who have in earnest questioned us as a couple about matters they felt we needed to reexamine. This should all be viewed as a healthy aspect of marriage and the healthy relationship of fellow Christians one to another. We indeed need other loving and good intentioned people to question our actions, motives, and words. It should always be done out of genuine compassion and concern and never in the spirit of final judgment as if speaking for God.

When speaking to the crowd gathered around to stone the woman caught in adultery, Jesus said in John 8:8, *He who is without sin among you, let him be the first to throw a stone at her* (NASB). We are all sinners; therefore, we are to help one another get back on the right road. Jesus didn't excuse the woman's sin, He brought the focus where it needed to be: we are all sinners. Judgment can be misused, and we would say that anyone who thinks of themselves as the "traffic cop" to judge everyone's actions is not balanced and should be subject to their own rebuke. Jesus final words to the woman caught in adultery was to *"go and sin no more"*.

Baby or a Grown-up?

The Bible admonishes us to mature in our faith and to move on from the basic understandings of our faith to the deeper things. In several passages the apostles describe new Christians as babies in their faith who can only take in the milk or simple things of the Christian walk. They expound that if we've been a Christian for any length of time we should have matured from the milk to the meat of God's word. Indeed one apostle strongly criticizes those who claim to have been a Christian for any length of time but has not grown up in their faith (Heb 5:11–14). In essence the apostle says: *You claim to have been a Christian for many years, why are you still drinking milk from a bottle and wearing diapers? By now you should be eating meat and teaching others how to walk, but instead you're still acting like a baby.*

I was an atheist prior to meeting Paige. Once I made a serious effort to examine the Bible, I found it to be a true and inspired book worthy of my attention. A Christian who is persistently reading the Bible, going to church, praying, and hanging out with other believers will be maturing, gaining wisdom and knowledge, and applying him or herself in helping others to mature in their faith. In essence a Christian will grow up from baby to adult, and will help to guide others.

We have to address this aspect because it factors so strongly in our Christian-based marriage relationship. When we first get married, we are an immature couple. We know very little, but if we apply ourselves we will grow and mature in our marriage. The tantrums and emotional outbursts we had in our first few years of marriage will no longer occur in our later years because we have matured. It is very important to understand. If you do nothing for your marriage relationship after your wedding day, if you do nothing to help your marriage grow, you might be older as far as age is concerned, but you'll always be a baby and still pooping in your diapers as a couple. We have seen couples who still fight over the same ridiculous things that they did when they were first married. Apparently neither spouse has been growing or building the marriage relationship so it becomes mature and vibrant.

The Next Step, Walking the Talk

For those of us who call ourselves Christians or followers of God, we need to understand God is not happy with our half-baked lifestyle of devotion to Him. He tells us to be one way or the other, but not lukewarm in our faith and relationship to Him. Will we do what God asks of us?

Revelation 3:15–17 I know your deeds, that you are neither cold nor hot; I wish that you were cold or hot. So <u>because you are lukewarm, and neither hot nor cold, I will spit you out of My mouth</u>. Because you say, "I am rich, and have become wealthy, and have need of nothing," and you do not know that you are wretched and miserable and poor and blind and naked. NASB

Titus 1:10 For there are many rebellious people, <u>mere talkers</u>. NIV

We believe in God's divine purpose, and to that end He is letting us (the world and all nations in it) prove that left to our own desires on this earth we as societies will pervert, fight, steal, lie, kill, and hate each other. For those willing to submit and love God now, God has promised a future kingdom where His peace and love will reign. It appears God is asking us to demonstrate our determination to love and follow Him in spite of all these earthy temptations and trials. If we don't want to follow God now, it would not be a stretch to say we would not be willing to submit later in an afterlife. Heaven is God's home and it is certainly His right to allow only those who love and seek to please Him into His home.

Right with God – Right with Your Spouse

If our relationship with God is right, if we are truly humble and open before God, if we are working to align our will with God's, our relationship with our spouse will also be correct. We cannot be right with God and not right with our spouse. Anytime we encounter a couple claiming to be Christian and yet talking about divorce, we know the relationship with God cannot be right because God hates divorce. Divorce is contradictory to God's will and we learned in one of the previously cited Scriptures that God only permitted divorce because of the hardness in our hearts. But God is a forgiving God, and He asks us to be a repentant follower. If you have committed adultery, been abusive, already been through one or more divorces, or rebelled in some other manner, return to God in repentance, and He will forgive you. But we must own up to our sin. He still loves us, but He wants us to obey Him and to put into practice His rules, which are actually for our own benefit. We do not live to obey the rules and become "right" before God, we use the rules to expose our rebellion and then seek God's forgiveness .

As Christians, we should already understand we do not clean ourselves up first, for that is an impossible task. Rather, we come to God with all of our faults as the Bible says "none are without sin, not one." It also says "none seek after God with their whole heart." I'm a sinner and so are you. However, we confess our failings to each other and to God and we are forgiven. Just like there are no perfect marriages, there are no perfect Christians. Coming to terms with our failures is not enjoyable; I hate the fact I do things I don't want to do. I struggle with some things over and over again, and I bet you do too. Forgiveness is at the heart of our relationship with God. He forgives our wrongs when we repent and try to do better. No matter how many times we fail, God forgives the repentant sinner. He demonstrates the love of a perfect loving father. I think that's a pretty good guide for marriages too. Forgiveness is perhaps one of the stronger expressions of love.

Couple's project—If you're a Christian, we'd like you to join with your spouse right now and one of you begin to lead by speaking out in a prayer asking God to help and guide you as a couple. This may be awkward for people who have never prayed out loud or never prayed with their spouse, but praying together is very normal for many of us and should be a normal (daily) activity in any Christian marriage. After the first spouse has prayed, then the other spouse can continue in the prayer. Regardless, finish this session with a prayer, even if you're reading this alone. Ask God to help change you and mold you into what He desires. Ask Him to forgive you for your previous sins and apathy regarding your relationship to Him and your spouse. Ask Him to help change you into a better spouse, a better parent, and a better follower of God. Starting this week, begin reading the Bible every day, join a good Bible-based church, and pray every day together as husband and wife. Each night put your children to bed with prayer, and grow your relationship with God. And know this, we have been praying for all the readers of our handbook from its inception. We believe in prayer, and we believe God hears our prayers on behalf of your marriage.

Angry or Humbled?

So here is the deal, some of you are going to receive this chapter and you are going to make a greater commitment to live your faith and to follow God's instructions for your personal and married life. You are like us; you admit that you have failures, but you pick yourself up and go again because you understand the love, grace, and mercy of God is unending for those who humble themselves before Him. However, there are going to be some of you who will be really upset with the term "casual" Christian. You may be really mad at us for asking you to live what you believe because that insinuates you are a hypocrite. You are ready to write us a letter or send us an email because we shouldn't be judging you. You are furious and consider this a bad chapter in what might otherwise be a great marital handbook.

As we mentioned earlier, take what you feel works and ignore what you feel does not. We do not know you and it's not our purpose to harm you; however, in every chapter we are asking couples to make changes and improve themselves in many areas of their life. This chapter is one area we also had to deal with. We'd remind you, we've never met "you," and thus we could not possibly pin this label on you. Could it be that the Holy Spirit or your own conscience is convicting you?

A person's faith can be a very dear and delicate topic to discuss. We have merely shared what we've learned and experienced when we ourselves are hypocrites regarding our faith. Bob's dad (an atheist) was the first to call Bob a hypocrite. It hurt, but it also motivated him to make a better effort at living what he espouses as his faith.

Finally, we all must understand that we are not only to love our spouse, but to be kind to our spouses too!

Ephesians 4:32 <u>Be kind</u> and compassionate to one another, <u>forgiving each other</u>, just as in Christ God forgave you. NIV

As you and your spouse interact with each other in discussing areas one or both of you have not aligned with regarding your moral code, be kind in your speaking and your responses. We hope that if you are of the Christian faith, this "pep" talk has stirred you to seek the deeper aspects of your faith. Every time we read this it stirs us to apply ourselves with more resolve. To be sure, we will have failures and so will you. But with our confession and repentance, our very loving heavenly father will forgive us and help us to change as much as we are willing.

All contractors are the same.	True / False
All trucks are the same.	True / False
All schools are the same.	True / False
All hospitals are the same.	True / False
All religions are the same.	True / False
All churches are the same.	True / False

We took you thru the statements above to make a point, all religions and churches are not the same, not only can they be very different, but some are downright bad. Just like all kinds of organizations, businesses, and people are different—so are churches. Ultimately if and what you believe is up to you and we have no desire to coerce you into our faith. Yet we are asked with some frequency what Christian faith and type of church we belong to and would recommend. As many of you have discerned, we cannot separate our faith from our marriage nor would we try. We believe serving and yielding to Christ is very beneficial to any marriage, and when we align ourselves with God's word we believe His provisions and blessings flow to us. We also believe our eternal destiny rests with having the correct belief system. So for those of you who would ask, we belong to a nondenominational, community, Bible-based, Christian church. We would suggest a biblically based Christian church that will help you grow in your devotion to God. The warning, however, is that just like there are good and bad examples of Christians, there are good and bad examples of Christian churches. Anything in which people are involved can be corrupted. Make sure you check around, ask a lot of questions, and make sure any church you join follows only the Bible lifting no other name other than Jesus Christ up, with no other allegiances to other so called prophets or inspired books. The ministry or church should not be focused on some current or past leader who is said to be divinely inspired. There have been no divinely appointed prophets since Jesus Christ.

Couple's project—Consider this a **SAFE TIME** and discuss the chapter in detail. Remember, it gets messy doing remodel work, but the work removes the stuff that doesn't function well and replaces it with new and better materials. Afterward the mess is gone and your home is far better for it.

Did you learn anything? Yes / No
Chapter personal benefit appraisal: **HER 1-2-3-4-5   HIM 1-2-3-4-5**
1=not at all, 2=a little, 3=some good stuff, 4=fairly helpful, 5=very helpful

www.u-build.com

CHAPTER 20

Marriage Statistics

Many technically minded guys like myself enjoy reading facts, data, statistics, etc. I find safety in knowing where I am compared to a group. Data lets me understand and quantify risk versus reward. If the data indicates that 50% of those who travel on smaller ships are going to get seasick and that only 5% who travel by large ships get seasick, I'm going to travel on a large ship or otherwise be prepared should I travel on a small one. Thus data can actually influence my life; I may make adjustments which support the data. This chapter is for those of you who, like me, want to know more about marriage and divorce with some actual data, polls, and studies. Perhaps you will find that some of the following data will alter your life too.

> *"Bad accidents, natural disasters, and crimes all make the leading sections of my newspaper, and perhaps rightly so, but rarely is my heart as broken as when I get to the legal notices section and see the names of all the couples getting a divorce. Why? Those people said they loved each other. Most divorces are preventable, but couples choose to self-inflict injury anyway."*

There is no real order to the following statistics; this is meant to be an informal but thought-provoking read. We have, however, arranged them into several subject headings we call "FASCINATING STATS." Not all of the statistics are in complete harmony with each other, which may reflect variations in the polling methods or data collection techniques of the various organizations. *(Note: Citations occur under the data.)*

FASCINATING STAT #1
Married people account for more than three-quarters of all Americans.

- One out of five adults (22%) has never been married.
- Four out of every five adults (78%) have been married at least once.
- The study discovered that one-third (33%) have experienced at least one divorce.

Barna Group, March 31, 2008. http://www.barna.org/barna-update/article/15-familykids/
42-new-marriage-and-divorce-statistics-released

FASCINATING STAT #2

Divorce has become much more prevalent since the 1900s when there was very little divorce. The last two to three generations have dramatically sought out more divorces. The higher divorce rates may indicate a throwaway mentality or less value placed on marriage. People may not be as willing to work through difficulties as they were previously. There will be approximately one divorce for every two marriages.

Year	# of Marriages	# of Divorces	% Divorce to Marriage
1900	709,000	55,751	8%
1950	1,667,231	385,144	23%
1970	2,158,802	708,000	33%
1998	2,256,000	1,135,000	50%

2008   Without providing actual numbers for the year 2008, the Center for Disease Control (CDC) describes a marriage rate of 7.3 with a divorce rate of 3.6 (based on total U.S. population), which equates to one divorce for every two marriages. This would appear to signify that the divorce rate has remained about the same since 1998.

U.S. Dept. of Health and Human Services, National Center for Health Statistics.
www.cdc.gov/nchs/   http://www.infoplease.com/ipa/A0005044.html#ixzz0zunZHU33

"Marriage is like going camping, it's supposed to be fun and indeed it starts out that way, but at some point while you're in it, unforeseen circumstances induce struggles you didn't plan for. The little space in the tent seems to be smaller than it was on the first day.
"But it's going thru those forced, close quarter dramas that later strengthen the family. We may disagree, but we are forced to disagree in the same tent, and remaining together at the end of the trip makes the family stronger.
"A marriage will force us into close-quarter struggles we didn't plan for, but later we will laugh at them. All we have to do is remain in the tent."

FASCINATING STAT #3

Apparently getting a divorce doesn't actually make most people happy afterward. And couples who were interviewed five years after having considered (but did not obtain) a divorce, were found to be much happier. This data (below) seems to suggest internal issues within a person need to be straightened out for a person to be happy, married or not.

- Unhappily married adults who divorced or separated were no happier, on average, than unhappily married adults who stayed together. Even unhappy spouses who had divorced and remarried were no happier, on average, than unhappy spouses who stayed married. This was true even after controlling for race, age, gender, and income.
- Divorce did not reduce symptoms of depression for unhappily married adults, or raise their self-esteem, or increase their sense of mastery, on average, compared to unhappy spouses who stayed married.
- The vast majority of divorces (74%) happened to adults who had been happily married five years previously. In this group, divorce was associated with dramatic declines in happiness and psychological well-being compared to those who stayed married.
- Unhappy marriages were less common than unhappy spouses. Three out of four unhappily married adults were married to someone who was happy with the marriage.
- Staying married did not typically trap unhappy spouses in violent relationships. Eighty-six percent of unhappily married adults reported no violence in their relationship (including 77% of unhappy spouses who later divorced or separated). Ninety-three percent of unhappy spouses who avoided divorce reported no violence in their marriage five years later.
- Two out of three unhappily married adults who avoided divorce or separation ended up happily married five years later. Just one out of five of unhappy spouses who divorced or separated had happily remarried in the same time period.

Report, "Does Divorce Make People Happy?" Linda J. Waite, Don Browning, William J. Doherty, Maggie Gallagher, Ye Luo, and Scott M. Stanley. of The Institute for American Values   http://www.americanvalues.org/UnhappyMarriages.pdf

- The National Center for Health Statistics released a report that found 43% of first marriages end in separation or divorce within 15 years.

Bramlett, Matthew and William Mosher. "First Marriage Dissolution, Divorce, and Remarriage: United States," Advance Data From Vital and Health Statistics; No. 323. Hyattsville, MD: National Center for Health Statistics: 2 1. http://www.divorcereform.org/rates.html

FASCINATING STAT #4
Living together is less likely to result in a lasting couple relationship, and living together prior to marriage slightly increases a couple's chance of

divorce if they later married after cohabitation. If a person does go through a divorce, they are very likely to remarry.

- Probability that 1st marriage breaks up in 15 years = 39%
- Probability that cohabitation breaks up in 10 years = roughly 68%
- Probability that a divorced person will remarry within 10 years = 68%
- Probability that 1st marriage breaks up for women who have had GAD (generalized anxiety disorder) within 15 years = 55%

From the CDC, Vital & Health Statistics, "Cohabitation, Marriage, Divorce, and Remarriage in the U.S., 2002."
 http://www.cdc.gov/nchs/data/series/sr_23/sr23_022.pdf

- Using a random telephone survey of men and women married within the past 10 years, the current study replicated previous findings regarding the timing of engagement and the premarital cohabitation effect (see Kline et al., 2004). Those who cohabited before engagement (43.1%) reported lower marital satisfaction, dedication, and confidence as well as more negative communication and greater potential for divorce than those who cohabited only after engagement (16.4%) or not at all until marriage (40.5%).

Galena K. Rhoades, Scott M. Stanley, and Howard J. Markman, Department of Psychology, University of Denver, *Journal of Family Psychology*, Volume 23, Issue 1, February 2009, Pages 107–111. http://www.sciencedirect.com

---

When my wife gets stressed I'll attempt to calm her down by using a technique we use to relax. It is a breathing exercise where I'll say: *"OK, breathe in the good air, and out with the bad."* Unfortunately, I might have used it at a time when I had been particularly exasperating to her, for not long after I said *"out with the bad,"* I found myself being led outside and left on the front steps while hearing the door close behind me.

FASCINATING STAT #5

Divorce rate for successive marriages are worse than for the 1st marriage.

- For the past decade, the overall American divorce rate has remained stable, at around **50%** for first marriages. The statistics become more depressing for each successive marriage, with **65%** of second marriages ending in divorce and even higher rates for third marriages and beyond.

http://www.divorceguide.com/usa/divorce-information/divorce-statistics-in-the-usa.html

> "The effects of the decline of marriage on society are striking. The failure of parents to marry and stay married leads to more crime, poverty, mental health problems, welfare dependency, failed schools, blighted neighborhoods, bloated prisons, and higher rates of single parenting and divorce in the next generation. *Nearly every major social problem has deep roots in the failure of adults to form and sustain healthy marriages.* There are other causes of these social problems, of course, such as economic dislocations and the decline of civic life and social responsibility in the United States, *but the disconnection of childrearing from marriage ranks high on the list of what ails our society and our communities."*
>
> Bill Doherty, Philanthropy Roundtable, 2006

FASCINATING STAT #6
People who truly practice their faith report high levels of satisfaction in many areas of their marriage.

From the book, "Couples Who Pray" the following data was uncovered for couples who pray frequently

0–2% "fear of divorce"
78% say their marriage is happy
92% say they are "satisfied with sex a great deal"
91% say "my spouse is my best friend"
75% "agree on how children should be raised"
69% see their agreement on financial matters as "very good"
86% try to make their marriage better
77% say "my spouse makes me feel important"
69% say "my spouse delights in me"
92% rate their confidence in the stability of their marriage as "very good"

"Couples Who Pray" by Squire Rushnell Louise DuArt
http://www.coupleswhopray.com

FASCINATING STAT #7

There is overwhelming evidence by multiple studies that couples who pray together daily decrease their chances for divorce by over a 1,000%. The following multiple studies provide truly amazing data. This data clearly establishes a line between two camps of people in Christianity, those who practice their faith *(dedicated Christians)* and those who don't *(casual Christians)*. The message is clear: if you really want your marriage to survive, you must be dedicated in practicing your faith and that must include praying together daily.

- "A Gallup Poll that was done in 1997 by the National Association of Marriage Enhancement in Phoenix, Arizona, showed the divorce rate among couples who **pray together** regularly, is 1 out of 1,152. That's a divorce rate of less than 1%" Greg and Erin Smalley.

http://www.liferelationships.com/resources/qa/viewAnswer.asp?articleid=200&categoryid=27

- Dr. Phil writes in his bestselling book, *Relationship Rescue*: *"...an interesting statistic shared by David McLaughlin in his wonderful series entitled* The Role of the Man in the Family *reflects that the divorce rate in America is at a minimum one out of two marriages. But the reported divorce rate among **couples that pray together is about one in ten thousand**. Pretty impressive statistic, even if you reduce it a thousand fold."*

http://www.familylife.com/site/apps/nlnet/content3.aspx?c=dnJHKLNnFoG&b=3842489&ct=5597805

- Retrouvaille International, a marriage-support organization, cites a 1980 study indicating the divorce rate for couples who attend church together regularly and also pray or read the Bible together on a daily basis is, remarkably, less than 1 divorce in every 1,100 marriages.

http://www.coupleprayer.org/CouplePrayerSeries.html

- "I have counseled with hundreds of married couples over the years. After seeing marriages improve, I use to ask what one piece of advice made the greatest difference. Over and over, I got the same answer...learning how to **pray together**." Doug Britton, author, marriage and family therapist.

http://www.dougbrittonbooks.com/onlinebiblestudies-marriageinformationandadvice/marriedcouplesprayers-praywithyourspouseeveryday.php

- When you add prayer into the mix, thoughts of divorce plummet. A 1998 survey by the Georgia Family Council found that among **couples who prayed together** weekly, only 7% had seriously considered divorce, compared to 65% of those who never prayed together.

http://www.focusonthefamily.com/marriage/strengthening_your_marriage/commitment.aspx

- Andrew Greeley working with *Psychology Today* and the Gallup Poll wrote, "**Whether they pray often together is a very powerful correlate of marital happiness**, the most powerful we have yet discovered."

http://divorce-buster.com/

FASCINATING STAT #8

Divorce can have devastating consequences for the children of broken homes. The statistics below are heart wrenching. It is imperative that we as a nation learn how to be married, not only for our own satisfaction but more importantly for the welfare of our children.

U.S. Marriage and Divorce Statistics (2002)
Fatherless homes account for:

63% of youth suicides
90% of homeless & runaway children
85% of children with behavior problems
71% of high school dropouts
85% of youths in prison
Over 50% of teen mothers

From the federal government website for the Center for Disease Control.
http://www.cdc.gov/nchs/data/series/sr_23/sr23_022.pdf

> *"It is instructive that 87% of those incarcerated in American prisons either don't know who their father is or have not had any contact with their fathers in years."*   Herbert London, Hudson Institute

FASCINATING STAT #9

The following are a few misc. tidbits of information:

From the CDC:

- Compared with unmarried people, married men and women tend to have lower mortality, less risky behavior, more monitoring of

169

health, more compliance with medical regimens, higher sexual frequency, more satisfaction with their sexual lives, more savings, and higher wages. (Page 3)

- Compared to married individuals, divorced persons exhibit lower levels of psychological well-being, more health problems, greater risk of mortality, more social isolation, less satisfying sex lives, more negative life events, greater levels of depression and alcohol use, and lower levels of happiness and self-acceptance. The economic consequences of divorce can be severe for women. (Pages 3&4)

- Single-parent families have lower levels of parental involvement in school activities and their children have lower student achievement compared to two-parent families. Children raised in single-parent families are more likely to drop out of high school, have lower grades and attendance while in school, and are less likely to attend and graduate from college than children raised in two-parent families. They are more likely to be out of school and unemployed and are also more likely to become single parents themselves, than children raised in two-parent families. Studies have found that, compared to children in two-parent families, children of divorce score lower on measures of self-concept, social competence, conduct, psychological adjustment and long-term health. (Page 4)

- Most separated women make the transition to divorce very quickly: 84% make the transition to divorce within three years and 91% do so within five years. (Page 22)

- Fifty-four percent of divorced women remarry within five years and 75% of divorced women remarry within 10 years. (Page 22)

The above five stats are from the CDC Report, Bramlett, MD and Mosher MD. "Cohabitation, Marriage, Divorce, and Remarriage in the United States." National Center for Health Statistics. Vital Health Stat 23(22). 2002.

From National Healthy Marriage Resource Center:

- Decades of research suggest that a stable marriage protects adult partners against premature death and illness, and provides children with the best physical health outcomes. The relationship of marriage to better health outcomes continues to be found in the most recent national health surveys and longitudinal studies. These studies indicate married adults live longer and enjoy better physical health than adults who are never married, divorced, separated, or widowed. In fact, these benefits seem to persist even when factors that affect health outcomes, such as health status prior to marriage, income levels and race/ethnicity are taken into account (Johnson et al, 2000; Kaplan & Kronick, 2006; Lillard & Waite, 1995; Wilson & Oswald, 2005; Wood, Goesling & Avellar, 2007). Also research suggests that married couples living in poverty have better physical health compared to their low-income peers who are unmarried, divorced, or widowed (Schoenborn, 2004).

- Research also indicates a man or woman's marital status at age 48—that is, whether married, divorced, widowed, or never married—strongly predicts their chances of either surviving to age 65 or dying prematurely. For example, as depicted in the charts below (Waite, 2005), divorced men have only a 65% chance of living to age 65, compared to a 90% chance for married men, and a never-married woman has an 80% chance of living to age 65, compared to a 95% chance for married women (Lillard & Waite, 1995, Waite, 1995).

- Research continues to show that divorce carries significant risks of illness and premature death for both partners, but especially for men (Lillard & Waite, 1995; Williams & Umberson, 2004). Men and women who have divorced have a greater likelihood of developing cardiovascular disease than adults who never marry or who remain continuously married without any disruption (Zhang & Hayward, 2006).

- Research findings on marriage are consistent with the extensive literature on the direct health consequences of social support and social isolation (Uchino et al, 1992, 1996). For many, a healthy marriage is the most intimate and enduring social network, providing the strongest and most frequent opportunity for social and emotional support. Also, a healthy marriage has been found to be the best protection for children's health and well-being. The research shows that marriage can have both negative and positive effects, depending on the quality of marital relationship. A recent national representative survey of adults has demonstrated that an unhappy marriage eliminates the health benefit of marriage (Brim et al, 2003). The research supports that a good-enough, healthy marriage, one that is low in negativity will provide cumulative, lifelong protection against chronic illness and premature death for both men and women as well as greatly increasing the chances that children will grow up healthy. And these benefits seem to only increase as couples grow old together.

- Our immune systems are also sensitive to the amount of discord or conflict in a relationship. Maintaining physical contact with a

171

spouse while under stressful experimental conditions lowered blood pressure and heart rate, and increased the hormone oxytocin, which prevents the body's stress responses from negatively influencing the cardiovascular and endocrine systems.

National Healthy Marriage Resource Center, "What is the Relationship of Marriage to Physical Health?" 2008. http://www.healthymarriageinfo.org

From Yahoo:

- In a study by Utah State University professor Jeffrey Dew, his research concluded that couples who argue about finances at least once a week are 30% more likely to divorce than those who only vent occasionally about money issues. Couples with no assets were 70% more likely to divorce compared to couples with assets of $10,000.

http://finance.yahoo.com/career-work/article/109813/when-fights-over-money-ruin-marriages?mod=family-love_money

- **Attitudes: Percent who agree that marriage is an out-dated institution**

U.S.	10.1%,
Canada	22.3%,
UK	25.9%,
France	36.3%,
Germany	18.4%,
Italy	17%,
Sweden	20.4%

"Marriage and Divorce: Changes and Their Driving Forces," Betsey Stevenson, Justin Wolfers, **DISCUSSION PAPER SERIES,** Institute for the Study of Labor, February 2007, http://ftp.iza.org/dp2602.pdf

Regardless of where you fit into these statistics, you have much of the information you need to keep your current marriage free from divorce and more importantly you have in your hands enough information to progress toward a great marriage. We've beat you up with this over and over, but if you do nothing to foster your marriage, it will likely end. There are many more statistics that we did not include in this brief overview, but you can visit the sources for more details if you like. Apply what you're learning, grow and strengthen your marriage, beat the odds, have a great marriage. It is really a choice; it's your choice!

Have you been divorced? Are you in your 2nd, 3rd, or 4th marriage? Obviously something is not working right for you in relationships. It appears you've not yet learned what it takes to have a lasting marriage.

Perhaps you have some major remodel work to do inside of you? The good news is you can turn it around. Let's work together to make the marriage you are in now <u>your last one</u>.

Couple's project—If you have been in more than one marriage relationship, we want you to do four things. **First**, say this out loud: *"I'm part of the problem; I need help to change."* **Second**, say this out loud: *"I need professional help, and I'm going to actively seek it out this week."* **Third**, say this out loud: *"This marriage is going to be a lasting marriage; I'll never consider divorce again."* And **Fourth**, if you actually verbally made the confessions, then <u>forgive yourself</u>. You still need to get help, you still need to make changes within you, but if you are indeed now determined to work on your stuff, then forgive yourself.

Our handbook is an attempt to turn around the rising tide of divorce that has occurred since the 1900s in America. To turn the tide, we need each one of you to work at your marriage, to value it, to make it grow and flourish. You can have a great marriage—what is it worth to you? You really want to be happily married, so let's change this, let's be happily married. It begins in your home, you must commit never to divorce except for one of the three A's, and then only if you've tried every possible way to salvage your marriage.

Imagine if every married couple fought for their marriage rather than fought with their spouse! In just one year we could cut the number of divorces from roughly 1.2 million to just 200,000 next year. The divorce percentages would fall from roughly 50% to roughly 10%.

Visit our website (www.u-build.com) after you have completed going thru our handbook; you'll find a downloadable copy of a marriage promise certificate. The certificate is something you and your spouse will print out and either post on your refrigerator (where ours hangs) or you can frame and hang it on the wall. It is a daily reminder of your promise to each other to have a great marriage.

20 | "President George W. Bush proposed, as part of welfare reform reauthorization, the creation of a pilot program to promote healthy and stable marriages. Participation in the program would be strictly voluntary, and funding would be small-scale: $300 million per year. *This sum represents one penny to promote healthy marriage for every five dollars the government spends subsidizing single parenthood*....The collapse of marriage is the principal cause of child poverty in the United States... Overall, some 80% of long-term child poverty in the United States is found among children from broken or never-formed families."

Robert Rector, Senior Research Fellow on Welfare
and Family Issues at Heritage Foundation 2003

Did you learn anything? Yes / No
Chapter personal benefit appraisal: **HER 1-2-3-4-5   HIM 1-2-3-4-5**
1=not at all, 2=a little, 3=some good stuff, 4=fairly helpful, 5=very helpful

www.u-build.com

174

The Blending of Husband and Wife

CHAPTER 21

The Two Become One

> *"I hate to be a failure. I hate and regret the failure of my marriages. I would gladly give all my millions for just one lasting marital success."*
> J. Paul Getty

That's quite a statement from Mr. Getty; we suspect many unhappily married couples would give up most of their fortune to enjoy an enduring and loving marriage. The good news is an enduring marriage is available to every couple.

This "two become one" concept is based in biblical Scripture and using that as our marriage guide, Paige and I sought to follow the road that led to this "oneness." A lot of people have heard or read the Bible passage about the two becoming one and smile without ever really thinking about it. Most people think it's talking about the act of intercourse, and indeed that is one aspect of it. Let's explore the concept and see if we can get an understanding of how we achieve this cohesive state of union.

Becoming one is not something that automatically happens when you are married, as the divorce statistics concede. Two becoming one is a willful act in which you each take **all** that you are and set that identity aside to change yourselves into something else. This doesn't go over with the new age psychologists; they say you shouldn't expect the other person to change. We say "**You have to change**!" If you didn't want to change you should have stayed single. It's that simple. We are not saying it's up to you to change your spouse, because that is not the case. The idea is you both must do your own changing.

It seems fitting to use the following example to get better understanding of how we lose (or should lose) our identity and become one when we get married. Consider the sperm and the egg in the "two become one" concept. Before joining together there is a separate sperm and egg. However, once the sperm penetrates the egg, the two lose their individual identities and now become a "zygote" (which means joined or yoked). The previous identities of the egg and sperm are lost, and they now have a new and completely different identity. Once joined it is impossible to un-join them—their previous individual identities are forever lost.

177

21 The genetic material contained in the egg and sperm have fused into something quite different than they were before.

It's also interesting to note that while the egg was open to advances from a sperm in the past, as soon as the first sperm penetrates the egg, the egg wall becomes hard and impenetrable to any other sperm that comes along. In an earlier chapter we shared the concept of putting up a fence to protect the marriage relationship from outsiders. Both the husband and the wife are no longer what they were; they have begun a new and fascinating journey of oneness, and a defensive wall is put up to protect the marriage from all other intruders. Pretty cool demonstration for a marriage, huh!

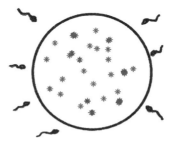

> *"Any married man should forget his mistakes—no use two people remembering the same thing."*   Duane Dewel

We briefly mentioned the following example of a pair of legs in an earlier chapter, but let's review again. Picture the human body with a right and left side. Picture one spouse as the left-side leg and the other as the right-side leg. You are one body 100% of the time while being two separate legs. As the body walks, each leg takes turns bearing all of the weight, and both legs are moving in the same direction. Sometimes the legs will stand equally bearing the weight and sometimes they will sit down and take a rest, but they always work together for the mutual benefit of each other and the body.

When you understand the concept of the "two become one," and, more to the point, when you work to achieve it, you keep unity thoughts before you and you make better decisions for the marriage unit. You're supplanting your own desires for the needs of the marriage. It's no longer about "your" needs; it's about the needs of the marriage.

Work thru your issues, giving the best you can give to help your spouse succeed. Do not be concerned if you think you are doing more than your spouse. One spouse having to bear the entire burden occurs with some frequency in all great marriages.

Ever see a great basketball or football team crumble in a crucial game? It seemed like everyone was in the wrong place at the wrong time. They miscued frequently, and it just seemed to snowball, getting worse and worse. Conversely, it's quite awe-inspiring when a team is working as a single unit, everyone is supporting the other, feeding the ball to the shooter, and blocking the advances of those opposing them. The team's owner will get the right coach and right support people until his team works as a single unit and comes out on top. The same holds true for a good marriage. The lesson for improving your marriage is the same; it's very beneficial to get support help when we need it and to always act as one.

> *"What counts in making a happy marriage is not so much how compatible you are, but how you deal with incompatibility."*
>
> Leo Tolstoy

The goal is to become one, to act like one and to represent your selves as one.

Couple's project—Let's do another exercise, but in this exercise we are going to get physical!

Tug of War Exercise

Right now we want both of you to take a tug of war rope (*please get a rope, or a belt, extension cord, or some other prop that will simulate a rope*) and pretend you're going at it. Put a knot in the middle if you like and assume your positions. Do this before you move on to the next page.

TUG - OF - WAR

Once you have the rope,

LOOK AT EACH OTHER FOR A FEW SECONDS AND THEN COME BACK

AND CONTINUE READING.

NO CHEATING!!

<u>GET THE ROPE!!!</u>

DO NOT TURN THE PAGE UNTIL YOU GET A ROPE —

LAST CHANCE!!!!!

**TAKE THE ROPE AND GET INTO YOUR TUG-OF-WAR
POSITIONS!**

**FOR REAL … DO IT NOW… WE DON'T WANT TO HAVE TO
HURT YOU!!! ☺**

**We are building a relationship here; it's built on trust.
We are trusting you <u>to do</u> what we've asked you to do.
Do you want help or not?**

21 We hope you both followed our instructions; if not you're both dead meat!!

The point we're trying to make here is, if you picked up the rope at *opposite ends, as though fighting one another* you haven't gotten the point. In all situations you are one! If there's going to be a battle, <u>any kind of battle</u>, no matter where it's coming from, you two are no longer two, <u>but one</u>, and that means <u>you ALWAYS fight on the same side, at the same time</u>.

We'd like to point out that we didn't tell you to pick up opposite ends, only to *"assume your positions."* If you went to opposite ends you did that all on your own. In spite of all the instruction you digested in the previous pages you're still not acting as one. You should be working together on the same end, the enemy—whomever or whatever the enemy is—is on the opposite end.

> *"Oh yes, I've **given in** thousands of times in our marriage, I'm proud to say it's a regular occurrence. Now please do not confuse that with **giving up**, that has never occurred, even once."*

Amazing! Let us say it with you. *"Boy, are we stupid!"* Yep, Bob and I have been right there with you! You see it takes a greater awareness and practice to apply what we've learned. Ninety-five percent of the couples we give this test to also pick the rope up at opposite ends. Don't berate yourselves for not passing this test; rather concentrate on ALWAYS acting as one from this day forward. Bob and I keep the tug-of-war rope on our bedroom dresser as a reminder to <u>never fight against each other</u>.

How Not to Become One

There are a few of you out there that own the title "princess" or "prince," not because you were born into royalty but because your parents raised you as if you were. You may know this already, but spoiling children is bad, it makes life tuff for these kids who become adults because life teaches us we don't get to have it our way any more than just some of the time. We see this struggle with the latest generation more so than all others. They are accustomed to having pretty much everything they wanted growing up and expect it now that they are adults.

While we are confident life will eventually beat this negative aspect out of most of these "it's all about me" men and women, it is paramount you do

182

not expect to be treated this way in your marriage. Your spouse is not your mom or dad who is going to tend to your every comfort. The "two become one" is not your spouse changing to be like you, you will in fact be doing much more of the changing if you've been accustomed to getting nearly everything your way. Your way is going away and so is your spouse's way, you both will be creating a new way. The goal is that none of your old selfish self will be left!

OK, let's play another game. Pretend you and your spouse are sitting around a table with 3 other couples playing a game of poker. When you play the game, are you playing against everybody including your spouse, or are you playing so that you **or** your spouse can win? Can you see the mindset we want you to have? Always consider you actions or efforts as joined to your spouse, never against them.

Couple's project—We'd like you to have a **SAFE TIME** discussion about how you can act more like one in your marriage and how you both can make a few changes that will foster becoming more like one. You may spend more time together, try to never disagree, learn to communicate better, and make other improvements.

FACTOID – Marriage requires learning a new lingo. "I, me, and my", language goes away, and a new language, "we, us, and our" become the new dialect. The sooner you learn the new way to communicate, the sooner you'll have better results.

Bob and Paige's tug of war rope and wedding jars that sit on our bedroom dresser to continually remind us we are never to fight each other and we are one.

21 Did you learn anything? Yes / No
Chapter personal benefit appraisal: **HER 1-2-3-4-5   HIM 1-2-3-4-5**
1=not at all, 2=a little, 3=some good stuff, 4=fairly helpful, 5=very helpful

www.u-build.com

CHAPTER 22

Personality Types

Relationship guru Gary Smalley teaches what he describes as the four personality types: *lions, otters, golden retrievers*, and *beavers*. Gary describes how each of us is a combination of these four main traits, and in the spirit of marriage unity, they all have value with no trait being better than the other. While each trait has positive and beneficial attributes, they also each have some negative attributes. Gary uses these animal types to help people relate to their personalities and they are much easier to remember than the sanguine, melancholy, and other professional psychological profiles.

I was so impressed with Gary's instruction and test on personality types that I routinely gave the test to people I was planning to hire to learn more about them. We also gave the tests away to friends and family to help them understand themselves and their spouses.

Gary's teaching about the four basic animal types was a huge breakthrough for me. Frankly, besides being a maxed-out lion type, I'm also a very organized beaver type. Paige is mostly an otter, she loves a party, socializing, and having fun. Can you see the differences between our personality types becoming apparent when we began to live inside the same four walls of our home? Deep cleaning the house was just not a big deal to her in the early years of our marriage. This disparity grated on me. I wrongly thought my wife was opposing me in having a super clean house. It was only after I watched Gary's videotape series that I understood my personality traits and my wife's personality traits were not the same; rather they contrasted each other, and I was attracted to her because she was not like me. Yet for years I wanted her to place the same value on the same things I placed value on. I was trying to make her into me…proving again that I am not right in the head!

FACTOID – Each of us has different aspects of personality types, each personality type has good characteristics and some not so good.

Once you understand we are designed to be different, you'll learn to accept your spouse as God created them. We've already established that you do not want to marry someone just like you.

22 Gary's teachings revealed that it's their contrasts we love, and yet those contrasts can also grate on us until we get an understanding of just how neat this all works out.

Gary has another technique he calls "word pictures." Using word pictures as a communication tool helps a person convey how they feel rather than using anger and resentment.

We didn't want to plagiarize Gary's work, so you'll have to seek his wisdom by picking up his marriage and family resources on your own. You can find the contact information in the last chapter and we highly recommend you check out his resources to help you understand each other more in depth.

"Do I look fat?" "Are my boobs saggy?" "Is my bottom bigger?" "Were you looking at her?"

Beware of these four questions. It is the <u>only time</u> I tell husbands it's actually mandatory that they lie if they would otherwise have to answer "YES" to any of those four questions.

Couple's project—Discuss between you that you have differences and contrasts and that is a good thing. You are not the same!

Did you learn anything? Yes / No
Chapter personal benefit appraisal: **HER 1-2-3-4-5   HIM 1-2-3-4-5**
1=not at all, 2=a little, 3=some good stuff, 4=fairly helpful, 5=very helpful

www.u-build.com

CHAPTER 23

How Much are You Going to Put Into It?

Let's imagine you and I are going to play a one-on-one game of B-ball or tennis, or a round of golf. The bet is going to be several thousand dollars, the winner takes all. The bet will be based on just one game with no warm-ups and no mulligans. So tell me, are you going to give it everything you've got to win?

Your marriage is much more valuable than a few thousand dollars but most couples act like it's a "just for fun" match and they don't put everything they have into it. One or both spouses have decided they only want to give it "some" effort and certainly won't work to the point of having to raise a sweat! They enter the game from a state of weakness almost ensuring they will lose.

Since there is so much at risk, why not give yourself the best shot by using every available tool you have and putting all your strength into it? Latch on, hold on, and give it everything you've got to win the marriage game so you will be standing in the winner's circle at the end!

Lack of effort in marriage reminds us of the instances when a person creates his or her résumé or goes in for a person-to-person interview. In general it goes something like this: they've never made a mistake, they'll always give 110%, and you can count on them when everyone else has dropped the ball, yada yada yada. We think most people genuinely want to do what they say, but sadly they often forget that it will take real effort to do what they promised. At some point, we should at least try to live up to all the claims we made during our dating and engagement period. And it may require much more effort than we originally thought would be needed. In the weeks leading up to the wedding day a couple will staunchly proclaim the marriage will work because they "will make it work," but as the months and years pass by, very little if any marriage building activity has occurred.

We need to clarify an area that seems to confuse many couples. We are sure that some of you are exhausted. You feel drained and when we tell you to put a focused effort into your marriage you are looking back at these words saying, "What the hell, I've got nothing left to give, I'm already spent!" You know what? We'd likely agree with you because you've just put too much of your energy in the wrong places.

23 As Americans we seem to fill our lives with tons of things we feel we need to do, but the reality is hundreds of millions of people are doing life without all this same busyness we cram into our lives. So while you may be exhausted, it may be that you've focused on the wrong areas of your life to put your energy. We can tell you this, if you put the energy into your marriage, it pays you back several times over in helping you get thru all the other stuff. Rearrange your priorities, and put the effort into the marriage. And don't get out of whack by ignoring all your other responsibilities; just make your marriage a top priority. If you do, when each day is over, you will be able to crawl into each other's arms and find comfort and peace. I think laptops, cell phones, and socials networks are competing with spouses in many homes today.

Some of the work we are asking you to do does not require more effort, it requires less. If you are a workaholic, we are asking you to work less. If you both have two jobs trying to make ends meet, how about doing with less and using more moneysaving practices so you can have more time together?

Couple's project—We'd like you both to think of someone you admire who you know of personally or someone you've heard about that has had these two qualities: a lasting and happy marriage. Who comes to mind?

Bob and I thought about Billy and Ruth Graham, Gracie Allen and George Burns, Ron and Nancy Reagan, and a couple of personal acquaintances. For those of you who were fortunate enough to be raised by the same set of loving parents, you included their names in your list. Others of you found it very hard to come up with any names at all. What we admire about these couples is they learned how to persist in a loving relationship. We included Ron and Nancy Reagan even though Ron had a prior marriage and was the only president to have been divorced. Ron and Nancy were married for over 52 years prior to his death and none of us will forget the pictures of Nancy refusing to leave Ron's coffin. We are not honoring Ron's divorce, but his enduring second marriage. It is irrelevant whether we agree or disagree with Billy Graham as an evangelist, or think George and Gracie's comedy was actually funny, or whether Ron Reagan was a good American president. For all of them their most important title was "spouse."

Let's Go Back in Time

We never look better than on our wedding day, and sadly for some couples, it's the happiest day of their lives because every day after that is filled with married misery. The reality is that when you have a great marriage, your wedding day begins to pale compared to all the days that follow.

In an interview Nancy Regan said she could not imagine life without Ronnie. She espoused that they were very much in love.

As you read the following wedding vows (which will apply to many of you who were wed in a traditional ceremony) think about the words you chose to speak.

"I, *[your name]*, take you, *[your spouses name]*, to be my lawfully wedded *(husband/wife)*. I promise to be true to you in good times and in bad, in sickness and in health. I will love you and honor you all the days of my life."

Or another version

"I, *[your name]*, take you, *[your spouses name]*, for my lawful *(husband/wife),* to have and to hold, from this day forward, for better, for worse, for richer, for poorer, in sickness and in health, until death do us part."

Perhaps the above reflection will take you back to what you felt and the depth of your commitment on your marriage day. Take a few moments and consider your thoughts back then.

The wedding day is another one of those sincere moments that we seem to quickly put out of our mind. It's not long before we've forgotten our vows and lost the sincerity that we swore before God and the witnesses. Recall that the basis of all the family and friends attending your wedding ceremony was to be witnesses who would *"hold you accountable."* Part of the solution may be to get your heads back to that original day and bring back to life that forever vision and the desire for a great marriage that developed during the courtship period.

So how do we live in this relationship we call marriage? We're going to suggest we live "fully & completely" by:

> Recalling our original intentions and vows and make every effort to live up to them.
> Putting into action the materials, tools, and other resources to foster our marriage.

Living and functioning as a happily married couple.
Resolving differences quickly, not letting them fester.
Living up to the moral code we profess to follow.
Living up to our title as father/mother to our kids.

We are asking you to put a renewed effort into having a great marriage. For real! We'd like you to commit to a 100% effort, nothing less. As we mentioned in an earlier chapter, we taught our daughter that her attitude and happiness resides in her head; if she wants to be miserable there is nothing we can do about it. We understand that right now your marriage may suck, and that the only way you see "is out." It is very likely you have some valid issues with your marriage, but if you're unhappy it is in part because you didn't help keep it on the right track. Some couples will feel it's easier to be unhappy than invest in the repair work to fix it. Prior to reading this handbook, you may not have had much of an understanding of how to foster and grow your marriage, but you are learning how now. Your happiness, your love and respect for your spouse, is something you alone control inside of your head, none of the rest of us is responsible for how you choose to feel.

Couple's project—We would like you both to agree to put more into your marriage than you have in the past. At this point in the handbook most of you are going to be willing to commit to 100%, but others of you still have stuff to work thru. That's OK, let's just agree to work on it.

We want you to step back here for a few moments and consider what is taking place here. You are reading a handbook from a couple who is asking you to have a great marriage. Somehow this handbook has ended up in your hands and a married couple who you've never met is trying to use a couple of hundred pages of their experiences, thoughts, and ideas to help you have an enduring and happy marriage. Sure we are going to make a couple of bucks, but what is in it for you? Why are you reading the handbook? Don't lose sight of your goal, to have the best marriage you can. It's all about your marriage!

Balance

Let's break down just the time aspect of balance. There are only 24 hours in each day, and a lot of things already take most of those hours away. Perhaps most important is sleep! That leaves about 16 hours for other tasks. If you work, minus another eight hours for work, minus two more for lunch and commuting and you're down to six hours. With three meals and personal hygiene activities taken off, most of you will only have three hours left of your day for spouse, kids, friends, and other activities. We can see that most of our time is already structured; there is not much we can do about it.

What we all need to understand is it's really only these three hours and our weekends we have to foster our relationships with our spouse and others outside of our work. If you work out at a gym that will usually take another two hours of the day. Hopefully you are getting an understanding of why we feel we have so little time and why we will all struggle with balancing our priorities. In all of the demands, our spouse needs to be very high on the priority list. So high if we need to make time for them we should be willing to cut time from some other activity. Besides balancing our time, we have to balance our responsibilities, we have to maintain other relationships, we may need to advance our education, and more. Overwhelmed yet? Make sure your marriage is a priority, but that doesn't mean following your spouse around like a puppy, which could also be out of balance.

> *"You've likely heard of S&M, how about M&M—Miserable & Married? The concept is the same, lots of pain and torture."*

Recap a Few Key Points

We've previously made the point that your desire to commit to your marriage is in part based on your desire to live up to your own moral code. After all why would you make much of an effort to build up your marriage and foster its longevity if your moral code doesn't require such devotion? We also told you how surveys found that nearly all Americans have a belief in God and the vast majority of Americans profess an adherence to the Christian faith and code of conduct. And we pointed out that while many people profess a faith, they often do not "walk the talk." We see this gap as fundamental to the reason there is little statistical difference between the marriage success and failure rates of people of faith. Given this chapter asks you how much you are going to put into it, it's time for you to answer that question. We'll lead up to it with several precursor questions.

23 **Couple's project**—On a scale of 1 to 10:
How strong is your desire to have a great marriage?

Him ____   Her ____

How strong is your belief in your moral code?

Him ____   Her ____

How well do you put into practice your beliefs with your day-to-day actions?

Him ____   Her ____

How much are you going to put into it?

Him ____   Her ____

A Few Indicators of a Healthy Marriage

- Healthy & regular sexual intimacy.
- Hanging out with people who encourage healthy monogamous relationships.
- Established boundaries to protect your marriage.
- Humility and an attitude of service to for each other.
- Humor, and lots of it; be silly sometimes!
- Sincere repentance and sincere forgiveness.
- Loyalty, coming to the aid and defending your spouse.
- Devotion to the marriage unit, in it for the long haul.
- Fun—some music, movies, dance, trips, etc.

Additional Indicators for Those Professing to Have a Christian-based Marriage

- Jesus is both Lord and Savior in your life.
- You are "doing" your Christianity, not being a "poser."
- You are praying together daily.
- You are reading the Bible daily.
- You are attending a local church.
- You have an awareness of Satan's influences.
- Your unconfessed sin is then confessed.

A Few Unhealthy Symptoms in a Marriage

- Cutting each other down, even if jokingly.
- Too little sexual intimacy.
- Putting children before spouse.
- Putting other family before spouse.
- Flirting with opposite sex.

- Spending beyond your means.
- Not spending time with each other.
- Working (job) too much.
- Talking to or spending more time in a day with your pet than your spouse.
- Pornography, romance novels, or other fantasy activity.
- Compulsive activity, eating, internet, drinking, etc.
- Harboring bitterness or being unforgiving.

23

"Grow up, buck up" these are words I need to hear with some frequency. Oh yeah, I can say it, but I need to regularly hear them too! I think we all have times when we lose sight of the real goal, and that is to have a great marriage. I'm not the best husband; I've gone up and down in the care of my marriage and wife. Thankfully, Paige has been forgiving. That is why many of us require constant reminders of what our goal is. Throughout our married life <u>most of us will frequently require being reminded about what is important.</u>

Are you Happy?

We cannot put this before you enough, so we'll ask you straight up, "Who is responsible for your happiness?" Is it God? Is it your spouse? Is it your parents? <u>No, it is "you."</u>

People and circumstances can make your life difficult, but it's still up to you to be happy. We've said this before: money, fame, power, none of these have made people happy for any length of time. Happiness is not about things, it's not about circumstances, it's not about the people we are with; it's about you and me choosing to be happy regardless of our circumstances. Some of the happiest people we know are poor by American standards. Some of the most miserable people we know are rich. You'll never be happy if you keep chasing after things that you think will make you happy. I just need a newer car, I just need a bigger home, I just need a new job, THEN I'll be happy. NO, your happiness is always available; it's up to you to take it right where you are. We can tell you this, if you make your marriage the best it can be, you'll naturally find it easier to be happy. Choose to be happy today!

Rekindle the Fire

It's a common complaint among couples who have become burdened with the hassles of life. So many daily demands have smothered that passion they once had. We've heard people say *"The fire has gone out of my marriage,"* and indeed that may be a correct observation, but let's discuss the mechanics of "fire" and see if we can relate that term to our marriages. There is something known as the "fire triangle." It is the basis for all combustion processes and all fire-fighting techniques in practice today.

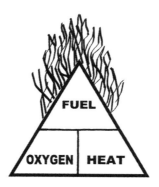

If you remove any one of the three components the fire is lost; if you want to restore or create fire all you have to do is make sure all three components are present and the fire returns. The three components are fuel, heat, and oxygen. The best fires are built using the best balance of all three components. Too much fuel or too little oxygen and the fire will be smoky and give less heat. Too much oxygen and too little fuel and the fire will burn too lean.

We'd suggest that if the fire has gone out in your marriage, there are at the most only three things missing to bring the fire back. Better yet you may only be missing two things, and very often it's just one thing. Can you visualize what is preventing the fire from igniting your marriage?

We want you to have hope here because we believe most troubled marriages are just 1–3 steps away from getting that fiery passion back. When you consider that many post-divorce people regret they got divorced, it appears the revelation of what was missing caught up with them after the divorce.

Sometimes a couple who has a lot of demands on their daily life will have to be persistent in keeping the fire going. If you've ever cleared land for pasture, you know there are a fair number of tree stumps that need to be burnt up, and it can initially take some serious effort to get those stumps burning. But you know what else is true? Once that stump pile finally gets going, it's nearly impossible to put out. It can rain and rain and those stump coals still keep putting forth heat. The stumps can burn for months afterward. Regardless, you have to keep adding fuel to have a fire, and you will have to keep adding passion, devotion, and love to keep your marriage going. We want you to work at keeping the fire alive in your marriage; if you ignore adding fuel, the fire will indeed go out. Don't stop courting your spouse after you have married. Present yourself as desirable, treat your spouse as special, smile to one another, touch one another, and meet each other's needs.

Say It, Do It, Live It

It's a little harder to beat up people and hold them accountable who profess no moral code, but for those who say they do follow a moral code it's a lot easier. We, like many of you, profess to follow the moral code contained in the Bible. As a result, it is the morals contained in it that we have to measure ourselves against. Thus I have to ask myself, "Am I a poser? Do I pretend to be something I am not? Do I play happily married couple out in public but go home in silence? Do I go to a great church but drive to and from church in a decaying marriage? Do I allege to have many close friends, but fail to nurture the love of my spouse?" We hate being posers, but as we've said before, we've been hot, cold, and lukewarm in following the moral code we say we adhere to.

> *"My wife tells me that if I ever decide to leave, she is coming with me."*   Jon Bon Jovi, when asked for his secret to staying married.

We bet you can think of some poser people. One couple comes to mind that we know. They attend church nearly every weekend. They are generally respectable and nice people, but they have had many years of a decaying marriage. They are M&Ms. We regularly have been the ear for one or the other of them as the drudgery in their marriage frequently boils up. The problem is not that they were once in love and now are not meant to be with each other. No, it's rather simple; they are going through the motions of simulating a marriage, but all the while they are too prideful to admit they need help. They have been shamed into accepting far less than they could have, so they let one miserable week roll into the next without getting help and working thru their stuff. They seem fearful of rebuilding into a loving relationship because they have become accustomed to the misery. It's really sad.

When we espouse a moral code of any type, we have to "do" the code, not just believe it. In the life of a Christian, it is the only really clear message

23 we send out that is heard, we are either doers of our faith or we are hypocrites. If we are not living to our moral code, why would anybody else embrace it? We are all going to stumble, that is a given, but where we as married believers should shine is in picking ourselves back up, confessing our mistake, and seeking forgiveness.

Jesus told us to love our enemies, yet 50% of professing Christian couples can't seem to love their spouses let alone anyone else. Christ told us to serve each other in love, but the word "serve" appears to be a curse word for many of us. Serve is a word that demands action.

Our daughter came home from school one day and she said something that we have never forgotten. She said, *"You guys are different than my friend's parents. The other parents talk like you, but you do it!"* Our daughter wasn't trying to make us feel good: she was making an observation that reflected not only the restraints we put on ourselves, but also on her. A marriage will require a huge amount of self-restraint, much more than when we were single because we now have someone living with us full time. And yet the truth for our household is we will occasionally fail in living up to our convictions. But we don't abandon our convictions—we strive all the harder to keep our faith and to allow God to be Lord and to climb down from the throne whenever we find ourselves sitting in the wrong chair. This striving was part of our marriage union and child rearing too.

Strive—*to devote serious or purposeful energy or effort, to contend, to fight for, to work hard.*

Paige and I consider ourselves frequent failures (a healthy self-appraisal for us) in a variety of areas because we frequently measure ourselves against our moral code and our own standards. No one asks us to be perfect, we were not created to be perfect, we were designed with faults, thus we will experience many failures, but we do not have to let ourselves or our families be destroyed because of them. Remember the first *Rocky* movie? Rocky didn't win the fight, but he picked himself up and came back again and again. We didn't admire Rocky because he won the fight; we admired Rocky because he picked himself up and kept going. We apply this same theme of persistence in our personal life and our marriage; we get back up, dust ourselves off, and rejoin life.

It is not enough to believe, it is not enough to declare, we have to put the pedal to the metal and follow our convictions. We have to fully commit to our marriage, to do or die.

No matter how tough the journey, we pick up and march on.

Remember chapter 11, the top three things discussion? Everything else comes after those three things. Sometimes we've had issues such as health push hard to break thru and dislodge something else, but we usually see what's out of balance and put things back the way they should be. For several years I made a great mistake in putting my work ahead of my child, and I repeatedly put it ahead of my wife. I was wrong! Learn from my mistakes.

We have a saying in our house, "It ain't Bosnia." It's a way to bring our heads back around to the reality that we have it really good, and truly have nothing to complain about.

> *"Then there was the guy who loved his wife so much, he almost told her."*
> Unknown

Every journey starts with a single step. With each additional step comes another and another until a person arrives at their destination. Your desire is to have a great marriage, so in this section we are going to have you take seven steps to practice and apply. Hopefully, you will take away many other points in this book, but we'd like your journey to start with these steps:

1. **No longer two, you are to act as one**. This requires practice, but in all things you two seek unity of heart and mind.
2. **Not the enemy.** From this day forward you'll not think of, nor speak to your spouse as "the enemy."
3. **Proper order of your house.** To put God 1st, your spouse 2nd, your kids 3rd, and to never change that order, and never to allow anything else (work, other family, etc.) to move up above #3. Since God is #1, you can't be.
4. **Never cut each other down.** No verbal abuse, not in public, not in private, or even jokingly. No more "jabs," no more curt jokes at the expense of your spouse.
5. **Have regular SAFE TIMES to talk.** At least every 3–6 months, you and your spouse can bring up whatever you desire with no condemnation or anger. This includes being able to bring up potential threats to your marriage.
6. **Give a smooch kiss every day.** Not a peck, but lips-to-lips kiss. Touch each other affectionately.

7. **<u>Value your spouse.</u>** Honor, cherish, and respect them. Prove your love by actions, hold hands, kiss, cuddle.

Don't be a poser person of faith, don't be a poser spouse, and don't be a poser parent. Live what you believe.

> *"Do not pray to marry the one that you love, but to love the one that you marry."*   Spencer Kimball

I have a friend, Kevin, who along with his wife, Keri, run a very successful business; it is Kevin's second successful business. What I admire most about Kevin is he is always moving forward no matter what obstacles come at him. His sheer desire to keep pressing forward makes his business ventures succeed. It is said that Thomas Edison tested 3,000 filaments for the light bulb before he found the one that worked. Imagine if he had quit at 2,900—we'd still be reading by candlelight.

Rocky, Kevin, and Mr. Edison are good examples for us with regard to persevering. Don't give up, keep pressing on, and make the effort to have a great marriage. If you do not press forward with this marriage, what makes you think the next marriage will be any better?

Reality check—when you say you've fought or would fight for your marriage, what would that long list of self sacrificing actions entail? We do not want you to discuss this between you, we want you to contemplate to yourself. Can you list all of the self-sacrificing, spouse building actions you think make you a champion who fights for your marriage. Hard stuff isn't it?

Did you learn anything? Yes / No
Chapter personal benefit appraisal: **HER 1-2-3-4-5   HIM 1-2-3-4-5**
1=not at all, 2=a little, 3=some good stuff, 4=fairly helpful, 5=very helpful

www.u-build.com

198

CHAPTER 24

Who's in Charge—How to Make
Decisions As a Couple

> *"When you were single all your decisions were entirely your own; however, when you married you made a profound proclamation that you didn't want to be single anymore. So what happens with the decision making; does one spouse lose it and the other becomes the ruler?*
> *This is so fundamental that I'm surprised you've already forgotten the practice drill you did when you made your wedding vows.*
> *You see, the wedding vows require that the two agree, and if they do, they become married. If they don't agree, they'd remain single. So don't be upset when your spouse doesn't agree with you and prevents you from doing this or that. Your very first decision required unity and serves as the model for every decision that comes after your first one."*

Let us consider the possibilities in a disagreement. Let's say that Paige has an issue with my spending. Let's dabble in how we can approach this in a <u>logical</u> manner.

Her "accusation" of me spending too much could be...
- right
- wrong
- partly right
- partly wrong
- exaggerated
- imaginary
- she may not have all the facts

Additionally it could be that I may...
- be unaware of any spending problems
- be unlearned in balancing a budget *(it is not taught in schools)*
- indeed be spending a lot, but on things that we both determined were necessary

24 Let's say she is right—*it's her favorite place to be!* And we agree I am spending too much.

- We have to consider, is she also guilty of spending too much and equally at fault?

Can you see how reasoning removes passion to determine the real issue at hand? One good skill in a great marriage is to practice good communication. Good communication is not about blame, it is a method of problem solving. It's not about loading up all the barrels in the gun to destroy our spouse; it's about identifying the real problem and finding a solution for it. Remember, two brains are better than one. When we bring up an issue it's far less about blame and far more about using two brains to come up with a solution. To put this in perspective, if I ask you to be on my football team and I fumble the ball, are you going to be all about blaming me or helping the team recover from the error?

FACTOID – Couples in healthy marriages make decisions together and never proceed without agreement.

In our early immature marital relationship years, the above issue might crop up like this: me bellowing, *"You're spending too much money on groceries and it has to stop,"* which is the way I tend to gravitate — *assigning the blame to someone else.* However, if I've matured at all, I'd rather decide it's better to repackage my thoughts and say, *"Hey hon, we're negative in the checking account. Can we take some time and see where the money is leaking out and where we can cut back?"* Do you see how we've reduced the confrontation factor significantly? While I may be 100% confident I'm going to show my wife that her spending is out of control, she might just as easily show me that she's spending it on certain foods I've requested that are never on sale and those premium no fat cuts of prime beefsteak I insist on are indeed costly. Do you see how two minds can be better than one? The couple joins their minds together working <u>with</u> each other <u>not against</u> each other.

> *"Only two things are necessary to keep one's wife happy. One is to let her think she is having her own way, the other, to let her have it."*
> Lyndon B. Johnson

The facts are that Paige is a very frugal spender and always has been. In previous years when she would do the shopping she was a coupon queen, sometimes getting our groceries for 30% or more off. I am also frugal in my spending, but not as good as Paige. Men tend to buy fewer items, but they tend to be more costly, while women tend to buy many items but they are less costly. Regardless, finances are one of those areas where men and women have to learn restraint. We help each other to be better disciplined.

Decisions are made jointly and in unity in a good marriage. Neither you nor your spouse should individually attempt to make big decisions on family issues you might otherwise disagree or fight over.

Here is how we work decisions thru. One of us will bring up something that we want, or do not want, or feel is not productive to our family. Let's say I want to buy a used backhoe (true story) and sell my plow truck, trailer, and tractor to pay for the backhoe. If Paige doesn't agree with me or otherwise expresses reservations that she's not sure it's a good idea, or a good time, then I do not do it. If we are in agreement then we proceed. If only one of us is on board with some major decision, it doesn't occur because we ALWAYS require both of us agreeing. Couples tend to gravitate to who is in charge and who is to blame; we like to turn that around and say decisions require agreement and let's not bother with blame, let's work on unity. No unity, no movement.

Here is a bonus in using this decision process. When we both agree and the decision turns out to be a bad one, another argument is avoided because no one gets to blame the other. We had agreed together, so we must also share the blame together. The only action we have at our disposal is to discuss how we might improve the situation and what other factors to include in the decision process the next time.

> *"Women get the last word in every argument. Anything a man says after that is the beginning of a new argument."*   Anonymous

Let's try a tougher topic. Let's say one of my sisters is having a tough time and she has asked if she can move in with us. Well if we hold to our unity theme, this decision requires a "joint" yes, not just one yes. We would also make it clear that we will be able to accommodate this arrangement as long as it doesn't threaten the stability and harmony of our marriage and home. We'd outline the rules and conditions beforehand. Truly we both believe that family should be there for family, and while sometimes it can be a drain, it is also a very natural aspect of families to help one another, and it can also be a very satisfying experience. BUT we preserve our marital unit above all others.

Thus we'd never allow an external issue or relationship to threaten our marriage harmony. Blood does not trump our marriage.

Families should be united in a similar way to marriages, but family relationships are subject to and subordinate to the couple's marriage health. Again, all things in balance. Many couples are forced to care for an injured or sick parent who is in their last years of life. This can be quite taxing emotionally and physically. Yet it must not continuously surpass the vitality of your marriage. If it does, finding some other solution is necessary. We discuss this kind of burden in chapter 28.

Let's say you both have something that you disagree about and neither side is willing to negotiate a joint solution. What are you to do? Well, we'd say you have to agree to disagree, and not be bitter about the disagreement even though one of you may be clearly wrong. Perhaps time will bring the other spouse around to your way of thinking somewhere down the road. Obviously, seeking the counsel of others or a marriage counselor may provide some settlement on an issue as well.

FACTOID – When you get married, you do not get rid of your problems, in fact you sleep next to another whole set of them.

Couple's project—Discuss how you can better make decisions as a couple. If you like, take one topic that you feel you could reach an agreement on and tackle it now. Then continue to practice unity on other topics as they come up.

Did you learn anything? Yes / No
Chapter personal benefit appraisal: **HER 1-2-3-4-5   HIM 1-2-3-4-5**
1=not at all, 2=a little, 3=some good stuff, 4=fairly helpful, 5=very helpful

www.u-build.com

CHAPTER 25

Grow Each Other, Teach Each Other

In chapter 24 we determined two minds were better than one. Our spouse's input should be viewed as beneficial. There are very likely many things that you can change and improve and we should view our spouse's input as helping us to be better. This is where you work with each other, talk things out, and get rid of things that weaken your relationship. You add or grow things that improve your relationship, thus always making the marriage better, stronger, and greater. Pick issues that are perhaps easier to find agreement on and work your way up to the tougher issues.

> *"I have no way of knowing whether or not you married the wrong person, but I do know that many people have a lot of wrong ideas about marriage and what it takes to make that marriage happy and successful. I'll be the first to admit that it's possible that you did marry the wrong person.*
>
> *"However, if you treat the wrong person like the right person, you could well end up having married the right person after all. On the other hand, if you marry the right person, and treat that person wrong, you certainly will have ended up marrying the wrong person. I also know that it is far more important to be the right kind of person than it is to marry the right person. In short, whether you married the right or wrong person is primarily up to you."*
>
> Zig Ziglar

Do you disagree on how to discipline your children? If so, that is an area you can begin to work out and if necessary seek help to get both of you working in unity. I rarely write an important document that I do not have Paige review for me; her input is invaluable.

Do you regularly help each other mature in your marriage? Do you really understand your spouse? Read the following two statements then discuss your feelings with your spouse.

For the man, how well does this statement apply to how you feel?
> *"I feel the most complete and strong when my wife is supporting me, and showing me admiration. I feel respected among my friends and family when you reach for my hand and lean on me in front of them. Show me by showing others that you are 'my girl.'*

Your affection makes me stronger."

For the woman, how well does this statement apply to how you feel?
"I never feel more complete than when my man cherishes me above all others and all things. I am special and he shows it. I love it when you look at me with adoration, affection, and desire. Choose me, pursue me, I need the security that you will always be there with me, show your love for me, call me a hot babe, help me at home, love me tenderly, ignore those "vamps" who flirt with you, hold me close, and touch me."

Did you learn anything new in just sharing with each other in the above exercise?

"I really want married people to understand this—if you do nothing to improve your marriage, nothing will come of it."

When Our Wives Speak, Play or Record?

Communication is a very important aspect of human interaction and it is essential in a great marriage; however, a certain kind of communication in marriage can be confusing to men. As men, we are never sure when we are supposed to fix it or just listen. Our women don't convey which action they are looking for from us.

This next help tool dates us, but in the "old days" we had various types of magnetic tape devices that played and recorded music or conversations. These were known as reel-to-reel, 8-tracks, and cassettes. The devices that used magnetic tape mediums came with buttons that a user pushed for actions such as "play," "record," and "fast forward."

Using this idea, one way women can communicate to men that they only want someone to listen, is to use the "play" button just prior to starting a conversation. When a woman just wants her man to listen, she can begin the conversation by saying, *"I'm pushing the play button,"* which means she doesn't want her man to try to fix it, she is not asking him to record what is being said, she only wants her man to listen. However, if she wants her husband to be involved in working out some issue, she can begin the conversation by saying, *"I'm pushing the record button,"* which means she is asking her man to not only listen, but remember what she is saying.

"I've noticed that happily married couples share their happiness, foremost with each other and if there's anything left over with people around them."

By seeking your spouse's input you grow and learn as a person. As you learn, you both see ways to improve and also see the error in some of your old ways. When you make corrections, you naturally grow closer and are no longer threatened when your spouse suggests a change. But some things will be beyond our ability to change.

Grant, a previous pastor of ours says there are some things that are *"God things."* These are events that are beyond our ability to handle, fix, change, or escape. We can do what we can do, but there are many things that we have to trust God to take care of. Did a child or very close relative just die? That's hard on a family, the grief can press in all around, and words do not seem to minister much relief. Only God knows the why. We are not capable of doing anything other than being there to support the one who is grieving.

Did you lose your job and are about to lose your home? You may not be able to fix those issues. Your marriage needs to be stronger now, more than ever, when going thru some of these tough trials. For a person of faith, the things you have no control over, you just have to trust God that everything will work out wherever that journey leads. While our spouses can help us in many areas, neither we nor they can be expected to solve every issue that crops up. Remember this: certain events will come at us in which the only thing we can offer is to go thru them with each other.

Perhaps one of you is saying, *"What do I get out of this, what if my spouse isn't responding or doing their part?"* Maybe you are willing but your spouse doesn't wanna go along? Well, we'd say you've missed the point; we've apparently not made it clear enough for you. Let us try another way to make it clearer.

Recall the farmer who took care of the peach tree? When the farmer took the time to till the ground (work), to water (more work), to fertilize (more work), to protect the tree from birds and insects (even more work), that was all BEFORE the tree gave him back any fruit.

So do not worry about what the other spouse is willing to do at this point, just do what you can to bless, encourage, serve, and love your spouse to bring out the best in them. Then after a little time, you're very likely going to be rewarded with some very good fruit that will bless the socks off you. When both spouses have this attitude toward each other, the very best lies ahead for them. Tend to the garden, and it will produce fruit.

> *"I've had far too many loves in my life and thinking about it I'm going to make a conscious effort to love less and I recommend that everyone join me in loving less. I must confess that I've loved things like money, cars, property, my job, my toys, and other "stuff," yet none of these things deserved my love nor did they love me back. What a foolish man I am."*

Couple's project—Communication exercise. We'd like each of you to write down at least one thing that irritates or aggravates you about your spouse and one thing that you really like about your spouse. Then discuss the results with each other.

Remember, this is a **SAFE TIME**, it's a time to share. Also remember that just talking about something does not resolve it. To resolve an issue you have to agree how it will be handled in the future or what changes will be made. It's only resolved when both spouses can express they have closure on the topic. We are not asking you to solve an aggravation issue now. In this exercise we are just asking you to talk about it. You're not mad (hopefully) at each other now, so you get to bring up an issue and just talk about it.

What I like about her most: _____

What aggravates me most about her: _____

What I like most about him: _____

What aggravates me most about him: _____

Resolve—*To reach consensus, to change by resolution, to find an answer to an issue, to work out the details.*

Did you learn anything? Yes / No
Chapter personal benefit appraisal: **HER 1-2-3-4-5   HIM 1-2-3-4-5**
1=not at all, 2=a little, 3=some good stuff, 4=fairly helpful, 5=very helpful

CHAPTER 26

Always Coming Closer

When Paige and I became engaged her pastor, Rob, would only conduct the marriage ceremony if we agreed to pre-marriage counseling. I do not remember the exact number of times we met, but it was several times for 1–2 hours discussing the various aspects of marriage and our obligations to work at having a Godly marriage. Truly Rob wanted to start us off on the right foot and wanted to give us some tools to make sure our marriage succeeded.

One of the tools he used to show us how our marriage should progress was using a triangle of sorts. Rob showed us how we were more distant from each other at that moment than we would be at any time in our marriage, but that if we worked at drawing closer to each other and to God, we would meet together and achieve oneness. Two variations below.

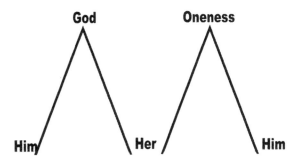

Rob also told us how two or three strands of rope are weaker apart than when woven together. He said that the woven strands can help share the load between each other. He suggested that we meld each other with God to form a 3-fold cord. Using an example like the following, he described how to braid ourselves into one common and stronger cord. He explained how three cords of rope woven together are stronger than three separate cords.

These very simple illustrations stuck with us and have provided good direction for us throughout our marriage.

FACTOID – If you're drawing closer together, you can't be drifting apart!

To help you in your quest at drawing closer together we have a few practices and activities that you can begin immediately. Areas we can all improve on are those periods of tension, disagreement, and fighting. We've already covered the need to fight fair, not to use condemnation, and no physical or belittling abuse. But there are a few other aspects that can make a home more peaceful.

A statistically inclined counselor would help solve a feuding couple's trouble by asking them the following: "What is the frequency, the duration, and the intensity of your disagreements and how quickly do you make up afterward?" It may sound a bit simplistic, but he would likely come back with statistical data to support ideas like the following.

> *"OK ladies, let me explain this: 'Lust' and 'Love' both start with 'L,' and they both have four letters. See why we men get them mixed up?"*

Argue Less

Bringing yourselves closer together includes minimizing the times you're further apart. If you previously fought five times a week, agree to only argue two times a week for the next three months. If you usually fight so passionately that you are yelling or getting angry, agree to turn it down more and more over time. After a few months of practicing this, you'll argue less and love more and be on your way to a much better marriage. Do not fail to reach resolution; just reach resolution in a manner that contains less confrontation.

Make Up Sooner

If your fights usually last overnight, agree to resolve them before you go to bed. Worse, some couples do not practice making up after a disagreement, rather hoping time will erase the unpleasant memory if they pretend it didn't happen. Thus the event remains unresolved, and doubtfully forgotten. This is not a good practice especially when emotions ran deep in the disagreement.

After we disciplined our child for a rebellious action, she'd receive a few swats on her bottom and a few minutes to think about it, then we'd come back to her and give her a hug, and tell her we still loved her. We'd let her know she's still valued, and that it was the act of disobedience that had to be dealt with. Sometimes the emotions run deep when a couple has a disagreement. We may not be able to manage much of a hug with our spouse, but giving a hug, saying to each other you love each other, and that you'll get thru it, is highly comforting. It confirms to each spouse, this is not a "deal" breaker, just a disagreement; the marriage is far stronger than any disagreement. It's an important key to end disagreement with affirmation, no matter the outcome. Make up even when it feels awkward to make up. Sure it was a serious fight, but are you going to let that be the fight that begins to build a wall between you?

"You have three choices after you're married:
(1) Spend a lot of time getting to know each other free of charge, at your own convenience, OR...
(2) Hire a marriage counselor and pay him/her a reasonable fee to get to know you, when you all can find the time to get together, OR...
(3) Don't get to know each other, then hire a divorce lawyer who will spend no time getting to know either of you, at an exorbitant cost and at the lawyer's convenience.
Am I missing something?"

Venting

It should be a given that spouses need to indicate when there is a real problem that needs to be dealt with or when they are just venting. We believe venting is something that we all need to do with some frequency. Bottling up our fears, concerns, and worries is never healthy. Venting lets us get it out, and is actually very therapeutic. Some spouses vent with each other, some vent with other people. Women tend to vent with other women. A close group of friends or a very close friend whom you trust and who will listen to you without transmitting your vent to others is a great way to get it out and feel better.

Here is an example of a vent: *"With my husband losing his job, I'm worried that we will lose all of our savings soon, and who knows what after that. I'm scared; I don't want to express my fears to him because he already feels bad about not providing an income. Everything is so uncertain these days. I don't know what we're gonna do."*

A hug, a cup of coffee, saying it will be all right, comforting touches, praying over it, all are responses a spouse or friend might do to let the vent go in and out and help bring some peace. Venting occurs with guys too. It might be coarser or shallower depending on the man. Both men and women can bottle it up, but again, that's not recommended. Venting is a great stress reliever. When you do vent, be it with your spouse or a friend, make sure that you convey to the listener that you are just venting. Use the "play" button you learned about earlier.

Venting is not condemnation and it is not complaining, it's just voicing a worry or concern, letting some feelings out, and afterward feeling somewhat better. It is a listening ear, it's therapy, and spouses should understand the difference. Venting does not fix a problem; it's not about solutions though a solution might be warranted. Sometimes it just helps us to feel better to say it out loud.

Practical Steps to Getting Closer to Each Other

Good marriage practices (nearly all should sound familiar) that bring you closer together:

- Same checking account
- Honesty, no secrets
- Knowing each other's passwords for computers/email accounts
- No concern for your spouse looking over your cell phone messages, phone number lists, etc.
- Confessing failures to each other
- Agreeing ahead of time to discuss (make it known) when you are tempted or afraid of being tempted by someone of the opposite sex
- Regularly getting marriage tune-ups: retreats, conferences, marriage improvement books, tapes, etc.
- Saying "I love you" to each other and meaning it
- Attending church + praying together daily + reading the Bible daily + being a sincere doer of the teachings of Christ
- Avoiding places, people, gatherings that can entice reckless behavior
- NEVER getting drunk or high, as these greatly reduce our inhibitions and invite trouble
- NEVER cutting one or the other down, not in public, not in private, not jokingly
- Encouraging one another, complimenting one another

- Touching each other while in bed, walking, sitting, driving, in public, etc.
- Kissing tenderly on the lips each day
- Holding each other, cuddling
- Regular sexual intimacy
- Discussing with each other how to make sex more enjoyable
- Listening to music together
- Dancing even if just in your living room
- Leaving little notes, Post-its such as "I love you." "Are you horny?" "You're hot!" "You're my one and only!" etc.
- Respecting each other's space, when needed
- Guys: Wooing her, seeking her out, pursuing her, choosing her, cherishing her
- Gals: Admiring him, honoring him, respecting him, and supporting him
- Regularly communicating needs, wants, and discussing problems
- Forgiving and forgetting wrongs, true "forgiveness"
- Doing things together, travel, eating out, picnics, movies, hikes, seeing a show, etc.
- Unity—an understanding that if you are not in complete agreement on a matter, then it's dead
- Ability to disagree, not take it personal, and to get over it
- Each day is a new day, no hold over grudges
- Truly believing that the marriage union is above personal wants, desires
- Not putting yourself into situations where interacting with the opposite sex could lead to emotional desires outside of the marriage. Guarding yourself against situations where adultery could be fostered
- No flirting with the opposite sex
- Living within your means, not spending more than you make
- Whatever "struggle" is facing you, you are fighting "**it**" not each other

The obvious repetition of points we've already covered is purposeful as we work thru the last few chapters. Perhaps you're starting to realize we are going to beat this into your head, over and over and over again, until you walk away remembering it. And even then, you are going to have to get refreshers every few months to keep yourselves on the right course. We call this a handbook because we expect you to pick it up again and again.

> *"I believe in Christianity as I believe that the sun has risen: not only because I see it, but because by it I see everything else."*
>
> C. S. Lewis

The captain of a ship doesn't look at the map once, he looks at it frequently during a voyage to make sure he is still on course. Married people need to follow the example of the ship's captain and frequently check to make sure they are headed in the right direction.

There is nothing as incredible as a couple that completely loves each other, and it is possible for every couple to enjoy this. Your marriage is what you make it, and what you make it begins with "today." What an example for your kids, what a testimony to others, what happiness you can have! What you seek <u>is</u> within your grasp, it is possible for <u>you</u>. One day you'll look back and understand that <u>only by caring for the marriage</u> will it produce the joy and happiness you both desire. This is a road we and others have traveled; we are sharing with you how to get where you want to go. The pages within this handbook are a map to lead you to your destination.

Couple's project—Take a moment and give each other a long, deep, sincere hug. Then decide what things you can do to draw closer to each other.

Did you learn anything? Yes / No
Chapter personal benefit appraisal: **HER 1-2-3-4-5   HIM 1-2-3-4-5**
1=not at all, 2=a little, 3=some good stuff, 4=fairly helpful, 5=very helpful

www.u-build.com

Sex and Love

CHAPTER 27

Sexual Intimacy

NOTE: Our publisher just patented a special reactive ink and offered to unveil it in our handbook for any one chapter we desired. This is very cool! On the following pages the otherwise invisible ink in this chapter will react with the phenol hormones our bodies secrete; these phenols are like a very subtle scent. By tweaking the ink compound they were able to get the ink to react only in the presence of our intimacy-based hormones. The text on the following pages will only be visible to those individuals who are secreting these intimacy-based phenols, which is an indication you're currently preprogrammed for sexual intimacy. Your hormones (if present) will react with the ink to reveal the text. Make sure you are close enough to the pages. If you can see anything below this line you've got what it takes to be intimate with your spouse.

Part 1 Basics

In dedicating one chapter on the subject of sex the way we have, we are likely going to upset just about every person who reads it. Why? Well, we are only going to

but accurate overview for couples so they do not have to go seeking information from distorted sources. Although this is a no win situation for

Be Open with Each Other

Between ourselves, we feel fully licensed to discuss all the aspects of our sexual experience. Our intimacy
some boundaries or inhibitions. We enjoy a very satisfying intimate

not sexually attractive, somehow

27 | **PART 1 Basics**

Oops! We had a printing glitch, it should be good now.
(That was close wasn't it?) ☺

Just to give you another laugh, Bob gave me this chapter and that previous page as part our back and forth editing and just like you I was rubbing the page trying to make the text appear! He can be such a shit sometimes!

In dedicating one chapter on the subject of sex we are likely going to upset just about every person who reads it. Why? Well, we are only going to discuss sex as it applies to marital intimacy. At the same time we are going to significantly explore the sexual intimacy side of marriage, challenging some couples to more deeply explore the sexual side of their union. We will venture well beyond the "lights out, missionary position" of cloistered marital intimacy and compel spouses to explore each other. We will try to offer a safe but accurate overview for couples so they do not have to go seeking information from distorted sources. Although this is a no-win situation for us as authors, we believe it is a topic that causes enough marital tension that we have to discuss it. We want to get those who are not moving into motion, and for those who are pushing away limits to perhaps consider reestablishing some limits.

Be Open with Each Other

Between ourselves, Paige and I feel fully licensed to discuss all the aspects of our sexual experience. Our intimacy is not perverted and it's not without some boundaries or inhibitions. We enjoy a very satisfying intimate union, we'd classify ourselves as "normal". Frankly, we believe we have a pretty good balance in this area and feel that we are also fairly well lined up with our moral compass. One only has to read the Song of Solomon and a few other biblical texts to see that God is not only the creator of our sexual being, He also set it up so we would enjoy sex. Again, everything including sexual intimacy should be in balance. However, we live in a culture where sex is not in balance and we will thus have to condition ourselves to stay within the boundaries of our moral compass.

Just so you know, we feel we are misfits when it comes to our marriage relationship, but the insanity we live seems to work for us. In a nutshell, we're sharing our insanity with you all, in the hopes you can be just as messed up as we are. Hopefully you'll have as much fun as we do, being misfits.

Unrestrained Sexual Freedom?

There is a simple law in politics; whoever has the most publicity ads wins. It's a pretty simple concept; bathe the citizens with your name and your cause more than the opponent and you will win. In our opinion this same principle is predominate in our society with regard to sexual liberty versus sexual restraint. The message (if any) of self-control and sexual maturity is drowned out by the super selling of sexual promiscuity. The pressures to remain faithful (and thus restrained) are overwhelmed when compared to all the TV programs, movies, and advertising promoting sexual expression with whomever and whenever you want.

By watching American television, an un-indoctrinated foreigner might think all Americans do is engage in promiscuous sexual adventures. This continuous bombardment of no rules, anything-goes sexual expression can threaten even the most determined of monogamous couples. At the very least it negatively impacts marriages by bringing too much focus on sex, and at worst by licensing promiscuity and infidelity, and creating a sex slave trade for the now hyped-up compulsive desires of men. This topic is important because husbands and wives need to be keenly aware of the not so subtle attack on your desire to remain faithful to each other. It's a flat-out war that will require diligence in honoring your marriage vows.

Sexual intimacy is an area of marriage that can induce the most uncomfortable feelings in one or the other spouse. We've seen people dodge the sexual intimacy sessions at marriage conferences. For some couples just talking about sex makes them feel like they are marching naked thru town with a hat on that says *"We are a joke, and everyone is laughing at us."* For others, the whole area of sex seems confusing, with medical terms that are hard to pronounce, fears that our penis or breasts are inadequate, our body is repulsive, we are not sexually attractive, somehow sexually inferior, or that our performance sucks and a feeling there's nothing that can be done about it. Others have wrongly been taught that sex is bad and all sexual expression should be rejected. For these and other reasons, it can be a scary topic.

You're not alone in this feeling and yet talking about sexual intimacy with your spouse is a really great idea. It should be a private time when no one is around so you can be real with your spouse. It should be one of those **SAFE TIME** talk periods, no condemnation, only supportive feedback where each spouse is sharing some of their inner thoughts, being vulnerable, but also drawing ever closer as a result. Getting to know each other in the context of marriage is like a giant exploration that lasts many years. We set out to learn, discover, and get to know each other. Sexual intimacy is just one of those aspects we need to explore.

This isn't a book about sex, but because sex is a very important aspect of a marriage, we want to devote a chapter to it. There are several fine books on sexual intimacy in marriage, and we'd highly recommend you pick up one or two, even if you're not having trouble in that area. I like to go up to the counter at our local book store and shout, *"Ya got any new books on sex?" (OK, I've never really done that, and wouldn't!)* Hey, God created it, and He made it to be pleasurable, and we are married, is there some problem?

We advise couples to stay away from pornographic type materials; you don't need to create new problems while trying to solve an existing one. We have the same view about bowel movements, i.e., it's not meant to be a public event. Keep the special in sex by keeping it personal; you don't need to have people watch you, nor should you watch others.

In covering this topic, we can only briefly hit on a few hot button subjects. We are not sex experts, and as we said we are not trying to write a book about sex. Thus much of it is going to be short and sweet and somewhat short on details allowing you to figure things out on your own. So let's have fun with this, embrace it, and don't run from it. In a nutshell, men and women are different. We are meant to be together, but we are different and in the following pages we will explore some of those differences.

> "Underline it, highlight it, or put big stars by it, but get it down: *Whenever we make orgasm the goal of sex, we will fail to experience godly sex.* In other words, the "Big O" of sex is not orgasm, it's oneness." Tim Gardner, *Sacred Sex*

Couple's project—Turn to each other and say: *"Let's talk about sex, and let's make it fun."*

Libido—*the desire for sexual intimacy, the urge for sex.*

Off to the Races! Men and Women Do Not Generally Operate on the Same Libido Frequency

I like to take difficult topics and find a way to break them down into a parable that is easier for everyone to understand. When it comes to sexual intimacy, men and women are usually not running at the same speed. Men have more testosterone than women and testosterone is an important hormone in the human sex drive. The fact that women have less and men have more testosterone seems to me to be a great design rather than a flaw. If men had the same amount as a woman does, the world's population might have disappeared a few thousand years ago. The fact that women do not have as much as men is good because we would have overrun the planet with children centuries ago. Thus with more libido, men are seemingly always *"willing if not ready"* whenever the woman is, and with her blessing a few more times to boot! It seems to be a nice balance even though it can be frustrating for the average male with regard to frequency. For obvious reasons we will be using generalizations. I'm sure you all know that everyone is not the same; some of you will not fit into a generalized group, and that's OK.

Here is how we'd explain the differences in libido: It is like being at a racetrack, the wife is in one car, the husband in the other. In keeping with the "oneness" theme, it's just you two and you're both on the same track and driving in the same direction. However, you are not driving at the same speed. The hubby is driving around the track at 100 mph while the wife might be going around at 50 miles mph. So while you are "one" with respect to both being on the same track, the frequency at which your sexual desires line up means you are not always driving next to each other. In this over simplified example, the male will desire sex two times more often than the female, and he will be coming up to the wife's car twice for each one of her laps.

It should be apparent that we are all different in this regard and in a relationship the referenced speed of either spouse may be different than the ratio we used above. But this is the point: the frequency at which a husband and wife will be together on the libido track can be vastly different. Normally that will mean the husband has to more frequently wrestle with his desire when his wife is not at the same place on the track as he is. And quite naturally husbands married their wives because they are indeed attractive, thus husbands are visually stimulated by their wives on a daily basis. There will be many times that the hubby's car comes up beside the wife's car and paces her, and at these times they are in sync, or both are in the mood. But the higher male testosterone levels will have the male libido racing harder; he will be wondering why his wife is driving so slow on the intimacy racetrack.

This parable is just an example to show that many males are often in the mood, but our spouses may not be, and we have to work this discrepancy out as a couple. In this example we are talking not only about the act of sex but also the desire for sexual intimacy. This topic is important to help men and women understand the apparent disconnect in the timing or desire for sexual intimacy. It may not be that there is any real intimacy trouble just the normal difference in libido between the sexes. This difference once understood can help both spouses to either accommodate the other's needs or not misinterpret the lack of desire as rejection.

Using the racetrack example, we'd like you both as spouses to take a few minutes here to discuss what your libido speed might be compared to your spouse's. This discussion will give you both an idea of your differences, if any, with regard to libido.

FACTOID – Sex is a very healthy function in every marriage.

> *"I've found when I want to get my woman interested in sex, all I have to do is stick a $25 prepaid factory outlet card in my waistband. It's not long before she's groping at me with both hands!*
> *Hey, whatever works!"*

Anatomy Basics

OK, in the previous paragraphs you learned your libido can be in sync but more often than not, the male usually has a stronger libido. Now we deal with another difference, that being your physical differences.

We don't care if you've been married thirty years or more, this lesson is worth running through if for no other reason than the fun of it. We are not going to insert diagrams or pictures here, although we admit that might be helpful. If you need more detail, check out various medically based texts. You do not need to have a medical understanding of sexual organs to have sex any more than you need a medical understanding of your teeth to eat. However, we do not share each other's teeth, but we do indeed share and enjoy each other's bodies in a healthy marital relationship.

We are going to provide a short anatomy lesson with each spouse repeating to each other a few body part terms to get more comfortable talking about sex. We will use medical terms. For the female terms, the wife should speak the term first and then the husband should repeat it back. Then go on to the next term. For the male body parts, the husband should first speak the term and have the wife repeat it. When you get into the bedroom, each spouse can take some time to show each other these body parts, explaining them in your own words. Each spouse should ask questions and touch each other's body parts, letting your curiosity roam. Depending on your degree of shyness, you may have to get to a point where you are even willing to be seen by your spouse with the lights on.

FACTOID – Sex should be enjoyable for both spouses.

Male

The male penis is the part that becomes erect when stimulated. Below the penis is a sack (scrotum) containing the testicles (or testes), which produce the sperm and testosterone. The penis may have been circumcised or not. Circumcision is frequently done on male babies. Circumcision removes a layer of skin (called the foreskin) that otherwise folds over and covers the forward portion of the penis. The scrotum will respond to temperature variations in the body, hanging low for cooling or pulling up tight against the body when needing to stay warm in an effort to keep the sperm within the testicles at an ideal temperature. The penis shaft is soft and bendable when placid; it thickens and becomes hard and significantly rigid when erect. As men age, their erections will not be as firm as they were in their youth. Bending the erect shaft of the penis can damage it and can be very painful, for this reason a couple shouldn't get into risky acrobatics where bending the penis could occur. The penis becomes hard by the dilation or relaxing of blood arteries *(normally constricted)* which allows blood flow into the penis at a rate significantly above the rate blood is returning to the heart via the veins. The resulting pressure buildup causes the penis to fill and become erect.

Husbands are deeper relationship thinkers….Therapist asks wife, "Name three great things about your husband." After thinking for a few minutes, wife responds, "Do you have anything in multiple choice or true/false?"
Therapist poses the same question to the husband. Smiling, he quickly responds, "Her breasts, and er, ah…her love cave, and er, ah…her booty!"

The triggering of the dilation occurs subconsciously in the male; it's not an on/off switch and sometimes acts as if it has a mind of its own, hence the huge market for erectile dysfunction pills. Yet it is very common for men to get erections during sleep and upon waking as this is a relaxed state. Sometimes a male may experience what is commonly called a wet dream where an orgasm occurs during his sleep. Generally erections will occur easily from either physical stimulation or by thoughts or by sight. The erection usually remains rigid through the time of stimulation and will go back to a placid condition some period of time after orgasm or sometime after stimulation (visual or physical) is stopped. A man urinates thru the same tube (urethra) that semen ejaculation occurs, which travels up to the tip from the base of the penis. The penis contains many nerve endings that convey the stimulation feelings to the man's pleasure center in his brain. The penis is typically fully developed by age 17. The testicles are tender and as everyone knows, can be easily bruised when hit, pinched, or handled too roughly.

Couple's project—OK guys, speak the following terms one at a time and have the wife repeat them back to you. This exercise helps you both get comfortable saying and talking about your anatomy.

<u>Male Parts Speaking Exercise</u>
Penis – "pee-nus"
Scrotum – "scro-tum"
Testicles – "test-i-culs" (slang: "balls")
Urethra – "U-reath –ra"
The area as a whole (in slang) can be called "the family jewels." ☺

A male form of birth control is getting "cut," medically referred to as a vasectomy. It is very effective when completed properly and the "in office" painless procedure does not affect any part of the arousal or stimulation activity. The doctor makes a small cut in the scrotum, and isolates each tube that carries sperm from each testicle to the tube leading to the urethra. The doctor is not cutting anywhere in the vicinity where a "mistake" could cause a man to have trouble with arousal. I highly recommend it and believe it's a far less invasive procedure than the choices women have. It's also a relatively low-cost procedure; mine cost about $250 in 1996. Some men report being slightly sore for a day afterward. Doctors will usually give the patient a mild tranquilizer a few hours before the procedure; however, I took no pain meds or tranquilizers and experienced nothing more than a little discomfort. (*Real men bite on a chunk of leather!*)

Female

Female vaginal area *(called the vulva)* can be a bit of a mystery to women as well as men, there's simply more going on in that area. The vulva contains a specific organ called the clitoris, which appears to have no other purpose than transmitting pleasure. *(Also known as the "clit" or "love button.")* The vaginal opening is not all that far away from the anus. Moving down from the belly button to the top of the mons, or pubic mound, which generally has pubic hair on it, the first thing you will encounter is the clitoris which may be slightly hidden under an upside down "V" shaped hood. Moving vertically downward, the next thing we will come to is the urethra where a woman urinates. As we move to either side of the vulva *(collectively the exterior vaginal area)* we find the labia major, which forms the outer sides of the vulva. They will appear as folds but not really distinct, and will typically be darker in color than the much smaller but brighter pink colored labia minor skin folds that may appear to be folding doors to the vulva area or vaginal canal. The labia minor will have no pubic hair on them but contain many nerve endings. The hymen is a fold of mucous membrane that crosses or partially covers the entrance to the vaginal opening. Tradition considers an intact hymen a sign that a woman has not had intercourse but in this modern age of tampons, the absence of an intact hymen or blood from initial intercourse is not a reliable indicator of virginity.

While the male penis is external, the female vaginal canal is internal. The vagina is a multipurpose channel serving as the birth canal, the passageway for blood during monthly menstrual periods, and the location the spouse's penis is inserted. Its interior surface contains nerve endings and slight folds or ridges. Generally, women can experience two types of orgasms (some say there are more)—one is via direct stimulation on the clitoris, the other is by internal vaginal stimulation.

While certainly separate from the vulva area, the breasts and or nipples serve to provide sexual stimulation for many women.

Couple's project—Gals, it's our turn to speak the following terms one at a time and have your husband repeat them back to you.

Female parts speaking exercise
Vagina – "veg-eye-nah"
Vulva – "vuhl-vah"
Mons – "mahns"
Clitoris – "clit-or-is" (slang –"love button")
Labia – "lay-bee-ah"
Hymen – "high-mun"
The area as a whole (in slang) can be called "the love cave." ☺

What is "Normal" Sexual Intimacy?

What we are describing here as "normal" should be discussed with your spouse so you can agree or disagree or share other concerns or desires. Obviously not everything applies to everyone and you should not engage in any activity you do not feel right about.

Man—visual and/or physical stimulation, arousal, orgasm—a three-step process.

A typical man (may vary) achieves an orgasm by stimulation that leads to arousal. A stimulation/arousal plateau is maintained while stimulation continues. However, at some point the stimulation crosses a line of heightened and increasing arousal intensity, where the intensity builds rapidly until the orgasm occurs, resulting in the ejaculation of semen that occurs with a series of spasm type muscle contractions resembling what feels like explosions inside of the male. An intense feeling of euphoria follows.

There is very little mystery in getting a typical male to orgasm, but that's not true for most females. One female gynecologist stated on a recent television program that many women do not even know what their own body requires to reach orgasm and they have to learn how to achieve an orgasm.

Woman—desire, stimulation, arousal, orgasm—a four-step process, and the first step is very important. Husbands have to help their woman get her head into sex before her body can follow.

A typical woman (may vary) achieves an orgasm by beginning with the initial and additional preparation step called "desire." The desire phase typically begins well before any clothing is shed, sometimes many hours before. Desire is fostered in a variety of ways, some of which may not be anything hubby can relate to, but he is indeed partly responsible in helping to get her frame of mind to the desire phase.

Where men easily transition from one compartment, figuratively speaking, to another *(fly fishing to sex is an easy jump)* a woman needs to have her spouse help her redecorate the room her thoughts are in.

Once she has that room *(a mental-emotional place)* cleared out of what was in there and looking more romantic like she wants it, she can move on to the stimulation phase and be reasonably expected to achieve arousal with sufficient stimulation.

Because women are not compartmentalized it can take some effort for a woman to switch gears, clear her mind of the day's distractions and bring desire to the forefront. Hubbies, this is when you can really help set the stage for your wife to get there. If you have been yelling, cutting your wife down, acting goofy, belching, farting, etc., and then turn to your wife and say, *"Let's get it on baby,"* do not be surprised when your wife says, *"I'm not in the mood."* That means the decorating you have been doing in her mental desire room is a turn-off. On the other hand, helping her get the distractions around the house off her plate, not having kid distractions, telling her she looks sexy, giving her some romantic kisses, etc., can help get her into the desire phase.

As your wife enters the stimulation phase she will have certain areas that will be unique to her, that lead to the arousal phase. It is very important that you stimulate the areas that cause arousal if she is to progress to orgasm. If not, she may enjoy the intimacy, but not get aroused, or get aroused but not reach orgasm. Information from medical experts indicates it is not uncommon that a woman has to be encouraged to explore just what and how these areas are aroused within her by experimenting.

When your wife proceeds into the arousal phase, she may be found concentrating solely on the stimulation action to help intensify her feelings, which helps her build to orgasm. She will build and build on these, usually stair stepping to a greater state of arousal until she reaches orgasm culminating in waves of euphoria. Orgasm will cause increased vaginal secretions, vaginal swelling, and increased vaginal sensitivity. Your wife may have difficulty in achieving her very first orgasm, but after the two of you learn each other's needs and improve your techniques, orgasms begin occurring more regularly to the point of being a regular and expected outcome.

> *"It's wrong that women accuse men of thinking about only one thing, afterward we think about beer too!"*

Some couples will perfect their technique [it is a team effort] enough to experience multiple orgasms. For most men, the initial orgasm will be better than any one that comes after and there may be a longer period of

225

recovery in between successive orgasms. For women, subsequent orgasms may be more intense than the first with successive orgasms coming much quicker than the first. Younger men are much more likely to go again soon after the initial orgasm. For older men multiple erections may occur less frequently or require a longer intermission between attempts if they occur at all. A woman may or may not desire more than one orgasm as they may be too sensitive and/or swollen to move on to another.

Some statistics relate that it takes on average about 13 minutes of stimulation and arousal for a woman to achieve an orgasm, but only about three minutes for the average man. It is interesting that during WWII, the prostitution houses set up in Hawaii charged $3 for three minutes and there were often long lines of men waiting for their turn. While men and women can climax simultaneously together, some surveys report that it is a rare event. Obviously every couple will be a variant of what average is espoused to be.

It is not uncommon for a spouse to accommodate the other spouse even though one or the other is not necessarily in the mood. Your wife may feel she just doesn't have the desire but replies with something like "It's just for you."

FACTOID – Sexual intimacy in a marriage union begins when both spouses are comfortable with their own bodies.

Frequency of Sexual Intimacy

There is a wide range of what might be defined as "normal" in a healthy marriage. There are also periods where sexual intimacy is temporarily set aside, typically during periods of grief, sickness, depression, or other life-changing events, as well as during the demands of raising a family or when both spouses are working outside the home. One recent medicine based TV talk show revealed that the average frequency for couples was determined to be three times p/week. Other studies put the average at two to three times p/week with those numbers declining with age. Couples should not feel pressured if they are under the so called average as long as both are satisfied with this area of their married life. In general the frequency is at the discretion of each spouse; however each should be endeavoring to accommodate not only their own desires, but the wishes of their spouse. Frequency might be several times a week in the younger years and taper off to once every month or so as couples age.

When sexual intimacy becomes all consuming, such as a desire for it every day or several times in a day, it should be evaluated to see if it has become a sexual addiction or compulsion. Sex is a small part of a couple's relationship; very important, but if kept in proper balance it will not be all consuming. Conversely, a couple who refrains from sex for long periods of time (several months or even years) should also discuss the reasons for such abstinence. Sex is a healthy aspect of a marriage and often an important gauge of how well the relationship is doing as it is rare that both spouses will become disinterested in sex at the same time unless the relationship is in turmoil.

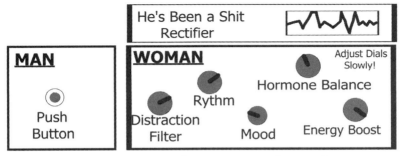

His & Her Orgasm Device

Couple's project—Take some time to discuss Part 1 with each other.

www.u-build.com

PART 2 TROUBLES

A study reported by JAMA in 1999 reported that sexual problems are common to both men and women; 43% of women and 31% of men reported some kind of sexual dysfunction. They also reported that for women, lack of desire *(remember, desire must come prior to stimulation)* was the larger problem, then difficulties in obtaining an orgasm, followed by pain. Most men can climax without much difficulty, but statistics say about one-third of women regularly have trouble or cannot achieve orgasm thru intercourse and require other types of stimulation. Our purpose here is not to solve any of these troubles, rather to open the door so you and your spouse can talk about them. Communication removes the tension, and the lack of communication induces fear, resentment, and avoids harmony. Remember we said we'd go before you, we'd be real, and we want you to be real too. Several of these have been factors in our marriage and we talked and worked thru them to restore balance and harmony. It is very likely that one or more of the problems listed apply to your marriage. So own it, talk about it, and agree to look for solutions.

Hormones: Cut Each Other Some Slack

It seems fitting to begin our troubles section with a brief overview of the biological difference between men and women. Men and women need to cut each other a little slack when it comes to understanding how their individual hormones play a huge role in each other's daily behavior. Our hormones do indeed affect our behavior and we both need to make allowances for this. We estimate that hormones alone account for a fair share of disharmony in a marriage and they play a bigger role with regards to libido. While a woman will defend her turf stating it's her time of the month, her hormones are raging and this is responsible for her disposition, many women will dismiss the fact that a man is filled with testosterone and his constant drive for sex is chemically driven. Likewise men need to understand that their wives will wrestle with hormonal changes, not only every month during her period, but also during and after pregnancy, and during menopause. These hormonal chemical changes and differences are very real and directly impact our behavior. This sets up an internal war within both men and women.

The so called "normal" testosterone levels vary between researchers, but a general guideline is roughly 30-90 ng/dl for females and around 300-1100 ng/dl for males. Think about it ladies, your husband may have 10 to 35 times more testosterone than you. This is what pushes his sex drive and his more aggressive behavior to the forefront. Men are often wrestling with this just like you wrestle with your behavior and emotions during your monthly period. Now with a better understanding of what we both have to struggle with, we can make greater allowances for those days when we are just not acting in the manner we should.

History of Sexual Abuse

If either spouse has been sexually abused, the road to fulfilling sexual intimacy will likely take a different route. When a person has been sexually abused they may require many months, sometimes years, of therapy to help them enjoy the act of intimacy. Any touch, music, smells, or even certain words by their spouse may bring back memories of a perpetrator or one of the abuse events. However, men and women can get beyond abuse trauma to have very fulfilling marriage intimacy. If you've never shared with your spouse that you were sexually abused, it's absolutely imperative that you share that information so they will not receive your timidity or recoil as rejection. Again, it's well beyond the scope of this book to help you work through abuse, but you should get the help you need to work through it. Do not let the perpetrator violate you again by stealing the intimacy from your marriage, fight back!

The Smiths returned to the marriage counselor's office after a one-month break in which the therapist had asked them to record every time they had sex on their calendar in order to settle who was right with regard to the number of times sex was occurring. The husband was thinking it was very rare and the wife was thinking it was occurring frequently. When the therapist asked what the results were, the wife quickly responded: *"Well, it turns out sex is occurring with a lot of frequency,"* to which the husband then chimed in, *"Yeah, but it turns out it's a rare event with each other!"*

Physical Troubles—Impotence

First we need to insert this caution: *"If our advice results in you maintaining an erection for longer than four hours, please seek immediate medical attention."* ☺

That statement alone is estimated to be responsible for a 25% increase in impotence drug sales. *(Men are actually hoping they might get four-hour-long erections!)* Obviously, this is a parody of the thousands of TV commercials we are being bombarded with every year. Ever wonder just how many of those pills are sold due to the constant showing of such commercials?

There are a variety of medical conditions that can interfere with either the man or woman's pleasure in the act of sexual intimacy. Consultation with a medical professional is certainly warranted for the following: pain of any kind during or after the sex act, allergic reaction to semen or vaginal secretions that cause burning or itching, peripheral nerve damage or numbness in the penal or vaginal area, trouble getting an erection, trouble keeping an erection, vaginal dryness, bleeding, and more. It's OK…REALLY, find a good doctor who has a reputation for treating sexually based conditions and see what medicine has to offer that may help you with any troubling condition.

Insignificant Stimulation or Technique

A common trouble for wives and husbands is the difference in the amount of time and type of stimulation each require to achieve orgasm. We've previously mentioned that women often must first learn for themselves how to achieve an orgasm, and then they will have to convey this information to their husbands. Premature ejaculation (PE) is perhaps the most common unreported condition among couples. Some men can become so over excited they climax before entry, shortly after, or still short of the time needed for their wife to climax. Men who suffer from PE will be frustrated with what they believe is an inability to delay climaxing before their spouse. Fortunately there are several options to treat this condition, such as numbing sprays/creams, letting your wife "drive" setting her own pace, wearing several condoms, practicing pelvic muscle contractions (as a distraction) just before each thrust, increasing the frequency of sexual intimacy, and more.

Disease

We are not medical experts, but there are many medical conditions and diseases that can inhibit or prevent sexual intimacy in either women or men or reduce the desire for sex. Low testosterone will reduce the desire in men and women. Thyroid issues can make either spouse too fatigued, and diabetes is a frequent cause of erection difficulties, etc. I have the disease Sarcoidosis, when it came on strong several years ago I had no libido what so ever. Everyone these days is aware that any person who has been sexually active prior to marriage has the possibility of having contracted an STD (sexually transmitted disease). STDs can interfere with the pleasure aspects of sexual intimacy. While many STD's can be treated and resolved, others can not.

Age and Life Changes

Frankly, as we get older most of us will have less interest in sex compared to our younger years. Men are said to peak in their sexual desire in their early 20s, and women in their mid-30s to early 40s. Aging men and women will naturally reduce the frequency of sex, which may or may not result in a corresponding reduction in desire for sex, and that's OK. Recall, the testosterone levels for both women and men declines as we age. It has been reported by some sixtyish couples that they may be more inclined to choose a good bowel movement over sex! There are, however, two gender-specific events that can put a significant spin on libido as a couple ages.

Menopause according to information from the Mayo Clinic is a biological process, defined as 12 months after a woman's last period, or removal of her ovaries. Some women proceed thru menopause with little emotional or physical changes. Many others report loss of energy, loss of sleep, los of libido, emotional swings, hot flashes, night sweats, and more. Many of these signs occur in the months before and after meeting the official definition of menopause.

There can also be a male menopause, or more correctly described by physicians "andropause." "Manopause" is another new term for it. This obviously doesn't have anything to do with the loss of menstruation in women; however, it is linked to the more often gradual decline in testosterone in men that for some men can really bring about changes in mood, energy, libido, and a general loss of motivation.

Both the male and female conditions above can be successfully treated with hormone therapy.

FACTOID – Not only should your spouse be able to bring up anything that interferes with your relationship, you should welcome it. Embrace communication that can improve your relationship bond.

27 | Midlife Crisis

Another age-related condition is often referred to as "midlife crisis" and is usually not associated with any physical changes in either the male or female, rather it can be brought on by various factors in life. After years of raising kids a housewife may feel the need to get sexy again. Having been confined to the walls of a home for years she may feel the desire to *strut her stuff*.

Likewise a male spouse may have become dissatisfied after many years of the 9–5 job and may be looking to add excitement to his life. Experiencing a divorce can also be a trigger. It's usually accompanied by a general feeling that life is not satisfying enough; the person becomes bored with life or feels too confined by family boundaries or perhaps financial debt or obligations. This seems to trigger a need to add excitement, take new risks, seek new adventure, press beyond boundaries, or add some other new stimulus that might invigorate their desire to live life to its fullest.

Just Too Tired!

This can be a common complaint by women, as we said before. Men tend to be more compartmentalized and can easily switch from putting the kids to bed to getting it on with Mama. Women and men can become emotionally drained when taking care of children, parents, work demands, or other tasks that require a huge emotional or physical effort.

FACTOID – Sexual intimacy is 90% mental and 10% physical.

All Is Not OK

Whatever is done in the bedroom must be agreeable to both the husband and the wife, and either spouse should be able to stop something they feel is not right for them, even if they agreed to it previously. While there is a whole cottage industry promoting "kinky," you'll find you and your spouse can have a great sex life without having to break new barriers. Sex has been going on for a long, long time and we are quite sure it will keep going on without the need for kinky. We've been married for nearly 30 years; we've kept the spice alive and intimacy interesting by being somewhat adventurous but without the need to go kinky.

Unable to Achieve Orgasm

Studies suggest that 95% of women can achieve an orgasm once they themselves know how to stimulate/achieve one. A small percentage of women and men cannot experience an orgasm for one reason or another; however, an orgasm is only one aspect of intimacy. If you otherwise enjoy the intimacy with your spouse, you may be content to leave things as they are. If not, seek a medical professional. As we said earlier, sex, although an important aspect of a marriage, is only a small part. Orgasm is an even smaller part, albeit a very fulfilling and highly desirable aspect for most men and women. But keeping it in balance, we'd all admit we'd trade orgasms away to keep the other intimacy and closeness we have with our spouses. Oh, you do not believe us? Take the following quiz. If you had to give up one of the three items below, which would you choose?

(A) Touching affectionately
(B) Orgasms
(C) Talking & listening

With an exception for a rare few, we'd say if you are not able to achieve an orgasm, seek medical help to determine why not. Orgasms are in a class all by themselves as far as a euphoric and pleasurable experience.

For the few individuals who are not able to achieve orgasms no matter what you've done or tried, don't lose your personal joy over it. Some people have never experienced the thrill of sky diving or swam in the ocean, and they still lead a very joyful and fulfilling life. Keep your joy; enjoy all the other things you have in life.

Mental Troubles

Big roadblocks can occur when our thoughts interfere with desire because of worries about:
  (1) becoming pregnant
  (2) getting caught or overheard by kids or others in the home
  (3) hearing a sound and not knowing what or who could be nearby
  (4) having the stereo or TV sound too high
  (5) being embarrassed to be seen in the light
  (6) self-performance, i.e., am I doing it right?
  (7) not being able to get to the point of orgasm, and thus suppressing their desire to prevent getting sexually frustrated
  (8) trying to get pregnant and having difficulty doing it

(9) feelings of bitterness or anger over unresolved issues toward the spouse

(10) lack of cleanliness in self or partner, the smell of body sweat, and other mental blocks

If you have one that was not mentioned, bring it up with your spouse.

Stimulant or Depressant

While alcohol typically causes our judgment to fail and reduces our inhibitions, alcohol actually depresses the sexual experience. This is confusing to most all of us because when we were younger we all knew booze helped a man get from "point A to point B." But that occurred as a result of reduced inhibitions—the alcohol actually works against the enjoyment of the sexual experience. Too much alcohol can actually interfere with your spouse's ability to achieve arousal or orgasm.

While libido drugs are viewed as sexual stimulants, they work by a relaxation process. As such, many men may find they can get the same benefits from a far less costly over the counter (OTC) sleeping pill. If you are having trouble getting an erection, try a couple of different brands of sleeping pills and see what happens. You'll sleep good too! A close friend of ours said a single sleeping pill worked for three days!

In any area that your intimacy is suffering for one or both of you, it is a good idea to seek medical or psychological therapy. When our eyes start to go bad, we seek medical help to restore our sight with glasses, contacts, or Lasik surgery. When our joints go bad we replace them or get the aid of a wheelchair or scooter. Thus, it seems reasonable that if our ability to get pleasure from sexual intimacy is hampered by a treatable condition, then we should seek help to treat that condition. If a prescription for erectile dysfunction will help the husband reclaim sexual intimacy with his wife, or if hormonal therapy or a personal vibrator will help the wife fully enjoy sexual intimacy with her husband, then it seems fitting to do so. We do not see it as a perversion to use medicine or aids to restore a fulfilling sex life between a married couple. The boundary line for us is based on motive. Is the desire based on restoring mutual intimacy, or just pushing boundaries away to obtain a new kinky experience?

Couple's project—Take some time to discuss Part 2 with each other.

www.u-build.com

PART 3 Application

Getting Your Woman Interested in Sex

It begins days or at least hours before. She is to be free from distractions such as kids and noises. Earlier in the day/week you have touched her tenderly, kissed her softly on the lips, you've been opening the door for her, making her feel special, and commented on how "hot" she is. *(Meanwhile you have not "groped" at her in the last several hours!)* You've held her, cuddled with her and helped her feel sexy. She has not caught you staring or flirting at other women, or watching programs or movies with perfect-bodied bimbos running around in swimsuits, and the house is warm or cool, as needed. You've made her feel desirable, sexy, and you've made yourself equally attractive to her.

Getting Your Man Interested in Sex—Show up!

Have You Given Your Man the Green Light Today?

Men are an optimistic bunch. I use to tell my daughter that men look for one of three signs. Men (young men especially) are always thinking about getting hooked up with a woman, and they have a pretty simple way to determine if a prospective girl might be willing to accept their advances. In this discussion, we are relating it to our marriage but this over simplification and generalization lesson is none the less relevant. With this lesson a woman will understand how something she does sends a message to her husband that she didn't know she was sending. It's something akin to a traffic light.

Yellow light—If you ignore a man, that's a yellow light. *(That's right, ignore means there's still a chance!)*
Green light—If you look at the man, talk with him or give any kind of body language that hints of being friendly, that's a green light.
Red light—The only way a man will see a red light is if you tell him off, or dress in a tent.

So let's take this into the home: A wife is always sending a signal to her husband, the signal will always be one of the three lights, so what signal have you sent your husband today? Did you climb out of the shower and walk past him? Change clothes where he was watching you? Now you wonder why he is in the mood? You're one hot woman!

It doesn't matter if you did it purposefully or not, your husband noticed! OK, now you understand our optimism!

Talking about and sharing what works and doesn't work is hugely important. Some husbands are embarrassed to ask you directly, so you, without being pushy, can "steer" your hubby to giving you what you need in the way of intimacy. Likewise, many women are embarrassed to actually speak during the act of intimacy to express what feels best. It can be a huge distraction for both, but working on getting to know each other's body is huge. Women especially should help their man know what is working and what is not. Set aside "sex" one evening and make it an *"explore our bodies night."* It's to be an instructional event rather than an intimacy event. A good lover, a good spouse, a good anything is rarely born, they are created and we get to create our own lovers in the marriage bed.

30 Years and Still Learning!

Very recently we discovered a communication glitch regarding our sexual intimacy after a marriage conference we attended. The woman instructing at this conference was explaining how she believed there were three distinct degrees of sexual intimacy for a woman. Using meals, she explained there are many times we share a plain sandwich, other times we will frequently share a pretty good meal, but there are those rare times when it's the "all-out luxurious five-course meal." Afterward, Bob and I were discussing what she had taught. Bob thought that my idea of a full-blown, luxurious five-course meal of intimacy was regularly being provided on many occasions. Bob's thoughts were focused on our mutually satisfying big O's. This began a discussion where I painted a new picture for him that having one or more orgasms is really great but that doesn't make it the top-of-the-line dining out event. I explained to him that it was all the trimmings that made intimacy an event that rated as a luxurious, all-out, top-of-the-line experience for me. Many women will express a similar contrast in marriage intimacy. For sure these events will be much rarer; but when the day is planned, when the candles are lit, when the music is on, when we slow dance in our own home, when we get dressed up and smell delicious from our best colognes, when we lay in each other's arms afterward and fall asleep, it is then that it's the best it can be.

If your wife wants you showered before, if she wants no kids around, if she wants the house warm and candles lit, then by all means help her make that happen. Set the stage for her; help her enjoy sexual intimacy by doing all you can to help her discover what works best for her.

FACTOID – Research indicates the best sex is between married couples!

About Men, a Short Read for Women

Ladies, for most men life seems to be only about sex, especially younger men; a young man's mind can be consumed by a quest for sex. If you are newly married, you're going to have to learn to deal with this as you may be amazed at the frequency your husband seeks your close company! It's your hot body that most likely drew your hubby in and the hopes of getting your hot body next to his started a chain reaction of events in which he was willing to don an alter ego personality that was nothing like the real him in hopes of getting you to accept the bait. *Note: Hot body does not mean it has to look like Barbie, we are fully convinced men and women come in all shapes and sizes because there are desires for each.*

As we discussed earlier besides testosterone, men are inundated with thousands of commercials and television shows using the opposite sex to sell us something. Advertisers say "sex sells," and they are using it to the hilt. Frankly it's getting way out of balance as sex makes up a small portion of our lives, but we are being bathed in it all day long no matter where we go. So ladies, it shouldn't be surprising that your husband thinks about sex or some aspect of it very often. Whether you hold to Christian or evolutionary moral codes, both agree that men are wired to seek sex. Some men will mature into a less self-centered balance in sexual intimacy; other men seem unaware or unconcerned that their wife has needs too.

The majority of men have a visually dominate, image-based brain, which explains why the pornography industry is so prolific. Unfortunately, many men including myself learned about sex from pornography when we were young boys. I can even remember way back when to the transition to live models in the clothing catalogs. Real women in their underwear! Yeowssa! In our modern American culture young and old men get hit with far more than that during prime time TV. The pornography industry is a multibillion dollar industry that depends on getting people addicted to it.

27 Men are stimulated by sight and when we can't see, we'll use some imagination. Our wives if not already aware, should be aware of a condition they can create in a man. It's known as being "worked up." A woman doesn't have to necessarily do much to get a man worked up, but once he is worked up, don't be surprised if he is on the hunt and looking to get a "pressure release." Of course many wives are aware of this worked-up condition because they very purposefully use their "wares" to see if they've still got it by baiting their man into getting all worked up. Vicious circle isn't it? We love you girls!

So what wives need to know about their husbands with regard to sex is very little, it's not too complicated, just show up. Indeed, most husbands want to provide you with gratifying intimacy too, but they are aware their own sex drive seems to be working overtime compared to yours. Because men can get so worked up, the unspoken fact is a good portion of married men will resort to masturbation to relieve the pressure when their wife is conveying signals they are not in the mood. A recent survey determined that married men will self-relieve several times per month. If this statistic is accurate, it means these extra pressure releases are in addition to the sex (said earlier to be two to three times per week) that husbands already enjoy with their spouse. Remember that we are not always in sync with regard to our desire for sex. Some husbands will feel it's just too much of a hassle to request that his higher libido needs be taken care of every time he is in the mood and his wife is not. If you will, masturbation can become the easy way out, with the husband feeling he is actually being very considerate of his wife by not pressuring her or having to work through all the interpersonal requirements of wooing a spouse into the desire phase. Unfortunately, some married men carry this further and seek out the services of a prostitute or other acquaintance when his needs are left unsatisfied.

Once a man is worked up, it may not be about "making love," it may be more about relieving the pressure. And yet a good share of husbands will take the eunuch approach patiently waiting for their wife to send them a signal when they too are ready for intimacy. While your man seems somewhat sex-craved, he very likely also has a deep desire to please you and wants you to help him navigate the path leading to your enjoyment. While you may not understand much about your body, your husband understands it even less and you both need to work thru the contrast in your libido and intimacy needs.

Couple's project—Take some time to talk about what you've just read. What we've written is less important than what your husband wants you to know about him.

"I spoke with a guy who has conducted tons of research and studies on human sexuality. He has interviewed hundreds of men and women, so I asked if he could sum up everything he has learned about sex and he replied, 'I like it!' The message: keep it simple."

What "No" Really Means

Some men do not take rejection well; it can be hard for some men to understand that when you say "no" you're not in the mood for sex, that you are not rejecting him. For indeed many men will take that as a direct dismissal against him. It can be very beneficial to help your man understand why you are declining his advances. To us girls, our "no" response means *"no, nothing in the day has moved me into the desire phase"* (remember husbands, your wife's libido has to start with desire) but our husbands are most likely hearing *"no, I have no desire for you."* Simply put, we are just not in the mood, but he may feel it is a personal rejection of him.

[Bob elbows in here] Ladies, let us relate this in a parable. Pretend you are at a senior high dance. It's like he chooses you from the bench to go dance, but then after getting out to the dance floor, he walks off, leaving you there standing by yourself. Would you feel rejected? Likewise your man can feel that he chose you, and declining his affection is a rejection of him personally. Thorough communication is huge in this area. Husbands need to understand that this occasionally occurs and it's not a disrespectful slap on their manhood. Remember, the racetrack libido example? Husbands need to be able to accept an occasional no, and accept that it is not a personal rejection of them. But men, remember, you can help your lady get in the mood more often by words and actions that foster desire.

Women have a lot to learn about themselves let alone trying to make it clear to their man. Truly a woman's hormonal changes and birthing capabilities make it much more difficult for them. And yet husbands want their wives to understand they are use to fixing things. When you have a problem, generally men will seek to fix it. But we will get very frustrated when we do make the effort to communicate and talk to you and we accidently say something that injures you or you take something wrong or get upset with us. Your man leaves feeling like he has made things worse rather than better. This frustration is what drives some men out of the home to the tavern because we start thinking nothing we do (with regard to communication) works. It is very important that couples continue to grant grace to each other and keep working thru these periods and come out closer on the other side. Do not give up on communication, continue in it until it harmony is restored.

About Women, a Short Read for Men

Women are not like men; they think there's more to life than sex. Oh, one more thing, women are more like a slow cooker and men are like a microwave in achieving an orgasm. Remember the picture of the orgasm device at the end of Part 1? About sums it up, doesn't it!

[Paige elbows her way back in] OK, now that you've stopped laughing, women are indeed complex creatures. But in fairness to us girls, there is really a lot more going on with us, so much more that we have a dedicated branch of medicine just for us that men do not have (gynecology). Given this complexity, guys can learn more about their wives by listening to them. If there is so much going on with our female anatomy that a special branch of medicine is required, it should be obvious that not only do we have a lot to figure out, but our husbands will too.

Your job, men, is to set up the conditions where intimacy can occur which will often begin early in a day long before the event, we then have time to get our heads into that frame of mind and set aside the hang-ups and distractions of the day. And after the room is cleared for desire, your woman has certain points, certain ways of being touched on those points, certain rhythms that require sensitivity on your part. Mashing a breast does little to turn on your wife in spite of what you've seen in the movies. Ask your wife what romance means to her; ask her to explain what you can do to be romantic with her to help build up the desire. Men it is very important that you make her feel that you really want to take the time to help her and you are not just hearing static from our lips. Don't be frustrated with your wife, don't give up, help her help you by showing you really want to know and you will work with her to get there.

If you think you are the master romantic seducer, and feel you've got all that down. OK, don't ask your wife what she needs, this is for all the other guys.

240

We men are generally able to receive satisfying stimulation while engaged in intercourse, whenever or whatever position it occurs. But your wife needs to be asked or prompted to convey to you what feels best to her. Depending on what the hubby is doing, the stimulation can range from painful, to uncomfortable, to feeling nothing, to sexually stimulating for the woman but interruptions or changes in the rhythm or techniques, can spoil the whole arousal phase for her. Sexual intimacy varies greatly from woman to woman, some are all about the intimacy rather than the act, some are indeed really into getting the big "O" (orgasm) and more than once. Women as well may use masturbation for relief, especially if she and her husband have had difficulties in keeping her stimulated. The best method to sexual harmony is to keep communicating to each other, to work thru differences, and to keep sexual harmony. Take care of each other's needs, convey them to each other and give no room for other temptations to enter your marital relationship.

Couple's project—Take some time to talk about what you've just read. What we've written is less important than what your wife wants you to know about her.

Jungle Gym?

What is "normal" can span the gamut of sexual positions and other interesting variations including mutual masturbation. However, we think there is a strong argument for the use of body parts as originally designed, i.e., penis goes into vagina both from a "design by nature" and/or a "design by God" aspect. There are many variations for vaginal intercourse, more than enough to keep couples interested. We personally believe that anal penetration should be avoided, as the rectum's sole purpose and design is to "extrude stuff," not to take in stuff. As for oral sex, all we're going to say is if you both agree to it, make sure you do not have cold sores or blisters in your mouth or lips (HSV-1) as your spouse as well as you can contract genital herpes (HSV-2), which has no cure.

Do's and Don'ts

What is OK in the bedroom? We're not going there—again, this is not a sex book; however, we offer the following advice that you can take or leave about sexual intimacy from our perspective, which may not be yours.

• Keep the sex aspect of your marriage in balance. It is a small part of your marriage; it shouldn't become the main aspect of your relationship.

- NEVER, EVER speak negatively about your spouse's body, especially during the act of intimacy.
- NEVER, EVER speak negatively about your spouse's performance, especially during the act of intimacy.
- Be careful how you word the need to change things, be sensitive to your presentation.
- Do not injure your spouse in what you say.
- Do help your spouse overcome any obstacles to sexual enjoyment.
- Do help your spouse understand what pleases you and how to stimulate you.
- While far less of a concern in a monogamous marriage, sexually transmitted diseases can be a concern. Some couples will be more relaxed and more in the mood if they and their spouse are clean, having recently showered or bathed prior to sex. Spontaneity should still be encouraged and enjoyed, as long as both spouses are willing. Washing afterward is also a desirable practice not only to clean up but you can use it as a form of "afterglow petting."
- Men, do not ask your spouse to perform acts you've seen in pornographic magazines or movies. Pornography has been described as "everyman's battle," but has made significant inroads with women. Many women feel cheated or that they cannot measure up to the women portrayed in pornography. Likewise, when women view porno most men feel they cannot measure up to the studs portrayed in the films. Pornography is not reality; it's a destructive perversion of marital intimacy.
- Do not use pornography to "get yourself in the mood" rather work on how you can help each other get there.
- During a small (<10) informal phone interview, Paige found that a significant portion of her married women acquaintances did own a clitoris stimulating vibrator. However, the vibrator was not meant to replace mutually satisfying sexual intimacy between the couple rather to enhance it. Indeed no one should use aids to the point that it leads to dependency on them, unless a medical condition requires such. Consult with your doctor if need be.
- Never use cameras; you never know what can fall into the wrong hands. Your home could be broken into and those films or computers stolen and fall into the hands of criminals who might be spurred on to bribe you or blackmail you. After a divorce, an

angry spouse could post such pictures or videos on the Web.

- In general terms, so called kinky sex is kinda like a drug, a drug that you need more and more of to feel satisfied. Stay far away from activities that are involved in fantasy, possibly painful, involve other participants, or something you'd be ashamed about if others knew.
- Do use lubrication gel, especially as the woman ages, but anytime there is vaginal dryness.
- Don't fake orgasm or fake any part of your marital relationship for that matter. It seems likely that this routine will become tiring and more importantly faking pleasure does not facilitate teaching your spouse how to mature in his or her technique. It may also be viewed as dishonest.
- Never use sex as a punishment to be withheld or only doled out as a reward when you get your way. Sex should never be used as a manipulative tool.
- Do set boundaries with regard to your sex life especially when your sex life is already very satisfying. This is one of the many troubles with the entertainment industry. People of wealth and fame start to feel they deserve to "experience it all" and press beyond what nature and God intended. Remember to stay on task, you are working to build a great marriage not experience every so-called pleasure that can be thought up in life.

Men usually say they "need" the pressure release that comes from intercourse. Men *(as they mature)* also have a deep desire to know they are giving their woman satisfaction in the bedroom. Some husbands may in fact have trouble getting an erection if they do not feel their wife is enjoying the foreplay or stimulation or if they are being pressured to perform "now." I have had friends express this erectile dysfunction condition especially when their marriage relationship is less than it should be. A wife that tells her man "Hurry up and get this over with," or "What's the matter, you can't get it up again?" is certainly acting with contempt and disrespect. Likewise, a man should never belittle or force his wife into sex or speak condemningly about her performance or timidity.

Couple's project—Take some time to talk about what you've just read; what we've written is less important than what your wife or husband wants you to know about their needs. Flip back and forth between the sections if need be.

PART 4 Mutual Care

Attraction is really in the eye of the beholder but it is also within us. Regardless of our actual looks, we should all embrace who we are and accept what we were born with. We all need to be comfortable in our own skin and people who are comfortable in their own skin are all the more attractive when they project that "I'm just fine with me" confidence. (Not to be confused with a conceited, arrogant-minded attitude.)

When we really look at ourselves and each other closely we may not paint a picture that is very attractive. For instance; Bob has a rather large birthmark on the back of his head, he is bald, has a spare tire, and his skin is abnormally dry and often inflamed. While I feel I have a long neck, a muffin-top waist, oily skin, and narrow shoulders. Bob feels I should gain weight, I feel I should lose some weight; we agree we both should get more aerobic exercise. We both have blemishes and pimples. That doesn't sound very attractive, but that is the reality. Imperfections and flaws are part of our humanity. We have preferences and desires, yet we all have to work with what we were born with and to that end, we should take care of the things we can take care of, and learn to live with what we cannot.

> *"It's one of life's mysteries to me, one that I hope never goes away, but what is it that makes a man act like a begging dog just to touch two globs of fat and tissue hanging from the front of his wife?"*

Add to that, that some men actually prefer their spouses without makeup, or significantly overweight or natural with regard to facial hair, underarm hair, and leg hair. But most of us have limits and boundaries in which any of these points, when crossed, move our thoughts from attractive to unattractive. On more than one occasion I have had a spouse tell me that they no longer find their spouse attractive. We really do have a responsibility to our spouses for our bodies. Once we are married, our bodies are not just our own any longer. Yet you should be able to deduce we do not consider divorce an option just because you no longer view your spouse as attractive.

We decided we needed to address this most sensitive topic to open the door to discussion. It is important for couples to remember this is a SAFE TIME and no condemnation should be inflicted. However, if your spouse's lack of personal care is getting in the way of your intimacy or attraction to them, then let's constructively use this section to work toward reaching some unity. Because we are married we should (within reason) desire to present ourselves in a manner that is, if not pleasing to our spouses at least not turning them off.

It can be helpful to take our thoughts back to our dating days when we went out of our way to make ourselves healthy and attractive to woo our future spouse into accepting the bait and getting them to consent to a lifelong committed relationship. Young girls daydreamed about the prince riding in to sweep them off their feet, and young boys had thoughts of being with the perfect girl. So we ask you, if you revisit those dreams, what did those make-believe characters in your dreams look like? What did you look like?

The questions we raise are these: Are we allowed to "let ourselves go" after we've been married? Do we have a responsibility to maintain our attractiveness, at least to some degree, for our spouses? If we do not keep up some degree of our health and appearance, can we then understand why our spouse may now have difficulty finding us still attractive?

For this discussion we are not talking about age, we are not talking about plastic surgery or disabilities. The neat part about growing old is we do it together, we will age and become frail together. Skin gets wrinkled, hair gets grayer and/or falls out, body parts start to succumb to gravity, and the teeth are not as bright as they used to be.

Bob and I love growing old together. It's not that we are happy with the aging process, but because aging is a fact of life, becoming less youthfully attractive, if you will, is just something we have to accept. We choose to put a better spin on this; we actually embrace getting old because it is a different attractiveness. We are enjoying it.

Our Health, Our Weight, Our Appearance

Do you and your spouse desire an enduring marriage? What if one or both of you are making a less than adequate effort at making sure you're still around for the long haul? Should your spouse put hard work into your marriage if you're doing your best to shorten the time you are on this round ball we call earth? The goal, remember, is to grow old together and then meet your maker *together*.

Attraction is a funny thing. We may not be concerned that our friends or coworkers are not exercising, or are easily tired or vastly overweight, but we are concerned for our family members in these areas, and we have to consider we look at our spouse with a different set *(sexual)* of eyes. Not to mention the example we set for our children when we want to avoid the "do as I say, not as I do" rule.

In this section we wanted to provide an opportunity to discuss health, weight, and appearance with each other, while in a SAFE TIME. We know both husbands and wives who have admitted to us that they are concerned about their spouse's health, that their spouse is too skinny or too overweight, or that their spouse is no longer working at keeping attractive.

Men are visual—we all understand that—but if women are honest with themselves, they are too, hence why there are so many mirrors in the house. Paige and I have had this conversation that if one or the other of us was vastly overweight, we would indeed still love the person, but likewise would be less attracted to each other. I want Paige to take care of herself and she wants the same for me. That includes my weight, my strength, and my endurance. Paige needs me to dress in something other than rags, to smell good, and to present myself as a man. I need Paige to look, dress, and act like a woman.

So how and when do we get the opportunity to tell each other how we feel without hurting or injuring each other? **Now!** Speaking for our relationship, Paige and I have been open with each other and have had this discussion before. We've both made personal goals to never become unhealthy or unattractive in what we have control over. I'm not saying we don't have some poor eating habits, digress from regular exercise, and have both put on a few pounds in the wrong places over 30 years of marriage, but what I am saying is we do not stray too far from our goal of being *reasonably* healthy and attractive for each other.

With the arrival of the BMI (body mass index) we have an industry standard to gauge if we are in a healthy weight range. The BMI doesn't work well for all people, for instance bodybuilders and other very athletic people might have a high BMI but be very healthy. But for most of the general population, the BMI will easily help us assess if we are in an unhealthy weight condition. The BMI will add a non-personal appraisal to our spouse's appraisal and will hopefully bring balance to it.

Couple's project—Agree this a SAFE TIME Using the BMI chart on the following page, find each of your BMI values, then discuss the health and appearance aspects of the results..

Height		Weight																												
FT In	inches	120	130	140	150	160	170	180	190	200	210	220	230	240	250	260	270	280	290	300	310	320	330	340	350	360	370	380	390	400
4 5	53	30	33	35	38	40	43	45	48	50	53	55	58	60	63	65	68	70	73	75	78	80	83	85	88	90	93	95	98	100
4 6	54	29	31	34	36	39	41	43	46	48	51	53	55	58	60	63	65	68	70	72	75	77	80	82	84	87	89	92	94	96
4 7	55	28	30	33	35	37	40	42	44	46	49	51	53	56	58	60	63	65	67	70	72	74	77	79	81	84	86	88	91	93
4 8	56	27	29	31	34	36	38	40	43	45	47	49	52	54	56	58	61	63	65	67	69	72	74	76	78	81	83	85	87	90
4 9	57	26	28	30	32	35	37	39	41	43	45	48	50	52	54	56	58	61	63	65	67	69	71	74	76	78	80	82	84	87
4 10	58	25	27	29	31	33	36	38	40	42	44	46	48	50	52	54	56	59	61	63	65	67	69	71	73	75	77	79	82	84
4 11	59	24	26	28	30	32	34	36	38	40	42	44	46	48	50	53	55	57	59	61	63	65	67	69	71	73	75	77	79	81
5 0	60	23	25	27	29	31	33	35	37	39	41	43	45	47	49	51	53	55	57	59	61	62	64	66	68	70	72	74	76	78
5 1	61	23	25	26	28	30	32	34	36	38	40	42	43	45	47	49	51	53	55	57	59	60	62	64	66	68	70	72	74	76
5 2	62	22	24	26	27	29	31	33	35	37	38	40	42	44	46	48	49	51	53	55	57	59	60	62	64	66	68	69	71	73
5 3	63	21	23	25	27	28	30	32	34	35	37	39	41	43	44	46	48	50	51	53	55	57	58	60	62	64	66	67	69	71
5 4	64	21	22	24	26	27	29	31	33	34	36	38	39	41	43	45	46	48	50	51	53	55	57	58	60	62	64	65	67	69
5 5	65	20	22	23	25	27	28	30	32	33	35	37	38	40	42	43	45	47	48	50	52	53	55	57	58	60	62	63	65	67
5 6	66	19	21	23	24	26	27	29	31	32	34	36	37	39	40	42	44	45	47	48	50	52	53	55	56	58	60	61	63	65
5 7	67	19	20	22	23	25	27	28	30	31	33	34	36	38	39	41	42	44	45	47	49	50	52	53	55	56	58	60	61	63
5 8	68	18	20	21	23	24	26	27	29	30	32	33	35	36	38	40	41	43	44	46	47	49	50	52	53	55	56	58	59	61
5 9	69	18	19	21	22	24	25	27	28	30	31	32	34	35	37	38	40	41	43	44	46	47	49	50	52	53	55	56	58	59
5 10	70	17	19	20	22	23	24	26	27	29	30	32	33	34	36	37	39	40	42	43	44	46	47	49	50	52	53	55	56	57
5 11	71	17	18	20	21	22	24	25	27	28	29	31	32	33	35	36	38	39	40	42	43	45	46	47	49	50	52	53	54	56
6 0	72	16	18	19	20	22	23	24	26	27	28	30	31	33	34	35	37	38	39	41	42	43	45	46	47	49	50	52	53	54
6 1	73	16	17	18	20	21	22	24	25	26	28	29	30	32	33	34	36	37	38	40	41	42	44	45	46	47	49	50	51	53
6 2	74	15	17	18	19	21	22	23	24	26	27	28	30	31	32	33	35	36	37	39	40	41	42	44	45	46	48	49	50	51
6 3	75	15	16	18	19	20	21	23	24	25	26	28	29	30	31	32	34	35	36	37	39	40	41	42	44	45	46	47	49	50
6 4	76	15	16	17	18	19	21	22	23	24	26	27	28	29	30	32	33	34	35	37	38	39	40	41	43	44	45	46	47	49
6 5	77	14	15	17	18	19	20	21	23	24	25	26	27	28	30	31	32	33	34	36	37	38	39	40	42	43	44	45	46	47
6 6	78	14	15	16	17	18	20	21	22	23	24	25	27	28	29	30	31	32	34	35	36	37	38	39	40	42	43	44	45	46
6 7	79	14	15	16	17	18	19	20	21	23	24	25	26	27	28	29	30	32	33	34	35	36	37	38	39	41	42	43	44	45
6 8	80	13	14	15	16	18	19	20	21	22	23	24	25	26	27	29	30	31	32	33	34	35	36	37	38	40	41	42	43	44
6 9	81	13	14	15	16	17	18	19	20	21	23	24	25	26	27	28	29	30	31	32	33	34	35	36	38	39	40	41	42	43
6 10	82	13	14	15	16	17	18	19	20	21	22	23	24	25	26	27	28	29	30	31	32	33	35	36	37	38	39	40	41	42
6 11	83	12	13	14	15	16	17	18	19	20	21	22	23	24	26	27	28	29	30	31	32	33	34	35	36	37	38	39	40	41
7 0	84	12	13	14	15	16	17	18	19	20	21	22	23	24	25	26	27	28	29	30	31	32	33	34	35	36	37	38	39	40

Diagonal category labels across the chart: Severely Underweight · Underweight · Normal · Overweight · Obese · Morbidly Obese · Super Morbidly Obese · VERY VERY HIGH RISK OF DIABETES, HYPERTENSION, and HEART DISEASE over 40 BMI

Paige and Bob's 30 year married life BMI ranges shown in bolded boxes. We individually set personal weight limit goals and stick to them.

National Averages for BMI, (20-29yrs) is 24.5, (30-39yrs) is 26.5, (40-49yrs) is 28, (50-59yrs) is 28.5, (60-69yrs) is 27.5

BMI is calculated the same for men and women because the health risks are the same.

27 One thing we women wrestle with far more than men is our weight and appearance. Bob has watched me stand in front of the mirror for the last thirty years criticizing myself and I believe that all women do the same unkind thing. Often these are not realistic self-appraisals, but it is true that Americans in general are overweight and in poor health due to being significantly overweight. Because weight, health, and attraction can be so closely tied together, and often a concern or topic in marriage relationships, we wanted to briefly make room for this discussion between couples. This is not a guilt or condemnation chat, this is a conviction chat.

We need to truthfully face the fact that we are not taking good care of ourselves. The truth is that a portion of us are more than just a little overweight and with that can come the hazard that we begin to care less about how we present ourselves to our spouses, especially around the house. The *Biggest Loser* show is very popular because this topic affects many of us and we also are cheering for the contestants as they come out the other side much healthier and disciplined than they were before.

Again we want to be clear, this is not about making women or men feel bad about themselves for being over or under weight. We do need to honestly deal with the fact that a lot of us are unhealthy with regard to what we eat, that we never exercise, and that our weight or reduced health may cause us to care less about how we look. It all adds up and the result is we not only know we are possibly becoming less attractive to our spouses, we have to admit it is our own decisions that have us in this condition.

> Initially we considered buying a stair climber, but after much thought, we bought a recliner. It was $20 cheaper and much easier to use.

If you or your spouse have a concern about your health, your attractiveness, or your weight then you need to seriously consider what they are telling you. Then, if necessary, optimistically and immediately begin a lifestyle change to improve your health, weight, or attractiveness. Real moment here: Bob has been concerned about my heart health for several years, and after reflecting on the truth I have to admit that I have become lethargic, which I know is not good for my health. So I have made a new commitment to regular aerobic exercise!

How does a lifestyle change take place? The process begins with (a) acknowledging you have a problem in one of these areas, (b) desire or resolve to change, (c) structure changes in lifestyle to accomplish the change, (d) substitution of another activity to avoid falling back into the same-ol-ways, and then (e) self-controlled effort to ensure the goals are always achieved.

Couple's project—Take some time here to discuss with each other the changes in your appearances (other than growing old) since your wedding day. This is an objective talk so discuss the changes in your health aspects followed by weight and then appearance. Help each other fill in the answers to the statements below.

This is a SAFE TIME

Since we married, the following changes have occurred: (True/False)

Wife's feedback for husband

> True/False He is not keeping himself physically healthy for his age.
> True/False He is not keeping himself as attractive as he could be with regard to hygiene, dress, or other.
> True/False He has gained a lot of extra weight, perhaps too much.
> True/False Some of these changes are not benefiting our relationship.
> True/False I'd like him to make some changes for us.

Husband's feedback for wife

> True/False She is not keeping herself physically healthy for her age.
> True/False She is not keeping herself as attractive as she could be with regard to hygiene, dress, or other.
> True/False She has gained a lot of extra weight, perhaps too much.
> True/False Some of these changes are not benefiting our relationship.
> True/False I'd like her to make some changes for us.

Husband's Response – *I agree with my wife's feedback and with her help and loving reminders, I'll make changes to be more healthy and attractive for her.*

Wife's Response – *I agree with my husband's feedback and with his help and loving reminders, I'll make changes to be more healthy and attractive for him.*

27 We hope you realize that this is not intended to be a demeaning exercise and that if your spouse is being loving and truthful then you should accept the honesty. Your spouse loves you, doesn't want to hurt you, and is trying to better your relationship. They are likely not telling you something that you didn't already know. It is normal to let ourselves go in any number of areas. It is also natural to be defensive when facing our shortcomings in these areas. Remember as we discussed in chapter 12 that everything decays unless we perform routine maintenance. Accept the fact you may need to work at making some changes not only in your marriage relationship, but in your physical appearance.

And for you California types that have been brainwashed into a warped, hard-body only view of what a spouse must be, stop it! That is not reality; do not force or try to shame your spouse into the Baywatch hunk or babe appearance.

Paige Has a Breakout Session about Mutual Care

I called upon my Posse Girls (*you know, that special group of friends that will talk to you about anything, no matter what the subject matter*) and some of my other girlfriends to bring in some additional perspectives and clarity to this very important chapter.

I'm sure most of you have heard about a woman's *love bank*. Men, you are told that you are either making deposits or withdrawals into your wife's love bank. My girls and I want to help you understand some of the rules for love deposits. The following is what we came up with.

Rule #1 Attention happens prior to and outside the bedroom. We wives need and desire touch without a goal (sex) during the day just for the sake of touching. And guys we really do need this on a daily basis. It can even make us grumpy if it doesn't happen (our minds wander into discouraging thoughts). Some ideas for this attention are holding our hand, a soft kiss while at a party, a kiss good morning or good night, soft purposeful touches, and cuddling (fully clothed or skin-to-skin). All this shows the world and us that you continue to choose us.

Rule #2 Communication must be thoughtful and deliberate. You might be getting tired of that word "communication," but it is huge for your wife. She desires both of you to express and guide each other to what your needs are, in a safe and non-belittling way. And the most important part of communication is that you listen attentively to what she says.

Rule #3 Romance equals foreplay to your wife. When you give her some of your attention during the day, when she feels pursued, she NATURALLY moves into the desire phase, actually wanting to be intimate later in the day. Not what you thought of as foreplay, is it? I'm not saying foreplay in the bedroom doesn't need to take place, but it really must begin many hours before. To some women romance can include flowers, cards, and love notes, hugs for no reason. Some of my girls thought your purposeful help around the house or with the kids was best. Cha-ching, deposits! When you help her clear her work load, then she has time to think about, prepare, clear her head of distractions, and get ready for expectant intimacy with you. And guys, I know this might be a special challenge for some of you, but try to refrain from digressing to the 13-year-old boy trying to cop a feel. DO NOT DEVIATE from the original plan!

Speaking of preparing and expectancy, some wives like to exchange advance clues if one of you wants to be intimate that night, by dropping clues or hints throughout the day that you would like some one-on-one time. She can mentally prepare and anticipate and this helps her heart and body be there for you and, just as importantly, also for herself. Clues can be: you wearing her favorite cologne, she might take a bubble bath, you help the kids with homework lessening her workload, you take her to lunch, or you exchange text messages. Discuss if one or both of you already drop hints and how it's working, and if you don't maybe this is a practice that can work for you.

Rule #4 Act the part! This can be different for some women, but most of us love it when you make plans and you take off that holey t-shirt and put on one of your best shirts and pants (ask her what you look hot in), walk us to the car and open the door for us, take us out to dinner (most of us agreed it doesn't have to be fancy), or otherwise treat us special. With these kinds of deposits you can almost always anticipate a large deposit back into your love bank!

Rule #5 Cleanliness. Guys this should be an easy deposit. Cleanliness in general is huge to us and to make larger deposits put on the cologne we like (find out which one makes HER crazy, and yes, there is one that will). We hang onto that smell for hours, and it reminds us of you all day. As one of my friends stated, sometimes the visual may be gone but the smell is always there. Most women really do respond to scents.

27 Rule # 6 True pleasure. When we are in our most intimate moments, we need to feel you are genuinely into us and that no matter how long it might take for us to get to the end result, you are committed, patient, willing, and enjoying it. Our minds can quickly sabotage the moment if we think you are getting tired, bored, or in any way sarcastic about the effort we might require.

Rule # 7 Appreciation. We need our husbands to tell us in words and actions that we are appreciated. We need you to be our number one fan. Value, enjoy, and cherish us. Husbands, when we gals feel appreciated, we are enthusiastic partners.

OK, I need to get real with us women too because we are not always considerate of our husband when he is trying to make us feel good. Do you value and embrace your husband's opinion when he gives it? Hopefully you said yes. Do you want your husband to compliment you and find you *hot*? What do you do with that gift when he actually expresses it? Do you embrace it and own it or do you ignore it and disregard it? Do you brush it off because you think he is just saying it? Why is it so hard to believe when it he tells you what you want to hear? What mixed-up message are we sending to our husband. How do you think this makes him feel? Ask him sometime (OK, right now works too) how he feels when you reject the compliments he gives you. HE REALLY MEANS THEM!

On that note, and to be real with you all, I needed to take my own advice and it was very revealing. For 30 years I have made my husband feel like his encouraging words about my looks didn't count, by rejecting his compliments about my attractiveness. By default, I was making him feel that everyone else's view about me mattered more than his. Yes, you heard correctly, Bob has told me almost every day of our marriage that he finds me attractive and HOT, to which I'd roll my eyes in unbelief and disregard him. Recently Bob told me that I have made him feel less valued than people that I don't even know. WOW, how that broke my heart. Well, no more! Hello world, you can think whatever you want about me and I don't give a rip, 'cuz my husband thinks I'm HOT! And I'm going to start wearing that. We need to look at *hot* as a favorite piece of clothing, each morning we must choose to put it on and own it. Go for it, ladies, it feels great. Embrace the truth that your husband thinks you're hot and then you can both enjoy your body.

Ladies, if you need a visual so you can see how your guy truly sees you, watch the Trace Atkins music video *One Hot Mama,* and ask your hubby if it's spot on. And if you need something to help get you into the "I'm hot" mood, try cranking up the tune *I Feel Like a Woman* by Shania Twain and see if a new confidence doesn't sweep thru you. You go, girl!

I gotta jump in here for my male buddies and put the romance/foreplay concept Paige and her friends discussed in words men can relate to. When the girls talked about foreplay beginning in the day not just in the bedroom, think about it as laying up firewood for the winter. We have to get that firewood before the snow comes. We prepare for winter by laying up the firewood before we need it. So the girls are telling us, that being attentive to them during the day is like laying up firewood for later on that evening. And the foreplay that takes place in the bedroom, is basically building the fire just before the stove starts putting forth heat. We have to arrange the kindling and get the fire going, then with the wood we've already laid up, it can put forth the heat we desire.

Time to Wrap up, or Unwrap?

Some of you are ready to get naked! But some spouses are not going to want to talk about this chapter, others will have acted goofy all thru the discussions, and still other spouses will be sitting straight-faced and carry on with a very generic and monotone voice. Let's put it in the proper perspective. Sex should be fun, it should be physically satisfying, and it should be emotionally satisfying, but it should also be free of tension, performance concerns, ridicule, and pain. Our goal is to make you feel more comfortable learning and exploring each other. We need to know each other when it comes to sexual intimacy; we hope you spend some time doing just that.

So in summary it is our opinion that sex is something special, we see it in a God-created perspective, and it is a union of two people that is not meant to be exploited. As a society, it seems to us that we are deep into a terrible experiment that is having horrible consequences. Restraint and self-control are words no longer echoed in the open—"anything goes" seems to be the mantra. But we as married couples can lead society back to the moral high ground by restoring sexual intimacy to the position it deserves. We can be monogamous while having so much fun being happily married and sexually satisfied couples that the rest of society will likewise desire an enduring marriage.

Indeed, the research already shows that married couples have better sex than non-married couples, so let's proclaim it from the rooftops, married sex is the best!

WOW! This has been a long chapter with many topics covered. For many couples it was very uncomfortable, stressful and hard to deal with. For others it was a yawn of sorts. What is important is that with regards to sexual intimacy that you resolve any issues that came up, don't set them aside because you do not want to deal with them, face them head on. Remember, this is a **SAFE TIME**. Discuss how you might improve your intimacy.

Later, in the comfort of your bedroom, one of you bring up the anatomy exercise and explore each other's bodies using the correct terms, asking questions, getting to know each other.

We'd like you to lay naked with your bodies next to each other in bed at least a couple of times over the next week and just cuddle and or fall asleep together. If it leads to sexual intimacy, that's OK, but what we want you both to experience is that very comforting feeling that affirms your attraction and love for each other as sexual beings. Your next assignment is to take a couple of showers together. Don't kid yourselves; men need this affirmation just like women do.

Couple's project—This is your chapter, its for your "mutual" benefit to take this subject matter and resolve any issues to make sexual intimacy a healthy, normal, and fulfilling part of your marriage relationship. Don't leave here until you have talked about all the things you want to talk about. If you have been hesitant, purpose to speak now. When we speak in love, and we are seeking what is best for our marriage, then its quite OK to talk about it. These conversations can take place over many weeks as you get to know each other more and more.

Did you learn anything? Yes / No
Chapter personal benefit appraisal: **HER 1-2-3-4-5   HIM 1-2-3-4-5**
1=not at all, 2=a little, 3=some good stuff, 4=fairly helpful, 5=very helpful

www.u-build.com

CHAPTER 28

Is Love a Burden?

Yes, absolutely yes, unequivocally yes, no question about it, <u>one aspect of love is a burden</u>. But it's a burden happily married couples desire to carry.

Burden (verb)—*To encumber, strain, bear down on, load, make heavy, obligate.*

In coming to the end of our marriage-building manual, we felt it was important to discuss one of the key components of marriage, "love." Society might describe love in various terms, such as euphoric, emotional bond, or romantic attachment. But love is much more; love emanates passion, intimacy, and commitment. Love is perhaps the strongest of all virtues. In the New Testament, the Bible devotes an entire chapter to love, describing not what love is, but what love <u>does</u>. Love is in motion.

FACTOID – Married couples like to say "we are in love," but the fact is they are really "in marriage." Love is just one component of what they "do" to stay married.

We are not linguistic majors by any sense of the imagination, but here is what we've learned. Love can be a noun, or it can be a verb. Verbs are action words, and it is vital that the "love" couples bring to their wedding day is the verb form of love. Marriage requires lots of love, but it is the action type of love not the static type of love that is needed. Spouses will have to give love and grow love and when they do, it is often returned to them.

It appears many people today do not want a great marriage if it means they will have to exert much effort. If someone says to you that they "feel in love" you might ask them if the feeling is from being tired because love requires effort and action. The action type of love should compel each spouse to do acts of love for the other spouse. The action type of love doesn't expect anything in return; it's an outward directional love. When your spouse does things for you, you are receiving their outward expression of love.

So hopefully you now understand that love carries with it some "burden activity" that when given to others demonstrates that love. But many couples will experience some period or periods of burdens that will demand an even greater dedication in expressing their love. While it's not unexpected that young, healthy couples focus on all the benefits of a marriage, the chances are that at some point one or both spouses can or will become disabled due to disease, injury, or as a result of the aging or near death process. Should it happen, or perhaps when it does happen, the strength of the marriage bond can be tested.

FACTOID – Love is an action word. It requires doing, it requires effort, and with some frequency love requires the sacrifice of your time and energy.

Bob and I are both workers, and when we work we put forth whatever effort is needed to complete the tasks in front of us. We have much laughter and joy in our home, not because we rely on the other person to make us happy, but because we choose to be happy. I do not wait for Bob to make me happy (although he works hard to make me laugh everyday), I choose to be happy. And yet I'll try to make him laugh or smile, and that in turn makes me all the happier. As a result we have much love in our home. Not only do we tell each other "I love you" several times every day, but significant portions of our daily activity conveys that love.

Love will have you doing things for your spouse even when you do not feel like it. Remember those "dating" days when you actually were excited to do stuff for each other? In a vibrant marriage, you keep doing those kinds of things with a similar joy and enthusiasm that you had when you were dating. Very often we've done them when we didn't feel like it. Love pushes us beyond our own comfort, to caring for the comfort of our spouse.

The Tale of the Critic and the Celebrated Sculptor

The tale is told of a snippy young art critic who was known for his blunt critique of even the most famous of artists. The critic was seeking a new target and had determined he would next take aim at a reclusive sculptor known to produce very fine works of art that powerfully and deliberately ignited passion and love by those who were lucky enough to obtain or view one of his works. Yet the artist was not well known and seemingly did little to promote his creations. The critic had only come across a rare few examples of the sculptor's works in his travels, but he heard much acclaim from all who had been moved by his work.

One early November day the critic set out to pay a surprise visit to the artist's home. The critic traveled for several hours until he came upon a quaint little cottage settled neatly into the countryside. Walking up the path the critic approached the entry to the artist's home and somewhat hesitantly knocked upon the door. While the critic was widely known for his bravado, he knew that many artists could be very eccentric and the reclusive types were usually the worst, he wasn't quite sure what might greet him at the door.

After a few moments the door swung open and the critic was greeted by a man of medium stature and a well-worn complexion. With a huge smile and without hesitation the man acknowledged himself as the artist and invited the young critic in. Responding in kind, the critic introduced himself explaining who he was and his purpose for dropping in unannounced and asked if he might have an hour or so of the artist's time. The artist explained he had a few immediate things to tend to, but if the critic didn't mind he would be free in a little while. The sculptor invited the critic to follow along if he wanted or otherwise take a seat out in his studio workshop. The critic responded he would enjoy tagging along, figuring he could make use of that time to get to know more about the reclusive artist and where the artist got his inspiration.

As they moved from the entry to the living room they came upon a woman propped up comfortably on the couch facing a large picture window looking out to the front yard. She was obviously unable to tend for herself. The artist smiled at his wife and introduced her to their new guest. As the artist completed tending to the needs of his disabled wife he explained they had been joyfully married for some 40 years describing a glorious courtship and that they were more infatuated with each other than the day they married. The couple engaged in a friendly banter about their early courtship days, each taking a turn in filling in the details of their romance and individual actions.

Following a brief pause in the bantering the artist explained that he and his wife had settled down for about seven years when his wife experienced a very difficult first pregnancy that resulted in the loss of their child and nearly cost the life of his wife. As a result of some mistakes in the operating room, his wife had become disabled but thankfully they had managed to save her life. His wife didn't seem to mind the telling of the story but rather smiled back at her husband as if she had heard the story numerous times before. Prior to leaving the room, the artist tenderly kissed his wife on the lips as she smiled endearingly back at him. She beckoned her husband to please go take care of his guest and told him she was quite comfortable and would be just fine. Waving his arms about, the artist jokingly acted like his wife was nagging him as he scurried to lead his guest out of his home and over to his studio.

The two men entered the studio together in silence as the sculptor began to set his tools out and prepared to work on his latest clay creation. He seemed to be waiting for the critic to begin the conversation with whatever had brought him out so far to see him. But now the critic, reflecting on the events he had witnessed in the last half-hour, was beginning to understand why the artist was known as a recluse and did so little to promote his work.

Even the gruff critic was humbled by the condition of the sculptor's wife and the artist's unselfish actions for his wife. He decided it would be inappropriate to ask the artist any questions related to self-promotion. Without saying a word, it was obvious the artist had a far greater devotion to his wife than anything he could make with his hands, yet what he created with his hands was what the artist was known for. A deafening silence permeated the air as the critic walked around the room looking at various pieces the artist had fashioned.

Yet the critic's thoughts were not on the sculptor's work, instead he continued to reflect on the interaction between the artist and his wife. He was overwhelmed with what he had just witnessed between this very loving couple. With two failed marriages behind him, the critic couldn't recall experiencing a spark of the love or caring he had just beheld. Gathering a little courage, he turned to the artist and uttered, *"What is a marriage?"*

Again the artist smiled. He knew that this question had nothing to do with why the critic came out to see him, but he was all the same pleased to answer. As he looked toward his clay creation he cleaned the clay from his hands. He momentarily pondered, gathering his thoughts, and then replied:

"Well, I think a marriage starts well before the wedding day, when a couple begins courting one another. At that time it's only an __idea__, it's the beginning of a vision. As they find themselves conforming to the idea, the couple will then proceed further to sketching out an __outline__ of their union, which naturally has them always together. I believe the outline is materialized on the day they get married.

"After a few years if they work at it, they will have filled in this sketch __with shades and highlights__ depicting a much clearer picture of their

bond. At times the eraser will have to come into play to fix mistakes, and some smudges will be found too. I think couples who are really in love are committed to work on helping each other to bring the original idea into greater clarity."

28

The artist elaborated further: *"As their cultivated love grows between them it will progress from a one-dimensional image on paper to a three-dimensional figure. A clay form **begins to take human shape,** which more closely resembles the couple in life-size form. However, this life-size form has not come without work, for along the way the clay has been kneaded, pushed, pulled, and gouged, until it conforms to the desired shape. As time passes and more work is applied the sculpture becomes complete, receiving all of the **expressions and fine details;** these too have been added by gentle cuts with a knife and pokes with needles and other sharp tools that clearly give definition to the original idea that the couple had. The two lovers' idea has now grown to closely resemble what they had envisioned and it is indeed a beautiful representation of what marriage is."*

Mesmerized at what he had heard, the critic contemplated what the artist had just described in the progression of a young couple's love, but he knew the artist had more to say. He could tell there was more passion to come but he didn't understand how the artist could improve on what he had just so beautifully expressed. The critic was determined to know more, so he asked, *"Can a marriage be better than what you just described?"*

Again smiling, the artist began cutting shapes into the clay model that was before him. Then he responded, *"Oh yes, sir, for we have not yet brushed on the colors nor applied the glazing. The colors and glazing will bring even greater depth to the vision; it will become much more **life-like and vibrant**. But the only way to complete this final step is by firing with intense heat, for it is only after that point that the sculpture is finished and folks from all around get to appreciate its beauty as a **completed work of art."**

Standing there with his jaw somewhat hanging down and his gaze fixed upon one of the artist's completed sculptures, the critic immediately understood the parable that the artist had presented. He had caught a glimpse of where the artist's passionate inspiration came from. It came from his deep commitment and love for his wife and his devotion to caring for her even when she could not return in kind. The sculptor's passion was for his wife and his love was fully present in tending to her

259

needs. At the same time their love and devotion was immersed in one of the most trying of fiery trails the critic could imagine, for the sculptor's wife had become totally dependent upon her husband for even the simplest of life's pleasures. The young critic discerned it was at this point that their marriage had become life-like; it was the heat of the trial that brought out the vibrancy that few other couples ever know. In spite of the trial, the sculptor and his wife came through the fiery furnace with greater love and passion than others could know.

It was now clear to the critic. The vows that we speak are not just for the wedding day, they are for all the days and the many years ahead. They are vows not of what you are at the time, but what you will become when you have kept them. The artist didn't "have" to take care of his disabled wife; he "gets" to take care of her.

Every Marriage is a Journey into the Unknown

Marriage is most certainly shared joy, but it is also shared pain and the best marriages will turn whatever pain besets them into joy. The artist and his wife took the loss of their child and the unfortunate disability of the wife and made their life nonetheless joyful. As the saying goes, they made lemonade out of lemons.

You have heard there are two things that are certain in life, "death and taxes." Some of us will pass on from this life violently, some suddenly, some slowly, some painfully, some will pass in their sleep with no pain, but death will meet us all in one form or another. Before ending our marriage manual we wanted to provide a brief overview of a topic rarely mentioned in marriage books; it deals with a situation in marriage where one spouse becomes totally dependent upon the other.

When a marriage begins, none of our visions contain the unforeseen path of a disabled spouse. Yet, no one knows what life has in store for us. Life is a path that we travel without knowing exactly how we will get there, nor what shape we will be in when we arrive. But when we marry we pledge that we are in this together, we will journey together, and we will arrive together. Along the way some couples are given the special opportunity to demonstrate and know love deeper and richer than others—for this love, this passion, and this intimacy is only known when one spouse is unable to care for themselves. It is then all the other trimmings of a marriage fall away and one spouse lives for two.

Yet what some people believe as a nearly unbearable hardship is really when love can burn the brightest. Many couples purpose to live for one another, but only when one spouse has become wholly dependent upon the other is the devotion brought into the light. The dependency of one brings out the devotion of another. Do you remember the picture of the adolescent boy carrying his brother on his back with the phrase under it saying "He ain't heavy, he's my brother"? This early drawing later became associated with the work of the Boys Town charities. It represented the kind of brotherly devotion that cared for one another.

Devotion—*selfless affection, dedication, loyalty, commitment, strong regard for another's well-being.*

If your spouse becomes disabled and there is nothing you can do to remedy it, then that is your reality. But just because your spouse is disabled doesn't mean your marriage has to be too. You still have each other even if it's just a portion of what you once had.

When Christopher Reeve became a quadriplegic, he and his wife still enjoyed a very enduring marital relationship while most of the trimmings had fallen away. In his 1998 book, *Still Me*, Reeve wrote that after considering his situation, believing that not only would he never walk again, but that he might never move a body part again, Reeve considered suicide. He mouthed to his wife Dana, "Maybe we should let me go." She tearfully replied, "I am only going to say this once: I will support whatever you want to do, because this is your life, and your decision. But I want you to know that I'll be with you for the long haul, no matter what. You're still you. And I love you." Reeve never considered suicide as an option again.

> *"Be selfish, stay married and keep your spouse to yourself!"*

Sometimes it is not a disability, it is the more trying test of solitude when a spouse is sent to serve overseas in military service for a year or more long tour. Or perhaps when a spouse is taken captive and held for several years. These trials are borne every day by tens of thousands of American families who faithfully bear burdens not unlike their spouses who are away serving in a foreign land.

Disability in Marriage

Some statistics report that nearly one in five Americans claim one type of

28

disability or another. If that's true, a lot of Americans are not fully capable of caring for themselves and it should be obvious that many married couples will experience this reality at some point in their marriage. Other research indicates that a very high majority of terminally ill patients are cared for at home.

FACTOID – Love is never "true love" until it's tested and found to be true.

The caregiver spouse—Spouses who care for an ailing or disabled spouse have many extra burdens that the rest of us do not. The caregiver spouse will have far less free or personal time and greater incidences of depression. They may also suffer loss of friends, loss of their lover, loss of other social activities, and more. Some caregiver spouses will complain of burnout and the lack of support from other family members. Some spouses are faced with attending a spouse who is of declining or terminal health, which can carry an even higher emotional burden. While a solider may watch his comrade die in a battle, the caregiver spouse may be forced to watch the love of their life die a little bit at a time over many weeks. It can be a very heavy burden.

The disabled spouse—Spouses who are disabled also have many extra struggles. Disabled folks have greater insecurities with doubts of self-worth and greater instances of depression. Often they are taking medications that in turn cause side effects both physical and emotional. Depending on the disability they will be very frustrated at the increased level of dependency on others, loss of social activities, possible loss of social interaction with friends and other family members, inability to get around, being less self-sufficient, the actual pain of the disability, the loss of bodily functions, and more.

Marriages of couples in which one or the other spouse is disabled—These marriages will typically have a greater strain on finances due to the extra costs associated with higher health care, including higher drug, doctor, therapy, and medical equipment costs. It is no wonder that there are statistically higher incidences of divorce when one or both spouses experience a disability. When Sarcoidosis hit me hard several years ago, not only was I not able to work or earn a living, I was not able to function well in many other areas. Thankfully my condition improved somewhat while being treated with some powerful (but toxic) drugs. Then in early 2010 after four years, I finally went into remission. While I was fighting the disease, Paige carried my weight with some frequency.

This needs to be said: Whether you are caring for a disabled spouse or for a disabled child, the stressors on the marriage are real and they must be recognized.

No one desires to be disabled; neither would anyone desire that their spouse or child be disabled. But the reality is this occurs frequently with many couples. When it does occur, how spouses handle it can be quite contrasted. There have been several studies done that have revealed two types of caregivers; one type becomes very stressed and burnt out and the other type seems to proceed through the added burdens with a joy and contentment. It's not clear what separates those who feel overburdened from those who do not.

The "caregiver's" checklist:

- Do not take on more than you can bear.
- Be willing to push beyond your comfort zone, but without overdoing it.
- Attitude is everything. Don't feel cheated—if you feel life is passing you by, then obviously you're not going to be happy.
- Do things outside of caring for your spouse. Enjoy bowling, golfing, knitting, or whatever other activity you would like. It's OK for caregivers to have enjoyable activities outside the home.
- Don't assume burdens you do not need to assume. In just about every task you have to do, there are ways to do it easier. Ask others to help you figure out alternate ways of doing things. If you are paying for a service that is depleting your savings, perhaps you can do without it. Again, ask for others to help you in deciding what your options may be.
- Accept the fact that death comes to us all. While understandable, the desire to keep your spouse with you should not overshadow God's desire to take them home. When it's time to pass on, allow them to pass on.
- When it gets too much, get help.

The "cared for" checklist:

- Do your best to do whatever you can do without injuring yourself. Push yourself to engage life.
- Stimulate your mind; keep it sharp by reading and other activities.
- Stay upbeat and positive; keep depression at bay.
- Keep in regular contact with other friends and family.

28

Paige and I have a very real expectation of death, there is no way to avoid it, and quite frankly it's a door we actually look forward to going through. We've discussed how we want to handle those last days and we have our living wills drawn up. My plan is to go standing or walking, but not lying on my back. If getting up kills me, then getting up is how I'll die. But we all know that rarely do we depart this world as we envision or plan for, and obviously Paige and I are looking forward to continuing our long life together.

Couple's project—Discuss the various aspects of how this chapter could come into play and how you plan to deal with it. If you need to draw up living wills, discuss making that happen.

> *"Do you think love dies? I think it may for the living but not for the dead. Just go to a cemetery and watch what goes on during any one day. You'll see lots of surviving spouses going over to the gravesites of their deceased spouse. They rearrange things, set up flowers, remove leaves, and talk to their loved one just like they did when they were still with them. I'm convinced love lives on after death, but up to the day we depart we have the power to kill love while our spouse is still with us."*

If you live near or know of, a military family who has an injured or deceased spouse, would you do us a favor and ask them what you can do to help them? The fact is, many of our service men and women have returned home with some form of disability, many of them could sure use a hand if you have any talent that could help make their life a little better. And a big **THANK YOU** to all the families who serve and have served in keeping our country free.

Did you learn anything? Yes / No
Chapter personal benefit appraisal: **HER 1-2-3-4-5   HIM 1-2-3-4-5**
1=not at all, 2=a little, 3=some good stuff, 4=fairly helpful, 5=very helpful

www.u-build.com

CHAPTER 29

BONUS

A Summation of 3,000 Interviews:
Married Men Share What They've Learned about Women

INCOMPLETE

(Mostly what we got was "deer in the headlight" blank stares from the husbands, it seemed like they were wrestling with the question. Some men opened their mouths but nothing came out, we had to tap chins up to return the jaw to the closed position. Several men started to speak until they saw that their wives were within listening distance, at that point it appeared all men went into full blown seizures followed by incomprehensible mumbling.)

29 *Hopefully you saw the humor in the last chapter, which contained no information. As men, we just don't understand our women, but we know we cannot live without you either!* ☺

CHAPTER 30

Links to Other Support

Will You Remember?

Some of you will need to write out the things you will begin changing "in you" as a list so you can glance at it every once in a while to keep yourself focused. Couples may decide to jointly write out a list about things you want to change in your relationship as a couple. Some spouses will be able to remember and keep focused on the items you want to change. But for others, you will need your spouse to call you or write notes to you until you work a new pattern into your life. The point is, nothing contained within the pages of this handbook will do anything for you unless you make the needed changes. Each spouse has to work these things into their life day by day. If you need help remembering, ask your spouse to help you, put reminders in your day planner or in your cell phone, whatever it takes to help remind you to improve your marriage. A house is never built or remodeled with thought alone.

Couple's project—Agree to revisit this handbook and your notes every month or so for the next few months.

Do Not Be Discouraged

Marriages are rarely standing still, they are either moving forward (improving) or going backward (degrading). Why? Because love is an action word. All thru your entire married life you will indeed be making changes to yourself and your marriage. Making changes and adjustments is a healthy part of marriage. Marriages should mature just as individuals should mature as they age, but it is entirely possible to get older without maturing.

> *"Marriage should come with a job description because it takes work and effort to keep it in good shape. You married another person, you made a promise on that day to love, respect, and care for the other spouse until death do you part. And while a marriage may not start off great, it can become great. When "u" consider this, "u" should come away with the understanding that to have a great marriage, 'u-build' it."*   Bob's cheap plug for our website

30 For most couples who have now reached the end of our handbook, you'll put this book down, look at each other, and you'll not see any changes. But remember the good farmer. It will take time for the tree to produce results; in the meantime the farmer continues to do everything he can to help the tree so when it's time, good fruit will come forth.

For a large majority of couples you will feel more stressed having discussed the various topics contained within these pages. Some of you will have had a few intense arguments working thru these chapters. That's a good sign! On any construction site you'll find workers with slivers in their hands, cuts, bruises, and some sore backs. Building and remodeling will have days of hard and heavy work. For existing marriages, remodeling makes the home messier during the initial phases of the construction work. It is to be expected. Just stay on task. Do not stop the remodel partway thru. Do not leave any issues unresolved. You might set something aside for another day, but do not ignore it. You have to make those repairs. Cut out the damaged sections and then progress to building in the good materials. If it seems like it is getting worse or stalled, get a professional counselor involved to help you move through the tougher stuff.

Sticking with our "be real" promise, Bob and I had a doggone good fight one Saturday morning in January, while writing this book. We had had about three hours of solid and meaningful communication that completely cratered over a few careless words. We gave each other some space, then we worked thru it over another couple of hours, and then we took our own advice later that night when we went to bed. We got naked and very solidly reestablished our bond. We cuddled and held each other and reaffirmed our relationship. OK, we had some great sex too! Fights, disagreements, misunderstandings, and other trials are going to occur, but just push thru them, steer yourselves out of the storm and back to safety.

FACTOID – All marriage relationships go through trials. Successful marriages just continue thru each trial as it comes along.

By building your marriage up, it becomes the home to protect you from the storms of life. And remember there are four seasons: winter, spring, summer, and fall. Every marriage will pass thru various seasons with none of them lasting forever. Cold wintery months should give way to a hot and passionate summer as you work on your stuff. Hot, passionate summers don't go on forever either, so don't fear periods of spring and fall. Take baby steps if need be, do not take on too much change at one time, then as you gain forward traction you can up the improvement pace.

"Pay It Forward"

Here in the Northwest, a couple of times a year a wave sweeps thru our coffee huts where the person in front buys the coffee for the person behind. At some coffee houses this has continued unbroken for days. One of the best things you can do is to be proactive in preserving not only your marriage but the marriages of friends and family. Giving other married couples a copy of this handbook for their anniversary, Christmas, or other special occasion would be a great way to share with people you care about. As an example, one year in which we were doing well financially we sent three books separate book titles to about 60 friends and family on what was normally our Christmas card mailing list.

How about all those soon-to-be-married people you know? If you want to really help them succeed in matrimony, why not pay it forward and give these newlyweds a lasting gift, a book or handbook such as this one that will help them get off on the right foot and provide the tools they need to build a great marriage? Sure, you can still buy them a wedding or anniversary gift, just package it with our handbook, you'll be giving them something that will far outlast a toaster or set of towels. Do you gather together with friends or lead a small group? This handbook would be a great focus topic. How about getting a copy for all of the employees in your department at work? On our website, we offer some huge discounts when you order six or more of our handbook so please visit our website if you are thinking about ordering multiple copies.

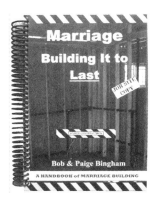

If this handbook has been helpful to you, if you feel you might have saved hundreds of dollars in marriage counseling or thousands in legal fees in what may have progressed to a divorce, please purchase copies and spread them around to other married couples. Leave a copy sitting out (not the one you've been marking up!) in your kitchen or living room. When you have guests over they will see it and ask you about it. You'll do a great service to your friends and family by giving them information that can greatly help them avoid the pain of divorce. Otherwise, spend a few bucks buying other books on marriage or going to a few marriage seminars. Couples should not only be willing to learn more, but be proud when they do. Share your newfound determination to have a better marriage with everyone you know. Don't hoard your gift, share it!

Couple's project—Talk about how you will share your gift and this or other marriage building aids with friends and family. Perhaps you will purpose to hand out just 6 handbooks over the next year.

> *"Some lobby for the protection of the institution of marriage, others say the fact we are in an institution means we need protection from ourselves!"*

We are not asking people to be M&Ms, we are asking people to be happily married. We want divorce to be a thing of the past, as healthy marriages become the norm. Wouldn't it be great to eradicate divorce?

Again, you must act; you cannot afford to just let things go as they have been. Change may indeed be uncomfortable at first; it may be messy exposing and tearing down the old parts of your marriage that were not working. It will definitely cost you some time and effort to rebuild the areas of your marriage that need to be rebuilt, but each couple must understand "just existing," just "letting it ride," and doing nothing to improve your marriage is to retain a miserable marriage. Be the first on your block to admit "we need help to build our marriage." Say it with pride!

When you work at rebuilding your marriage remember this, you do not have to take from your spouse to build up yourself. The building materials are obtained from the "marriage depot building materials store," included within this handbook, and there is an endless supply. So build up your spouse, encourage your spouse. By doing so, you're making them better, which in no way reduces your own self. When you build each other up it costs you nothing, but greatly improves you both.

Please log onto our website, **www.u-build.com** and add your name to the growing list of other couples who have decided to build their marriage and never to divorce. All you need to do is enter your name and the city and state you live in and the serial # found on inside cover of this book. You'll be making a public declaration much like you did on your wedding day that you are committed to each other and will build your marriage to last. There is an optional box to enter an email address (which will be kept private) if you would like to receive occasional updates and information. As our website grows over time, we plan to add a membership area that will provide additional resources to help you in your marriage building. We also plan to create a list of "couple recommended marriage counselors," providing a resource that will be available to all our readers.

Helping Others or Meddling?

Butt in or butt out? Let's say you have a family member who is really struggling to maintain their marriage, should you get involved? How about a neighbor who has similar marriage struggles? What if it was someone you know at your church, your health club, or golf club? Should you get involved? Well our opinion is going to be "YES" for most of the time. We have opened the marriage remodel doors with our own family, friends, and even people we barely knew. Why? Well, we care…for real. We really want to help folks have a great marriage. But we want you to know that being involved in other peoples marriage remodel work is messy. When you get involved, be ready to see it through, to keep your own opinions in check while providing helpful information and resources to the couple. You have to use humility, tact, and be very sensitive to the fact that you only know what you have been allowed to know. Most of the time the issues are much deeper than what is being conveyed and you're likely only getting one biased opinion. It's best that you do not try to act as a marriage counselor but rather direct the couple to such professionals. Frankly, we really enjoy seeing marriages rebuilt and changed as people get the tools and help they need to nurture a great marriage. One sad aspect of our modern culture is we don't place a high priority on relationships anymore. So if you care about someone, care enough to get involved.

Couple's project—Agree that you as a couple will get involved to help those around you anytime you become aware they may be struggling with their marriage.

30 | Links to Other Tools

The very last thing you should do, as a couple, is to consider this handbook the end all for helping you build a better marriage. In fact, if you have learned anything it is that you should always be seeking to grow your marriage-building skills. A carpenter never stops learning his trade because there are always new products, new tools, and new methods in building and remodeling, and the same is true for rebuilding or maintaining your marriage. To that end, we've listed several good resources to help you.

There is no test at the end; instead we asked you to rate your marriage at the start of this handbook. After having read this handbook, you have gained some (not all) knowledge, but that knowledge will be useless unless you put it into action. It is important to note that the change does not take place in the marriage before it takes place in you. <u>You</u> each have to change. For many couples, you will need more help than we have given you within these pages.

Your outlook is hopefully brighter; we've detailed the concepts, given you materials and tools, asked you to create a plan for the success of your marriage, informed you about the order of building up your marriage, and told you to seek the help of others. From this point on <u>you must put into practice daily all you have learned.</u>

You're on a journey that may have just started or has been going on for awhile. You are not alone in this journey; you have a spouse that at some point in your past you pledged to love. We do not know what lies behind you, but we know a great marriage lies in front of you. It's your dream, take it; don't let it get away, make the best of what you have. Tear down the things that do not work, rebuild them, remodel the areas needing remodeling, use new materials and tools. Take this vision and make it happen; do not let it decay any further. Make it a goal to re-read this book again in a month or two.

You must investigate other helpful marriage aids and build your marriage into a glorious working union. These recommendations are made without compensation or commission, and reflect only what we knew in the year our book was published. This is by no means a complete list, there are very likely many other great resources out there. While we at one time or another found the following helpful, we are not responsible for changes in the information or the integrity of any organization, individual, or resource listed.

You will see by the wide range of marriage building resources listed below that we truly want to make available to you everything that can help you build a great and enduring marriage. Many publishing companies and authors will refrain from promoting books and resources outside of their own because of a fear that you will spend your money elsewhere. We are hoping that you do! We really want you to have the best marriage you can have and we encourage you to get that support and help wherever it can be found.

Couple's project—From the list below, agree to individually or collectively to check into finding more resources to build your marriage.

Helpful Internet-Based Resources

- *U-build* – Is our Internet-based portal to connect with us and other resources we offer. You will find bulk purchase handbook discounts here for those of you wishing to give copies to family and friends. **http://www.u-build.com**

- *Family Life* – We volunteer at and highly recommend that you attend one of these marriage conferences. "Family Life" was founded by Dennis & Barbara Rainey. They conduct marriage conferences (called "Weekend to Remember") in nearly every major city thru-out the year using biblically based principles. **http://www.familylife.com**

- *Dr. Phil* – Who hasn't heard of Dr. Phil? His nationally syndicated reality/talk show is broadcast across America and deals with behavioral and relationship issues. His advice is usually right on; however, he needs to come out of the closet and shave the rest of that hair off. *Dr. Phil McGraw produces a TV program and holds a B.A. from Midwestern State University and an M.A. and Ph.D. in clinical psychology from North Texas State University with a dual area of emphasis in clinical and behavioral medicine.* **www.drphil.com**

- *Focus on the Family* – We've listened to their daily radio programs and read several of Jim Dobson's books on family and marriage relationships. They provide great insight, especially for parents.

"Focus on the Family" was founded by Dr. Jim Dobson, and is a global, non-profit Christian organization with a vision for healing brokenness in families, communities, and societies worldwide through Christ. We endeavor to inspire and equip married couples to live out God's design and intention for biblical marriage and to help parents raise children who know, love, and serve God. **www.focusonthefamily.com**

- **Smalley Relationship Center** – Gary's teaching on personality types was a breakthrough for me; it came as part of an 18-video-tape package.
  Gary Smalley is a family counselor, and is the president and founder of the Smalley Relationship Center. He is the author of books on family relationships from a Christian perspective.
  http://www.garysmalley.com/
  http://www.dnaofrelationships.com/

- **Crown Financial Ministries** – is a really great tool for helping folks get their finances in order. We have listened to their radio information for years.
  Crown Financial Ministries, founded in 1976, is an interdenominational ministry dedicated to equipping people around the world to learn, apply, and teach biblical financial principles. **http://www.crown.org**

- *Marital resources of all types –*
  http://www.marriagebuilders.com

- This is a great resource to help mothers of preschoolers – **http://www.mops.org**

- Marital resources of all types – **http://homebuildersministry.org**

- A Catholic based marriage building organization.
  http://foryourmarriage.org

- **Couples Who Pray** An organization based on a book and theme that couple prayer. **http://www.coupleswhopray.com**

- **Biblicalbeliever.org** is a website that accepts no advertising and seeks to provide the basics of what Christianity should be for individuals. **http://www.biblicalbeliever.org/**

Some Good Marriage Books

- *Sexual Intimacy in Marriage* by Cutrer Glahn
- *Fight Fair* by Tim & Joy Downs
- *For Women Only* by Shaunti Feldhahn
- *For Men Only* by Jeff & Shaunti Feldhahn
- *20 rules for a Great Family* by Dr. Steve Stephens
- *Home Remedies* by Gary Smalley & John Trent
- *The Proper Care and Feeding of Husbands* by Dr. Laura Schlessinger
- *The Smart Step-Family* by Ron Deal

Books Dealing with Adultery
- *Living with your Husband's Secret Wars* by Marsha Means
- *Torn Asunder* by Dave Carder

Wrap-up, a National Vision

Ideally we would like to help promote a strategy that sweeps across America to build strong, healthy marriages. After we get strong marriages at the forefront, we would then seek another movement to build stronger families. This would be followed by another movement to build stronger communities. From strong communities we could build stronger states. With strong states, we could once again have a stronger nation. Our politicians seem to be going at this backward.

We'd like couples to understand there is a lot more at stake than just a married couple trying to get along. Healthy marriages are the foundation building blocks for a strong and healthy nation. If every married couple reading this handbook would reach next door or across the street and touch 2–3 other neighbors by spreading the message of building strong marriages, we indeed would have a movement that is far nobler than anything our Congress has ever achieved, and it will have been born by "we the people."

When a couple learns how to be kind to and with each other, they will naturally have a better disposition toward others. That will reverberate into our communities and neighborhoods. Compassion for our spouses does indeed set the tone for not only our family relationships, but also our nation as a whole. At the time we were writing our book, our nation had been deeply divided for the last 20 years or so. Our politicians are breeding contempt between us; just maybe we can turn it around and

30

foster greater national unity at a grassroots level. It's sure worth a try!

Community Marriage Initiatives

Many of our readers may not be aware that there are several national movements underway to support the building of enduring marriages. There is even a government-funded Department of Health and Human Services project dedicated to supporting healthy marriages. All of these organizations are working to promote enduring marriage initiatives in cites, counties, and states. Ideally, every person reading our handbook would petition their local clergy, city, and governments to create healthy marriage initiatives requiring that people obtain premarital and pre-divorce counseling and to have them sign a pledge to work continually on their marriage.

Couple's project—Agree that one of you will become active in promoting local marriage building activities in your community, neighborhood, and/or church.

National Marriage Movement Organizations

- (NAME) The National Association of Marriage Enhancement – is a organization seeking to help churches set up marriage enrichment public awareness campaigns in their communities. **http://www.nameonline.net**

- Stronger Families Fuel a grassroots movement to change the culture around marriage, so that more kids grow up with their mom and dad. **http://www.strongerfamilies.org**

- **Marital resources of all types** – http://www.smartmarriages.com

- **U.S. Dept. of Health and Human Services, Administration for Children and Families** (Federally funded) **http://www.acf.hhs.gov/healthymarriage**

- **The National Healthy Marriage Resource Center** (NHMRC) is a clearinghouse for high quality, balanced, and timely information and resources on healthy marriage. The NHMRC's mission is to be a first stop for information, resources, and training on healthy marriage for experts, researchers,

276

policymakers, media, marriage educators, couples and individuals, program providers, and others. (Federally funded) **http://www.healthymarriageinfo.org**

- **A Nationwide network of Marriage an Relationship Educators.** National Marriage Centers in association with the National PreMarital Institute is an independent, non-partisan, non-sectarian, non-discriminatory, not for profit, Educational and Coaching service.
  http://www.marriagecenters.com/index.htm

- **AM/FM** The vision of AMFM is to see Christ's love reflected through healthy marriages and strong families. We are committed to building up marriage and family champions in churches and communities and facilitating a spirit of collaboration between all those who share our vision. **http://www.amfmonline.com**

- **The Relationship Institute** serves the online community, as well as communities in southeastern Michigan, We provide marriage counseling, relationship therapy, couples counseling, premarital counseling, singles and couples workshops, help with divorce, relationship advice, as well as help with dating, love and communication. **http://www.relationship-institute.com**

- Founded by Dr Gary and Barb Rosberg they promote America's Family Coaches to directly address the needs of marriages and relationships. **http://www.thegreatmarriageexperience.com**

- **RemarriageWorks.com** is dedicated to providing you with information, community, and products to enhance your experience of remarriage and stepfamily living. **http://remarriageworks.com**

Did you learn anything? Yes / No
Chapter personal benefit appraisal: **HER 1-2-3-4-5 HIM 1-2-3-4-5**
1=not at all, 2=a little, 3=some good stuff, 4=fairly helpful, 5=very helpful

www.u-build.com

Feedback Page

Book Serial # _____

Dear Readers,
As our last **Couple's project,** we would really like to know your thoughts on our first book and we are really looking forward to getting your feedback. So thank you in advance for answering these questions, which can also be completed on our website at www.u-build.com. Your email address or other contact information will not be shared or sold. Please try to keep responses brief and to the point, use another sheet of paper if needed.

1. On a scale of 1–10, how helpful to you were the marriage building concepts and the book over all? _____

2. How well received was the book by your spouse?

   Very well – went along – hasn't yet read it

3. Do you feel your marriage will improve from reading this book?

   Yes / No

4. What chapters do you consider the best? _____

5. Where or how could we improve?

   _____

   _____

6. Would you consider buying copies of the book in bulk to give to friends & family?   Yes / No

7. Would you like to be part of a future marriage survey we are planning?   Yes / No

   If so, please supply your email address? _____

8. How long have you been married in your <u>current</u> marriage? _____

9. How many times have you been married? _____

   # of times your spouse has been married? _____

10. Are you male or female? _____

11. Had you considered getting a divorce prior to reading this handbook?

    Yes / No

12. If you had considered divorce prior to reading this book, how determined are you now not to consider a divorce in the future? Never going to consider it / much less likely / still may / going to divorce anyway

13. Do you think you would be likely or not likely to purchase our next book?   Likely – Not Likely

14. What are the top 3–6 issues you and your spouse have struggled the most with in your current marriage?

_____

_____

_____

15. Any other comments you might want to provide that would be OK to publish on our website, or on our next book cover? If you provide a comment, we will only use your first name and last name initial and we reserve the right to use all, none, or a portion of your comments, without compensation to you. If you like, think of your comments like a critic's review. Overall was the handbook good or bad and why?

_____

_____

_____

_____

16. If we were to offer a 1–2 day weekend marriage boot camp in your area, would you be likely to attend if the registration fee was around $100–$150 per couple?   Likely – Not likely – Depends

17. Please name other resources you've found to be beneficial in helping your marriage grow and endure.

Thanks! You can mail the survey and/or any comments to:
U-build, P. O. Box 1510, Spirit Lake, ID   83869 or email them to info@u-build.com.

Mail Order Form

You may order online **www.u-build.com** for the most current and best possible direct purchase pricing. Shipping costs will be more precise when ordering online. The shipping costs stated below may be higher depending on significant (10% or more) adjustments implemented by major shipping carriers like: USPS, FedEx, or UPS. Please enclose your check for the cost of the book and shipping charges. Money orders should be made out to "U-Build". Delivery to Idaho residents must add 6% sales tax. If you enclose cash, we cannot be responsible for lost or misdirected mail, nor will we make change when filling your order.

Marriage, Building It to Last (each) . . . . $ 21.99
Shipping & Handling (1-3 books) . . . . $ 8.00
$ 29.99

For Credit Card Orders   We accept - Amex/Visa/MasterCard

_____
Your Name as it appears on your credit card

_____
Your complete address as it appears on your credit card

_____   _____
Your phone number   Credit card expiration date

_____   _____
Your credit card type   Your credit card number

Your credit card security code _____

Your signature _____

Shipping address if different than your credit card address:

To: _____

         _____

_____ zip _____

Mail this form to: U-Build Enterprises LLC, PO Box 1510, Spirit Lake, ID 83869   or call **1-208-963-6914** with this information handy.